Patricia Smith's

DOLL VALUES

Antique to Modern

Series VI

COLLECTOR BOOKS

A Division of Schroeder Publishing Co., Inc.

The current values in this book should be used only as a guide. They are not intended to set prices, which vary from one section of the country to another. Auction prices as well as dealer prices vary greatly and are affected by condition as well as demand. Neither the Author nor the Publisher assumes responsibility for any losses that might be incurred as a result of consulting this guide.

Additional copies of this book may be ordered from:

Collector Books
P.O. Box 3009
Paducah, KY 42001-3009

@ $9.95 add $2.00 for postage and handling.

CREDITS

We wish to thank the following for their help in getting this volume completed: Hazel Adams, Sandy Johnson Barts, Sally Bethscheider, Arthur Bouliette, Kay Bransky, Irene Brown, Joanne Brunkin (H.C. Tims, photos), Sylvia Bryant, Barbara Earnshaw-Cain (P.O. Box 14381, Lenexa, KS 66215), Betty Chapman, Marlowe Cooper, Lee Crane, Renie Culp, Sandra Cummins, Bessie Dorsett, Shirley Dyer, Marie Ernst, Frasher Doll Auctions (Rt. 1, Box 72, Oak Grove, MO 64075), Beth French, Carole Friend, Maureen Fukushima, Martha Gragg, Green Museum, Karen Heidemann, Phyllis Houston, Genie Jenright, Karen and Paul Johnson, Beres Lindus, Margaret Mandel, Marge Meisinger, Jeannie Mauldin, Lynn Motter (John R. Ross, photos), Kay Moran, Carmen Moxley, Pam Ortman, Nancy Prestosh, Doris Richardson, Cindy Ruscito, June Schultz, Betty Shelly, Jeannie Shipi, Pamela Smith, Henri and John Startzel, Bonnie Stewart, Betty Tait, Pat Timmons, Turn of Century Antiques (1415 S. Broadway, Denver, CO 80220), Mike Way (Cindy Wolff, photos), Jane Walker, Ann Wencel, Patricia Woods, Glorya Wood and "Dutch" Voss.

Cover Photo:

Courtesy Karen and Paul Johnson:
Rare Bruno Schmitt child, "Wendy."

PRICES

This book is divided between "Antique" and "Modern" by sections, with the older dolls in the first section and the newer dolls in the second section. Each section is listed by maker alphabetically or by type of material or by name of the doll. (Example: Bye-lo or Kewpie.) This is done to try to make a quick reference for the reader. An index is provided for locating a specific doll.

The condition of the doll is uppermost in pricing. An all original modern doll in excellent condition will bring a much higher price than those listed in a price guide. A doll that is damaged or without original clothes, is soiled and dirty, will bring far less than the top price listed. The cost of doll repairs and cleanup has soared, and it is wise to judge the damage and estimate the cost of repairs before you attempt to sell or buy a damaged doll.

With antique dolls, the condition of the bisque, or material the head is made from, is the uppermost importance, as is the body in that it does not need repairs and is correct to the doll. Antique dolls must be clean, nicely dressed and ready to place into a collection and have no need of repair in any way for them to bring book price. An all original one with original clothes, marked shoes and original wig will bring a lot more than any prices listed. Boxes are very rare, so here again, the doll will have a higher price.

It is very important to show the "retail" price of dolls in a price guide and to try to be as accurate as possible for insurance reasons. This can be referred to as "replacement cost" as an insurance company or a postal service must have some means to appraise a damaged or stolen doll for the insuree, and the collector must have some means to judge their own collections to be able to purchase adequate amounts of insurance.

No one knows your collection better than yourself and in the end, in relation to what to pay for a doll, you must ask yourself if the doll is affordable to you and do you want it enough to pay the price. You will buy the doll, or pass it up - it is as simple as that!

Prices shown are for dolls that are clean, undamaged, well-dressed and in overall excellent condition with many prices listed for soiled, dirty, re-dressed dolls also.

ANTIQUE AND OLDER DOLLS SECTION

French all-bisque dolls will be jointed at the necks, shoulder and hips. They have slender arms and legs, glass eyes and most have kid-lined joints. The majority of the heads have a sliced pate with a tiny cork pate. French all-bisque dolls have finely painted features with outlined lips, well tinted bisque, and feathered eyebrows. They can have molded-on shoes, high top boots with pointed toes, high top buttoned boots with four or more painted straps. They can also be barefooted or just have stockings painted onto the legs. Any French bisque should be in very good condition, not have any chips, breaks, nor should there be any hairline cracks to bring the following prices:

Swivel Neck: (Socket head.) Molded shoes or boots. 4½" - $750.00; 6-6½" - $950.00.

Bare Feet: 5-6" - $900.00; 8-9" - $1,600.00; 11" - $2,600.00.

With Jointed Elbows: 5½-6" - $2,200.00.

With Jointed Elbows and Knees: 5½-6" - $3,200.00.

S.F.B.J., UNIS, or other late French all-bisques: 5-6" - $425.00; 7" - $575.00.

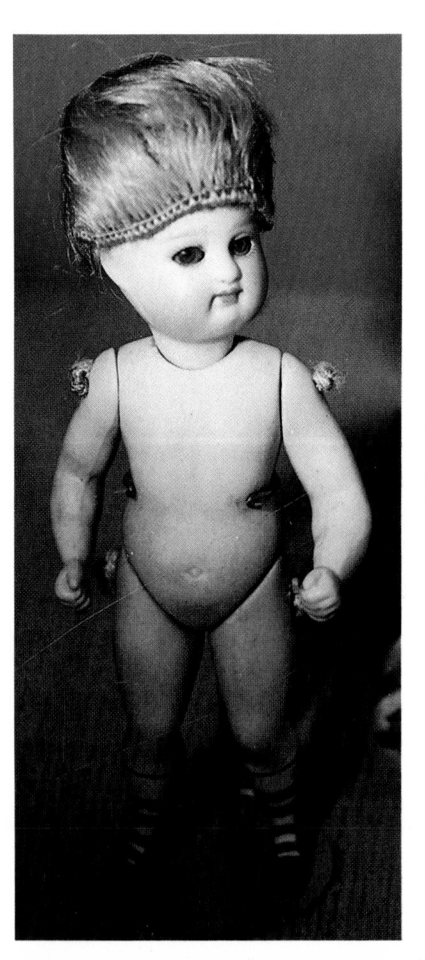

5½" French-type all bisque with swivel head and early excellent quality bisque. Molded and painted on high top boots, glass eyes, string jointed and both fists are clenched. Courtesy Frasher Auctions. 5½" - $900.00.

German-made all bisque dolls run from excellent quality to moderate quality. The following prices are for excellent quality and condition with no chips, cracks, breaks or hairlines. Dolls should be nicely dressed and can have molded hair or a wig. They generally have painted-on shoes and socks.

Swivel Neck, Glass Eyes: Open or closed mouth, good wig, nicely dressed, painted-on shoes and socks. 4" - $325.00; 5" - $450.00; 7" - $565.00; 9" - $950.00 up.

Swivel Neck, Painted Eyes: Open or closed mouth, one-strap shoes and painted socks. Nice clothes and wig. 2" - $165.00; 4" - $225.00; 5" - $265.00; 7" - $425.00; 9" - $600.00 up.

One-Piece Body and Head, Glass Eyes: Excellent bisque, open or closed mouth with good wig and nicely dressed. 3" - $245.00; 4½-5½" - $285.00; 7" - $425.00; 8-9" - $600.00-700.00.

One-Piece Body and Head, Painted Eyes: Open or closed mouth with good wig or molded hair and nicely dressed. 2" - $85.00; 4½-5½" - $185.00; 7" - $265.00; 8-9" - $385.00; 11" - $950.00.

Marked: 155, 156, 162: Smiling, closed or open/closed mouth, glass eyes and swivel head. 6" - $775.00.

Molded-on Clothes or Underwear: Jointed at shoulders only or at shoulders and hips. No cracks, chips or breaks. 4½" - $165.00; 5½" - $225.00; 6-7" - $365.00.

Marked: 100, 125, 225: (Made by Alt, Beck and Gottschalck.) Closed mouth or open/closed, sleep or inset glass eyes, chubby body and limbs and molded-on one-strap shoes with painted socks. No chips, cracks or breaks. Has one-piece body and head: 5" - $225.00; 6½" - $350.00; 8" - $500.00; 10" - $800.00.

Marked 150: (Made by Kestner or Bonn.) One-piece body and head, painted-on one strap shoes with painted socks. Glass eyes, not damaged and nicely dressed. 4" - $275.00; 6" - $365.00; 9" - $850.00.

Marked 150: With painted eyes and molded hair. 4½" - $250.00; 5½" - $300.00.

Marked 150: With swivel neck and glass eyes. 5" - $475.00; 9" - $975.00.

Mold 155: Smile face, glass eyes. 5½" - $550.00. Painted eyes: 5½" - $325.00

Molded Hair: One-piece body and head, painted eyes, painted-on shoes and socks. Excellent quality bisque and artist workmanship. No chips, cracks and nicely dressed: 5" - $200.00; 6½" - $325.00.

Marked: 886, 890: (Made by Simon and Halbig.) Or any all-bisque with marks S&H. Painted-on high-top boots with four or five straps. No damage and nicely dressed. 6" - $965.00; 8" - $1,500.00.

Black or Brown All-Bisque: see Black Section.

Molded-on Hat or Bonnet: All in perfect condition. 6" - $450.00 up; 8" - $600.00 up.

With Long Stockings: (To above the knees.) Glass eyes, open or closed mouth; jointed at neck and stockings will black, blue or green. Perfect condition: 5½" - $625.00; 7½" - $800.00.

Flapper: One-piece body and head, wig, painted eyes, painted-on long stockings and has thin limbs, fired-in tinted bisque, one-strap painted shoes. 5" - $300.00; 7" - $400.00. Same, but with molded hair: 5" - $300.00; 7" - $400.00. Same, but medium quality bisque and artist workmanship: 5" - $175.00; 7" - $265.00.

Marked With Maker: (S&H, JDK, A.B.G., etc.) Closed mouth, early fine quality face. 7" - $985.00; 10" - $1,800.00. Same, with open mouth and later quality bisque: 5" - $425.00; 7" - $600.00; 8" - $800.00.

Pink Bisque: 1920's and 1930's. Jointed shoulders and hips with painted features, can have molded hair or wig. All in excellent condition: 3" - $80.00; 5" - $110.00; 7" - $185.00.

Bathing Dolls: see that section.

6" all-bisque twin characters; incised 156/4 Germany. Probably made by Kestner. Sleep eyes, open/closed mouths. Jointed at neck, shoulders and hips. Painted-on shoes and socks. Both have original clothes. Courtesy Frasher Auctions. 6" - $545.00 each.

All-bisque babies were made in both Germany and Japan, and dolls from either country can be excellent quality or poor quality. Prices are for excellent workmanship to the painting and quality of bisque. There should be no chips, cracks, or breaks. Dressed or nude.

Germany (Jointed Necks, Shoulders and Hips): Can have glass eyes or painted eyes, wigs or painted hair. 3½" - $175.00; 6" - $285.00; 8½" - $425.00.

Germany (Jointed at Shoulders and Hips Only): Well painted features, free-formed thumbs and many have molded bottle in hand. Some have molded-on clothes. 3½" - $95.00; 6" - $185.00.

Germany (Character Baby): Jointed shoulders and hips, molded hair, painted eyes with character face. 4" - $185.00; 6" - $300.00. Glass eyes: 5" - $375.00. Swivel neck, Glass eyes: 6" - $500.00; 10" - $1,000.00.

Germany (Toddler): Jointed neck, glass eyes, perfect condition. 6½" - $600.00; 9" - $900.00; 12" - $1,400.00. **Japan:** Of poor to medium quality. 3½-5" - $5.00-40.00. Very nice quality: 3½-5" - $15.00 to $65.00.

"Candy Babies": (Can be either German or Japanese.) Generally poorly painted with high bisque color. Were given away at candy counter with purchase. 1920's. 4" - $65.00; 5-6" -$90.00.

Pink Bisque Baby: Jointed at shoulders and hips, painted features and hair, bent baby legs. 1920's and 1930's. 2" - $50.00; 4" - $75.00; 8" - $135.00.

8½" all-bisque toddler with sleep eyes, open mouth with two teeth and marked "Germany 47/2" on back and on head "231/G.B./A 9/0 DGRM/248/1." This mold number is same as "Fany," an extremely rare Armand Marseille baby, but this doll does not look anything like the incised "Fany" 231 mold. Courtesy Bessie Dorsett. 8½" - $900.00 up.

All bisque with character faces or stances were made both in Germany and Japan. The German dolls have finer bisque and workmanship of the painted features. Most character all-bisque dolls have jointed shoulders only, with some having joints at the hips and a very few have swivel heads. They can have molded-on shoes or be barefooted. Prices are for dolls with no chips, cracks, hairlines or breaks.

Baby Bo Kaye: Made by Alt, Beck & Gottschalck. Marked with mold number "1394." 6-6¼" - $1,800.00.

Baby Peggy Montgomery: Made by Louis Amberg and marked with paper label. 6" - $525.00.

Bonnie Babe: Made by Georgene Averill. Has paper label. 5" - $750.00; 7" - $1,000.00.

Bye-Lo. Made J.D. Kestner. Has paper label. Jointed neck, glass eyes, solid dome. 4" - $525.00; 6" - $700.00. Jointed neck, wig, glass eyes: 4½" - $675.00; 6" - $875.00; 8-8½" - $1,400.00. Painted eyes, molded hair and one-piece body and head: 5" - $375.00; 6" - $450.00; 8-8½" - $625.00.

Campbell Kids: Molded-on clothes, "Dutch" hairstyle. 4½" - $265.00.

Chi Chi: Made by Orsini. 5-6" - $1,400.00.

Chin-Chin: Made by Heubach. 4½" - $300.00.

Didi: Made by Orsini. 5-6" - $1,400.00.

Googly: Glass eyes: 6" - $600.00 - 800.00. Painted eyes: 4" - $300.00; 6" - $485.00. Glass eyes, swivel neck: 5½" - $675.00; 7½" - $850.00 Jointed elbow and/or knees: 6" - $2,100.00; 7-7½" - $2,800.00. *Marked with maker (example K*R): 6½-7" - $2,400.00.

Grumpy Boy: Marked Germany: 4" - $185.00. Marked Japan: 4" - $85.00.

Happifats: Boy or girl. 5" - $300.00 each and up.

Hebee or Shebee: 4½" - $350.00-$375.00.

Heubach: Molded hair, side glance eyes: 6½" - $775.00. Molded ribbon: 6½" - $850.00. Wigged: 7" - $925.00.

Bunny Boy or Girl figurine: 5" - $575.00.

Little Imp: Has hoofed feet. 6½" - $500.00.

Kestner: Marked mold number 257, 262, etc. 10" - $875.00; 12" - $1,200.00.

Mibs: Made by Louis Amberg. May be marked "1921" on back and have paper label with name. 3½" - $250.00; 5" - $375.00.

Mimi: Made by Orsini. 6" - $1,200.00.

Molded-on Clothes: Made in Germany. Unjointed, painted features. 4" - $200.00; 7" - $345.00. Jointed at shoulder: 4" - $275.00; 7" - $485.00.

Orsini: Head tilted to side, made in one piece and hands hold out dress. 2½" - 3" - $450.00.

Our Fairy: Molded hair and painted eyes. 9" - $1,400.00. Wig and glass eyes: 9" - $1,750.00.

Our Mary: Has paper label. 4½" - $475.00.

Peek-a-boo: By Drayton. 4" - $275.00.

Peterkin: 9" - $425.00.

Peterkin, Tommy: Horsman. 4" - $265.00.

Quesue San Baby: Various poses. 5" - $285.00.

Scootles: Made by Cameo. 6" - $975.00.

Teenie Weenie: Made by Donahey. Painted one-piece eyebrows and features. 4½" - $225.00.

Tynie Baby: Made by Horsman. 9" - $1,700.00.

Sonny: Made by Averill. 5" - $850.00.

Wide Awake Doll: Germany. 7½" - $325.00. Japan: 7½" - $125.00.

Veve: Made by Orsini. 6" - $1,600.00.

"Wrestler": (so called.) Fat legs, painted high-top boots, glass eyes, closed or open mouth, no damage. 8" one-piece body and head - $900.00. 8" swivel neck - $1,400.00. Bare Feet: 8" - $1,800.00; 11" - $2,600.00.

** K star R Mold 131: 9½" at auction - $6,100.00 and $6,900.00.*

ALL BISQUE - NODDERS

"Knotter's" are called "Nodders" as when their heads are touched, they "nod." The reason they should correctly be called "knotters" is due to the method of stringing. The string is tied through a hole in the head, and they can also be made with cutouts on the bodies to take a tiny rod that comes out of the side of the neck. Both styles were made in Germany and Japan.

Santa Claus: 6" - $145.00.

Teddy Bear: 6" - $145.00.

Other Animals: (Rabbit, dog, cat, etc.) 3½-5" - $30.00 - $85.00.

Comic Characters: 3½-5" - $125.00 up.

Children/Adults: Made in Germany. 4½-5½" - $55.00-100.00.

Japan/Nippon: 4½" - $25.00; 5½" - $35.00.

Sitting Position: 8" - $285.00.

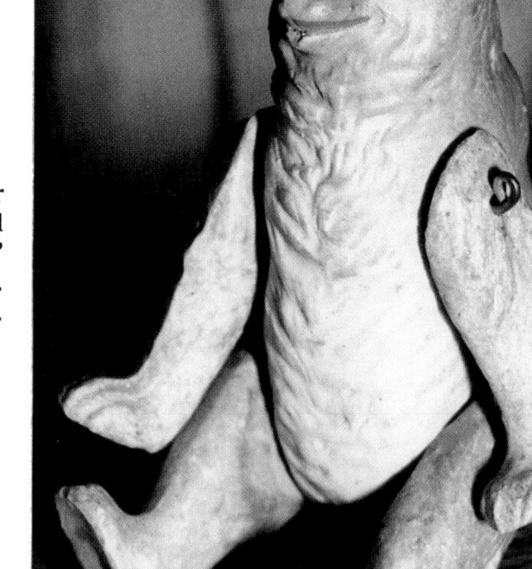

4" all-bisque German bear with pin joints, painted features with brown-tan "fur." Courtesy Frasher Auctions. 4" - $495.00; 7" - $900.00.

ALL BISQUE - JAPAN

All bisque dolls from Japan vary a great deal in quality. Jointed at shoulders (may have other joints). Good quality bisque and well painted with no chips or breaks. (Also see all-bisque characters and nodder sections.)

Marked Nippon: 4" - $35.00; 6" - $80.00.

"Betty Boop": Style with bobbed hair, large painted eyes to side and one-piece body and head. 4" - $20.00; 7" - $35.00.

Child: With molded clothes. 4½" - $35.00; 6" - $55.00.

Comic Characters: See "All bisque - Comic Characters" section.

Occupied Japan: 3½" - $12.00; 5" - $15.00; 7" - $25.00.

Figurines: Called "Immobilies" (no joints). Children: 3" - $45.00. Teddy Bears: 3" - $60.00. Indians, Dutch, etc: 2½" - $45.00. Santa Claus: 3½" - $85.00. Adults: 5" - $85.00.

Bent Leg Baby: May or may not be jointed at hips and shoulders. See "All Bisque - Babies" sections.

Original box holding 10 all-bisque immoblies with painted features and clothes. 2½" tall and marked on backs "Japan." Courtesy Sandra Cummins. 2½:" - $25.00 each. 10 in box: $300.00.

ALL BISQUE - COMIC CHARACTERS

Annie Rooney: Made in Germany. 4" - $325.00.

Aunty Blossom: Made in Germany. 3½" - $60.00.

Baby Tarzan & Gorilla: $75.00.

Betty Boop: With musical instrument. Made in Japan. 3½" - $60.00 up.

Betty Boop: Fleisher Studios. Made in Japan. 3½" - $45.00 up.

Dick Tracy: Made in Germany. 4" - $250.00.

Herby: #C82. Made in Japan. $55.00. Nodder - $75.00.

Johnny: "Call for Phillip Morris." Made in Germany. 5" - $125.00.

Lady Plush Bottom: Made in Germany. 4" - $65.00.

Mickey McGuire: Fontaine Fox. Made in Germany. $95.00.

Mickey Mouse: Walt Disney. 5" - $175.00 up.

Mickey Mouse: With musical instrument. $175.00 up.

Minnie Mouse: Walt Disney. $175.00 up.

Moon Mullins and Kayo: 4" - $85.00.

Orphan Annie: 3½" - $60.00. Nodder - $85.00 up.

Mr. Bailey, The Boss: Made in Germany. 3½" - $65.00.

Mr. Peanut: Made in Japan. 4" - $45.00.

Our Gang: Boys: 3½" - $75.00. Girls: 3½" - $80.00.

Popeye: 3" - $95.00 up.

Seven Dwarfs: Walt Disney. 3½" - $75.00 each.

Skeezix: 3½" - $75.00.

Skippy: 5" - $100.00.

Snow White: 5½" - $100.00. In box with Dwarfs: $725.00.

Winnie Walker: Banner. Made in Germany. 3½" - $165.00.

All-bisque 5½" Snow White and 4" Dwarfs in original box. Each incised with own name in front and "Walt Disney" on the back. Unjointed and painted features and clothes. Box: "1938 Distributors Geo. Borgfeldt Corp. N.Y./Japan." All in box, no damage: $725.00.

ALL BISQUE - PAINTED BISQUE

Painted bisque has a layer of paint over the bisque which has not been fired. Molded hair, painted features, painted-on shoes and socks. Jointed at shoulder and hips. All in good condition with no paint chips.

Boy or Girl: 4" - $55.00; 6" - $85.00.

Baby: 4" - $70.00; 6" - $90.00.

Alt, Beck & Gottschalck was located near Ohrdruf at Nauendorf, Germany. The firm was the maker of both the "Bye-lo" baby and "Bonnie Babe" for the distributor, George Brogfeldt. The leading authorities in Germany, and now the United States, have assigned nearly all the turned-head dolls as being made by Alt, Beck & Gottschalck, with the bodies being made by Wagner & Zetzsche. It is claimed that this firm produced dolls with tinted bisque and molded hair (see that section of this book), as well as wigged turned head and shoulder head dolls and also dolls made of china. There is a vast variation to the eyebrows among these dolls, which is just one variation listed here, but "offically" almost all these dolls are being lumped under Alt, Beck & Gottschalck.

Marks:

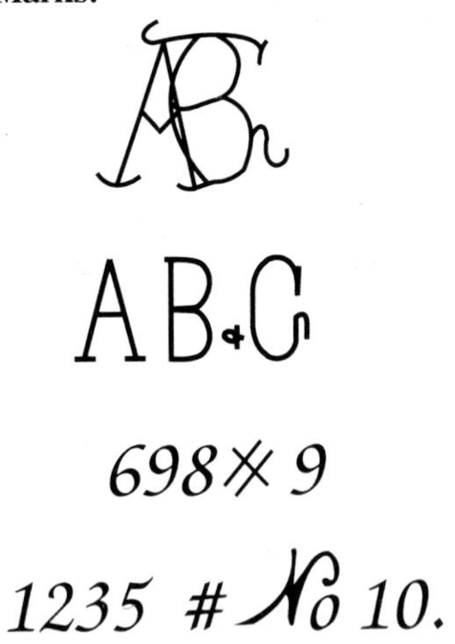

Babies: After 1909. Open mouth, some have pierced nostrils, bent leg baby body and are wigged. Prices will be higher if on toddler body or has flirty eyes. Clean, nicely dressed and with no cracks, chips or hairlines. 12-13" - $395.00; 17" - $550.00; 21" - $800.00; 25" - $1,400.00.

Child: Socket head on jointed composition body, sleep or set eyes. No crack, chips or hairlines. Clean and nicely dressed. 12" - $400.00; 14" - $450.00; 17" - $500.00; 21" - $625.00; 25" - $750.00; 31" - $1,400.00; 36" - $1,800.00; 40-42" - $2,700.00.

Character Child: Ca. 1910 on. Socket head on jointed composition body, sleep or set eyes, open mouth. Nicely dressed with good wig or molded hair with no hairlines, cracks or chips. **#1322:** 15" - $495.00; 19" - $700.00. **#1352:** 12" - $395.00; 16" - $495.00; 21" - $800.00. **#1357:** 14" - $625.00; 18" - $900.00. **#1358:** 14" - $1,700.00; 18" - $2,900.00. **#1361:** 12" - $395.00; 16" - $495.00; 21" - $800.00.

Turned Shoulder Head: Bald head or plaster pate, closed mouth, glass eyes, kid body with bisque lower arms. All in good condition with no chips, hairline and nicely dressed. Ca. 1870's and 1880's. Some have the Wagner & Zetzsche mark on head or paper label inside top of body. Some mold numbers include: 639, 698, 870, 911, 916, 1044, 1123, 1127, 1234, 1235. 16" - $750.00; 20" - $900.00; 24" - $1,200.00.

Turned Shoulder Head: Same as above, but with open mouth. 16" - $475.00; 20" - $575.00; 24" - $700.00.

20" lady style doll marked "639." Pale bisque turned shoulder head with closed mouth, kid body with bisque lower arms. Attributed to Alt, Beck & Gottschalck. Courtesy Frasher Doll Auctions. 20" - $900.00.

22" baby marked "ABG 1361 58." Bisque head with sleep eyes, open mouth and on five-piece bent limb baby body. Courtesy Frasher Doll Auctions. 22" - $900.00.

28" Marked "A.B.G./1362/Made in Germany/4. Socket head on jointed body, open mouth and pierced ears. Courtesy Arthur Bouliette. 28" - $1,400.00.

Louis Amberg & Sons were in business from 1878 to 1930 in New York City and Cincinnati, Ohio.

Marks:

L.A. & S. 1926

AMBERG
DOLLS
THE WORLD
STANDARD
MADE
IN
U.S.A.

AMBERG
L.A. & S. 1928

Prices for dolls in perfect condition, no cracks, chips or breaks, clean and nicely dressed.

Baby Peggy (Montgomery): 1923 and 1924. Closed mouth, socket head. Mold numbers 973 or 972: 18" - $2,900.00; 22" - $3,200.00.

Baby Peggy: Shoulder head. Mold numbers 983 or 982: 18" - $2,900.00; 22" - $3,200.00.

Baby Peggy: All bisque. See "All Bisque" section.

Baby Peggy: Composition head and limbs with cloth body, painted eyes, closed mouth, molded brown short bobbed hairdo. 1923. 12" - $350.00; 16" - $550.00; 19" - $800.00.

Charlie Chaplin: 1915-1920's. Portrait head of composition with painted features, composition hands, cloth body and legs. Black suit and white shirt. Cloth tag on sleeve or inside seam of coat. 13-14" - $475.00.

Newborn Babe: Bisque head with cloth body and can have celluloid, composition or rubber hands. Lightly painted hair, sleep eyes, closed mouth with protruding uppper lip. 1914 and reissued in 1924. Marks: "L.A.&S. 1914/G45520 Germany." Some will be marked "L. Amberg and Son/886" and some will be marked "Copyright by Louis Amberg." 9-10" - $475.00; 14" - $675.00; 18" - $1,200.00.

Newborn Babe: Open mouth version. Marked "L.A.&S. 371." 9-10" - $325.00; 14" - $500.00.

Mibs: Marked "L.A.&S. 1921/Germany" and can have two different paper labels with one "Amberg Dolls/Please Love Me/I'm Mibs," and some with the same label, but does not carry the name of Amberg. Molded hair with long strand down center of forehead. Composition head and limbs with cloth body, painted eyes. All in good condition. 12" - $500.00; 16-17" - $800.00.

Mibs: All bisque. See all bisque section.

Sue (or Edwina): All composition with painted features, molded hair and with a waist that swivels on a large ball attached to the torso. Jointed shoulders, neck and hips. Molded hair has side part and swirl bangs across forehead. Marked "Amberg/Pat. Pen./ L.A.&S." 1928. 14" - $475.00

Twist Bodies: (Tiny Tots) 1926, 1928. All composition with swivel waist made from large ball attached to torso. Boy or girl with molded hair and painted features. Tag attached to clothes: "An Amberg Doll/Body Twist/ Pat. Pend. #32018." 7½"-8½" - $195.00.

Vanta Baby: Marked "Vanta Baby-Amberg." Composition head and limbs with fat legs. Cloth body, spring strung, sleep eyes, open/closed mouth with two teeth. Made to advertise Vanta baby garments. 1927. 18" - $275.00.

Vanta Baby: Same as above, but with bisque head. 22" - $1,400.00; 26" - $1,850.00.

26" Vanta baby marked: "Amberg 1927." Glass eyes with hair lashes, open mouth with molded tongue and upper teeth, molded hair and a five-piece bent limb baby body. Courtesy Barbara Earnshaw-Cain. 26" - $1,850.00.

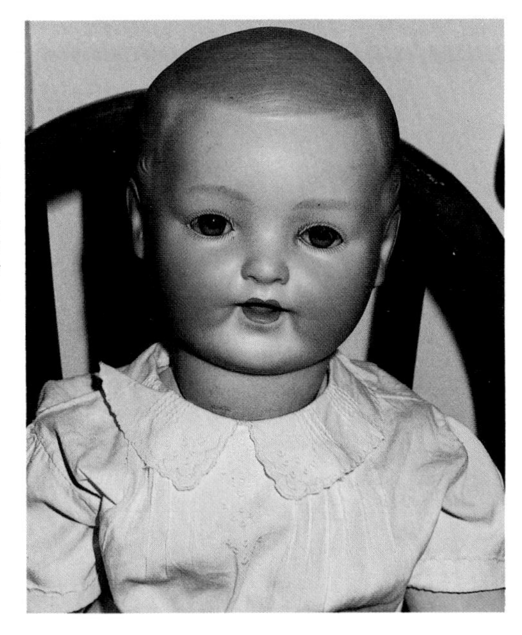

16" Amberg's "Mib." All composition, jointed neck, shoulder and hips, painted features. 14" "Edwina" 1928 Amberg doll that is all composition, painted hair and features. Marked "Amberg Pat. Pend. L.A.&S. 1928." Courtesy Jeanne Mauldin. 16" "Mibs" - $800.00. 14" "Edwina" - $475.00.

Center baby: 8" marked "L. Amberg & Son." Dress tagged "The Original Newborn Babe, Amberg Dolls." Sleep eyes, cloth body and composition hands. Tall girl is a Kestner marked "f½ Made in Germany 10¼ 167," and infant in chair is marked "11 HS Germany" and was made by Herm Steiner. Cloth body and composition hands. Courtesy Frasher Doll Auctions. 8" - $365.00. Kestner - $675.00. HS 12"- $350.00.

AMUSCO

Amusco dolls were made by August Moller & Sohn with the bisque heads being made in Germany. The name Amusco was registered in 1925.

Baby or Toddler: (Allow more for toddler body.) Bisque head, wig, sleep or set eyes and with open mouth (most marked with mold number "100.") 16" - $475.00; 20" - $700.00.

Baby or Toddler: (Allow more for toddler body.) Composition or painted bisque head and limbs with cloth body. Can have sleep, set or flirting eyes, closed mouth. 16" - $275.00; 20" - $425.00.

Prices are for perfect doll with no chips, cracks, breaks or hairline cracks, and needs to be clean and nicely dressed.

Armand Marseille made the majority of their dolls after the 1880's and into the 1920's, so they are some of the most often found dolls today. The factory was at Kopplesdorf, Germany. A.M. marked dolls can be of excellent to very poor quality. The finer the bisque and artist workmanship, the higher the price. This company made a great many heads for other companies also, such as George Borgfeldt, Amberg (Baby Peggy,) Hitz, Jacobs & Kassler, Otto Gans, Cuno & Otto Dressel, etc. They were marked with "A.M." or full name "Armand Marseille.

Mold #370, 326, 309, 273, 270, 375, 376, 920, 957: Kid or kidaleen bodies, open mouths. 15" - $250.00; 21" - $375.00; 26" - $550.00.

Mold #390, 266, 300, 310, (not "Googly"), 384, 391, 395: Socket head, jointed body and open mouth. 6" (closed mouth) - $225.00; 10" (crude 5-piece body) - $165.00; 10" (good quality jointed body) - $225.00; 14" - $275.00; 16" - $350.00; 18" - $400.00; 22" - $465.00; 24" - $525.00; 26" - $575.00; 28" - $650.00; 32" - $900.00.

Large Sizes Marked Just A.M.: Jointed bodies, socket head and open mouths. 36"- $1,500.00; 38" - $1,800.00; 42" - $2,500.00.

Mold Number 1776, 1890, 1892, 1893, 1894, 1896, 1897 (which can be a shoulder head or have a socket head); **1898, 1899, 1901, 1903, 1909:** Kid or kidaleen body, open mouth. (See below for prices if on composition bodies.) 12" - $165.00; 15" - $250.00; 18" - $325.00; 20" - $375.00; 22" - $400.00; 26" - $550.00.

Same As Above, On composition jointed bodies: 12" - $285.00; 15" - $400.00; 18" - $485.00; 20" - $550.00; 22" - $675.00; 26" - $785.00; 30" - $850.00; 36" - $1,500.00; 40" - $2,200.00.

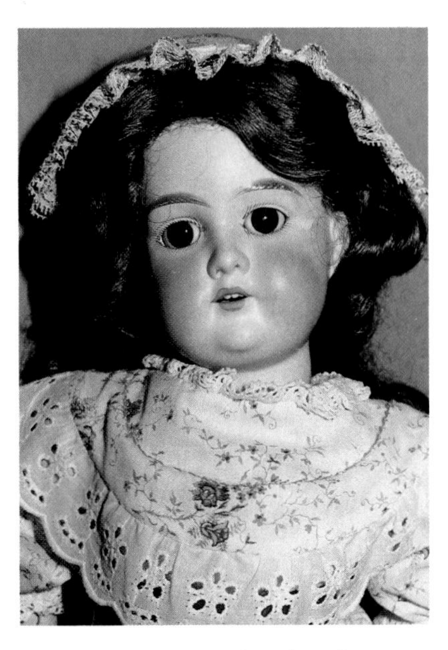

24" marked "Made in Germany Floradora." Fully jointed composition body, open mouth and sleep eyes. Courtesy Frasher Doll Auctions. 24" - $565.00.

Alma, Floradora, Mabel, Lilly, Darling, My Playmate, Sunshine, Dutchess: 1890's. Kid or kidaleen body. 9" - $165.00; 14" $225.00; 16" - $265.00; 18" - $350.00; 22" - $400.00; 25" - $500.00; 28" - $800.00; 32" - $1,000.00.

Same As Above, On Composition Body: 14" - $275.00; 18" - $400.00; 22" - $465.00; 25" - $565.00; 28" - $675.00; 32" - $925.00.

Queen Louise, Beauty, Columbia, Jubilee, Majestic, Princess, Rosebud: Kid or kidaleen body. 10" - $150.00; 12" - $175.00; 14" - $250.00; 16" - $300.00; 18" - $375.00; 20" - $400.00; 24" - $500.00; 28" - $850.00; 32" - $1,100.00.

Same as last listing, on composition body: 14" - $275.00; 18" - $375.00; 24" - $1,100.00; 28" - $825.00; 32" - $1,100.00.

Babies (infant style): Some from 1910; others from 1924. Can be on composition bodies, or have cloth bodies with curved or straight cloth legs. (Add $100.00-150.00 more for toddler babies.)

Mold #340, 341: With closed mouth (My Dream Baby, also called "Rock-A-Bye Baby.") Made for the Arranbee Doll Co. 6-7" - $185.00; 9" - $250.00; 12" - $365.00; 14" - $550.00; 16" - $650.00; 20" - $750.00; 24" - $1,000.00; 28" - $1,400.00.

Mold #345, 351: With open mouth. Same as above, but some will also be marked "Kiddiejoy" or "Our Pet." 7-8" - $195.00; 10" - $265.00; 14" - $550.00; 20" - $750.00; 28" - $1,400.00.

Mold #340, 341 or 345, 351: Twin puppets in basket - $850.00 up. Hand puppet, single doll - $350.00.

Mold #341, 345, 351 ("Kiddiejoy" or "Our Pet): With fired-on black or brown color. See Black section.

Babies: 1910 on. (Add $100.00-150.00 for toddler bodies.) **Mold #256, 259, 326, 327, 329, 360, 750, 790, 900, 927, 971, 975, 980, 984, 985, 990, 991, 995, 996, 1321, 1333:** 10" - $275.00; 14" - $400.00; 16" - $450.00; 18" - $565.00; 22" - $675.00; 26" - $900.00. **Same mold numbers as above, but painted bisque:** 14" - $200.00; 18" - $350.00; 26" - $500.00.

Character Babies: 1910 on. (Add $100.00-150.00 for toddler body.) Composition jointed body. Can have open mouth or open/closed mouth.

Mold #233: 10" - $325.00; 14" - $585.00; 18" - $900.00.

Mold #248: With open/closed mouth: 14" - $1,600.00. With open mouth: 14" - $775.00.

Mold #251: With open/closed mouth. 14" - $1,600.00; 16" - $1,750.00.

Left:
17" marked "Germany G 327 B DRGM 259 A.9 M." On five-piece bent limb baby body, open mouth with two lower teeth. Holds a 5½" Shuco Teddy Bear with original banner "Berliner Teddy-Bar."

Right:
18" Baby by Kestner marked "JDK Z 226 Z." Courtesy Frasher Doll Auctions.
17" A.M. - $500.00; 18" Kestner - $800.00; Bear-$125.00 up.

19" Character Armand Marseille mold number 800. Large eyes and wide open/closed mouth with molded gum and tongue. Large cheek dimples an excellent quality bisque. Courtesy Barbara Earnshaw-Cain. 19" - $2,500.00.

Left: 15" marked "Germany 550 A 4 M DRGM. Closed smile mouth, sleep eyes and on composition jointed body. Right: 16" unmarked except for the number "28." Closed mouth with red accent line between lips. On jointed composition body. Courtesy Frasher Doll Auctions. 15" A.M. - $2,900.00. 16" unmarked - $2,000.00.

With open mouth, 16" - $800.00.

Mold #328: 10" - $265.00; 14" - $425.00; 18" - $600.00; 22" - $800.00.

Mold #346: 16" - $500.00; 20" - $650.00; 24" - $800.00.

Mold #352: 10" - $265.00; 14" - $365.00; 18" - $550.00; 22" - $800.00.

Mold #362: 10" - $275.00; 14" - $550.00; 20" - $800.00.

Mold #410: Two rows of teeth, some are retractable. 14" - $1,000.00; 16" - $1,400.00.

Mold #518: 14" - $550.00; 18" - $650.00.

Mold #506a: 12" - $450.00; 15" - $600.00; 18" - $800.00.

Mold #580: Has open/closed mouth. 16" - $1,500.00; 20" - $1,800.00.

Mold #590: Has open/closed mouth. 16" - $1,500.00; 20" - $1,900.00; Open mouth, 16" - $950.00.

Mold #970: 16" - $475.00; 20" - $700.00; 26" - $1,000.00.

Baby Gloria: Mold #240: 10" - $400.00; 14" - $600.00; 18" - $1,000.00; 24" - $1,400.00.

Baby Phyllis: Heads by Armand Marseille. Painted hair, closed mouth. 12" - $450.00; 16" - $700.00; 20" - $1,100.00.

Baby Florence: 12" - $450.00; 20" - $1,100.00.

Baby Betty: 1890's. Jointed composition child body, but few heads found on bent limb baby body. 16" - $525.00; 20" - $750.00.

Fany Baby: Mold #231 along with incised "Fany." Can be baby, toddler or child. With wig: 14" - $3,800.00; 18" - $6,800.00.

Fany Baby: Mold #230 along with incised "Fany." Molded hair. 14" - $5,200.00; 18"- $8,000.00; 25" - $9,800.00.

Melitta: Baby: 16" - $575.00; 20" - $800.00. Toddler: 20" - $1,000.00.

Character Child: 1910 on. May have wig, molded hair, glass or intaglio painted eyes and some will have fully closed mouths while others have open/closed mouth. For these prices, doll must be in excellent condition and have no damage.

Mold #250: 16" - $1,000.00.

Left: 13½" marked "251 G.B. Germany A. 0 M. DRGM 248." Open/closed mouth and on five-piece toddler body. Right: 21" marked "K*R Simon & Halbig 117n," open mouth and flirty sleep eyes. On fully jointed composition body. Courtesy Frasher Doll Auctions. 14" "251" toddler - $1,850.00. 21" "117n" - $2,200.00.

Mold #345: 12" - $1,200.00; 16" - $1,900.00.

Mold #350: Socket head, glass eyes, closed mouth. 10" - $1,400.00; 16" - $2,400.00; 20" - $3,600.00.

Mold #360: 14" - $395.00; 18" - $725.00.

Mold #372: "Kiddiejoy." Kid body, molded hair, glass eyes. 14" - $675.00; 17" - $925.00; 20" - $1,200.00.

Mold #400: Glass eyes, socket head and closed mouth. 14" - $2,600.00; 17" - $3,200.00; 24" - $3,800.00

Mold #449: Painted eyes, socket head and closed mouth. 10" - $500.00; 16" - $1,250.00.

Mold #450: Socket head, glass eyes and closed mouth. 19" - $1,200.00 up.

Mold #500, 520: Molded hair, intaglio eyes, open/closed mouth. 10" - $500.00; 16" - $950.00; 20" - $1,400.00.

Mold #500, 520: Wigged, glass eyes and open/closed mouth. 10" - $750.00; 16" - $1,100.00; 20" - $1,800.00.

Mold #550, 600: Molded hair, painted eyes. 10" - $1,200.00; 16" - $2,200.00. Glass eyes: 10" - $1,600.00; 16" - $2,900.00; 20" $3,800.00.

Mold #570, 590: Open mouth: 12" - $600.00; 16" - $950.00. Open/closed mouth: 16" - $1,700.00.

Mold #700, 701, 711: Glass eyes, closed mouth. 10" - $1,400.00; 16" - $2,800.00.

Mold #800, 820: Glass eyes, open/closed mouth. 16" - $1,900.00; 20" - $2,600.00.

Mold #950: Painted hair and eyes, open mouth. 12" - $500.00; 16" - $950.00.

Character with Closed Mouth Marked only "A.M.": Intaglio, 18" - $4,800.00 up. Glass eyes, 18" - $4,200.00.

Googly: See Googly section.

Just Me: See Googly section.

Black or Brown Dolls: See that section.

Adult Lady Dolls: 1910-1920's. Adult face with long, thin jointed limbs. Knee joint is above knee area.

Mold #300: 10" - $1,000.00.

Mold #400, 401: Closed mouth. 14" - $1,850.00; 16" - $2,300.00.

Mold #400, 401: Open mouth. 14" - $950.00; 16" - $1,200.00.

Painted Bisque: Mold #400, 401: 14" - $775.00; 16" $1,000.00.

Painted Bisque: Mold #242, 244, 246, etc. 14" - $300.00; 18" - $500.00; 26" - $750.00.

Biscoloid: Like painted bisque but material under paint more plastic type. (Mold #378, 966, etc.) 14" - $400.00; 18" $600.00.

29" marked "A 12 M 390." Sleep eyes, inset fur eyebrows, open mouth and on fully jointed composition body. Courtesy Aurthur Boutiette. 29" - $700.00.

Left: 9½" boy marked "Made in Germany 390 A 11/0 M." On five-piece body with painted shoes and socks. Set eyes. Right: 9" marked "Made in Germany 390." Five-piece body, painted-on shoes and socks and glued-on fur costume. Courtesy Frasher Auctions. 9-9½" - $225.00.

14" marked "Germany 970 A. 5 M." Unusual solid dome baby, sleep eyes, open mouth and on five-piece bent limb baby body. Courtesy Frasher Doll Auctions. 18" Steiff monkey, all straw stuffed, button in ear. 14" - $400.00. Monkey - $250.00 up.

Left: Baby marked "S & Q 201" and made by Schuetzmeister & Quendt. Rear: Baby by Kammer and Reinhardt marked "K * R 126." Right: Armand Marseille baby marked "346 A.M." Character face with sleep eyes, open mouth and solid dome with painted hair. Five-piece bent limb baby bodies on all dolls. Courtesy Turn of Century Antiques. 17" S&Q 201 - $585.00. 15" K*R 126 - $750.00. 20" A.M. 346 - $650.00.

A. Thuillier made dolls in Paris from 1875 to 1893 and may be the maker of the dolls marked with "A.T." A.T. marked dolls can be found on wooden, jointed composition or kid bodies and can range in sizes from 14" to 30". The dolls can have closed mouths or open mouths with two rows of teeth. The following prices are for marked A.T. dolls on correct body, clean, beautiful face, dressed nicely and with no damage, such as a hairline cracks, chips or breaks.

Closed Mouth: 14" - $45,000.00 up; 18" - $50,000.00 up; 24" - $58,000.00 up; *26" - $65,000.00 up.

Open Mouth: **14" - $8,000.00 up; 18" - $18,000.00; 24" - $26,000.00.

** 26" - $68,000.00 at auction.*
*** 14" - $47,000.00 at auction.*

Marks:

A.T. N°3

A N°6 T

A. 8 T.

Above photo:
25" marked "A 12 T." Beautiful bisque head that is a socket head on jointed body with straight wrists. Courtesy Marlowe Cooper. 25" - $65,000.00 up.

Right photo:
14" A.T. with large expressive eyes, closed mouth and on jointed body with straight wrists. Courtesy Marlowe Cooper. 14" - $45,000.00 up.

AVERILL, GEORGENE (MADAME HENDRON)

Georgene Averill used the business names of Madame Georgene Dolls, Averill Mfg. Co., Georgene Novelties and Madame Hendron. Averill began making dolls in 1913 and designed a great many for George Borgfeldt.

First prices are for extra clean dolls and second for dolls with chips, craze lines, dirty or soiled or with part of or none of the original clothes.

Baby Georgene or Baby Hendron: Composition/cloth and marked with name on head. 16" - $195.00, $70.00; 22" - $285.00, $100.00.

16" Averill-Hendron whistling doll of 1929. Straw stuffed body and legs, molded hair, painted eyes and open whistling mouth. Lower arms are composition. Replaced clothes. Courtesy Jeannie Mauldin. 16" - $265.00.

Baby Yawn: Composition with closed eyes and yawn mouth. 17" - $300.00, $100.00.

Body Twist Dolls: Composition with large ball joint at waist, painted hair and features. 15" - $400.00, $100.00.

Bonnie Babe: Bisque head; Mold #1368-140. Cloth body, open mouth/two lower teeth, molded hair and composition arms/or hands. 14" - $700.00, $350.00; 22" - $1,400.00 up, $500.00. Celluloid head: 15-16" - $450.00 up, $100.00.

Bonnie Babe: All bisque: see "All Bisque" section.

Cloth Dolls: Mask face with painted features, yarn hair, cloth body. Clean condition for first price, second for soiled dolls.

International: 12" - $85.00, $30.00; 15" - $100.00, $45.00.

Children: 15" - $150.00, $65.00; 20" - $200.00, $80.00; 25" - $250.00, $95.00.

Tear Drop Baby: One tear painted on cheek. 16" - $250.00, $100.00.

Children: Composition, cloth body. Perfect and original. 18" - $350.00; less than mint - $145.00.

Comic Characters: All cloth with mask faces and painted features. Includes Little Lulu, Nancy, Sluggo, Topsy & Eva, Tubby Tom. 1940's - 1950's. 12" - $450.00, $175.00; 14" - $525.00, $250.00.

Dolly Dingle (for Grace Drayton): All cloth. 11" - $400.00, $150.00.

Fangel, Maude Tousey: All cloth. Marked "M.T.F." on tag. 12" - $485.00, $150.00.

Dolly Record: 1922. Composition with record player in back. 26" - $575.00, $300.00.

Googly: Composition/cloth. 14" - $275.00, $95.00; 16" - $325.00, $125.00; 19" - $550.00, $185.00.

Indian, Cowboy, Sailor, Soldier: Composition/cloth, molded hair or wig, sometimes yarn hair, painted features. 14" - $300.00, $100.00.

Snookums: Composition/cloth. Smile face, character from George McManus's "The Newlyweds." 14" - $375.00, $125.00.

Vinyl Head, Laughing Child: With oil cloth body. 28" - $200.00, $85.00.

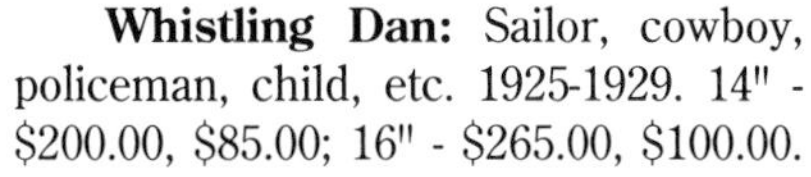

Whistling Dan: Sailor, cowboy, policeman, child, etc. 1925-1929. 14" - $200.00, $85.00; 16" - $265.00, $100.00.

Whistling Rufus: Black doll. 14" - $400.00, $125.00.

Whistling Dolly Dingle: 14" - $400.00, $125.00.

Babies, Infant Types: 1920's. Composition/cloth, painted hair, sleep eyes. 14-16" - $175.00, $70.00; 22-23" - $245.00, $100.00.

18" "Krazy Kat" made of felt and has cut out face that is machine stitched on, red felt tie and footpads. All straw stuffed and unjointed. Tag: "Krazy Kat Manufactured under special arrangement with Geo. Harriman, patent applied for, Averill Mfg. Co. Union Square W. N.Y." Appeared in Nov. 1916 "Playthings," selling for $12.00 a dozen. 5½" "Ignatz Mouse," all wood. Courtesy Margot Mandel. 18" - $500.00. 5½" - $175.00 up.

Beautiful 18" child doll by Averill-Hendren. Cloth body and composition shoulder plate, head and limbs. Open mouth with three upper teeth. Molded and painted hair, original clothes. Sleep eyes. Ca. late 1920's or early 1930's. Courtesy Jeannie Mauldin. 18" - $350.00.

24" marked "Barclay Baby Belle Germany." Sleep eyes, open mouth, excellent quality bisque. On fully jointed composition body. Made and sold by Bawo & Dotter 1908 to 1910. Courtesy Frasher Doll Auctions. 18" - $750.00. 24" - $1,000.00. 30" - $1,800.00.

Bisque heads were made by Alt, Beck & Gottschalck in 1925. Celulloid heads were made in Germany, and composition heads were made in the U.S. by Cameo Doll Company. Designer of the doll was Joseph L. Kallus, owner of Cameo Doll Co.

Bisque Head: Molded hair, open mouth, glass eyes, cloth body. In overall good condition with no damage. 19-20" - $3,000.00.

Celluloid Head: Same as "Bisque Head" description. 16" - $800.00.

Composition Head: Same as above description. 16" - $675.00. Light craze: 16" - $500.00. Cracks and/or chips: 16" - $200.00.

All Bisque: 4½" - $1,400.00; 6½" - $1,800.00.

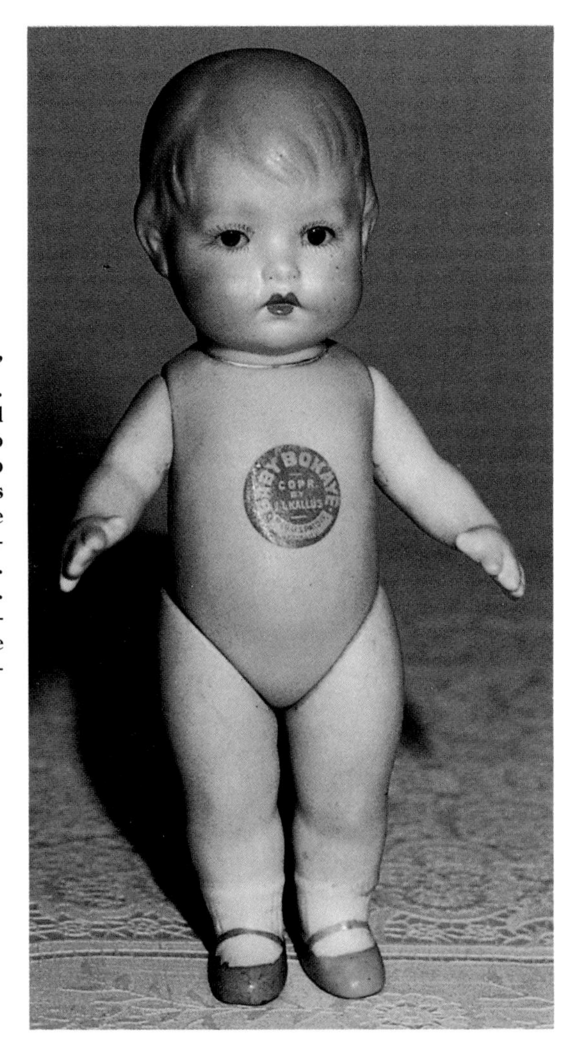

All bisque "Baby Bo-Kaye," 1925, made by Cameo. Jointed neck, shoulders and hips, open mouth with two upper teeth, glass sleep eyes and painted-on shoes and socks. Can also have pink shoes. Unmarked except for paper label. Courtesy Joanne Brunken. 4½" - $1,000.00. 6½" - $1,800.00. 20" bisque head and cloth body - $3,000.00.

Bahr & Proschild operated at Ohrdruf, Germany from 1871 into late 1920's. They also made dolls with celluloid (1910).

Character Baby: 1909 on. Bent limbs, sleep eyes, wigged and open mouths. Allow $100.00-150.00 more for toddler body. Clean, nicely dressed and no damage.

Mold #585, 587, 604, 624, 678, 619, 641: 13" - $500.00; 16" - $595.00; 19" - $685.00; 25" - $1,200.00.

Mold #169: 12" - $450.00; 16" - $650.00; 20" - $800.00.

Character Child: Can be on fully jointed composition body or toddler body. Ca 1910. Nicely dressed, clean and no damage. Can have molded hair or be wigged.

Mold #520, 526, 2072: Open/closed mouth. 16" - $4,200.00; 20" - $6,500.00.

Mold # in 200 and 300 Ser-ies: Now attributed to Bahr & Proschild. Can be on French bodies. Open mouth, jointed composition bodies. Ca. 1880's. Prior to recent findings, these dolls were attributed to Kestner.

Mold #224, 239, 246, 309, 379, etc.: As described above. 15" - $750.00; 18" - $825.00; 23" - $1,000.00.

Mold #224, 239, 246, 309, 379, etc.: On kid bodies, open mouth. 20" - $595.00; 25" - $725.00; 29" - $1,200.00.

Mold #224, 239, 246, 309, 379, etc.: Closed mouth, dome head and socket head on composition or kid body with bisque shoulder plate. 15" - $1,300.00; 20" - $1,900.00; 25" - $2,200.00.

Mold #2025: Painted eyes, closed mouth. 19" - $3,700.00 up.

Marks:

Beaporit

BP

B P

33" tall marked "(BP) 585/15/Germany." Open mouth with two upper teeth, flirty eyes and on very large, chubby five-piece toddler body. Voice box in torso. Courtesy Joanna Brunken. 33" toddler - $2,000.00

20" marked "8." Could be a Kestner or a Bahr & Proschild. Closed mouth, kid body with bisque lower arms. Baby is 14" and marked "585 6. By Bahr & Proschild." On five-piece bent limb baby body, open/closed mouth and sleep eyes. Courtesy Frasher Doll Auctions. 20" - $1,900.00. 14" - $500.00.

Bathing dolls can be in any position, including standing on base. They are all bisque and will have painted-on bathing costumes or be nude. They were made in Germany and some in the United States. Prices are for ones with no damage, chips or breaks, and must be clean.

Excellent quality bisque and artist workmanship: 3" - $225.00; 5-6" - $525.00; 8-9" - $800.00 up.

Fair quality of bisque and workmanship or marked Japan: 3" - $85.00; 5-6" - $125.00; 9" - $185.00.

Left Photo:
Foreground: 6" Bathing Beauty with wig and painted-on shoes. Marked "Germany."
Background: 9" all-bisque lady on base. Has solid dome and wig, molded-on necklace and shoes. Courtesy Frasher Doll Auctions. 6" - $525.00. 9" - $800.00.

Bottom Photo:
Bathing Beauty that is 3½" long. Bisque with pebble bathing suit. Marked "5684" on leg. $225.00. Courtesy Bonnie Stewart.

"Belton-type" dolls are not marked or will just have a number on the head. They have a concave top to a solid uncut head with one to three holes for stringing and/or plugging in wig. The German dome heads have a full round solid uncut head, but some of these may even have one or two holes in them. This style doll was made from 1875 on, and most likely a vast amount of these dolls were actually German made, although they must be on a French body to qualify as a "Belton-type." But since these dolls are found on French bodies, it can be assumed the German heads were made for French firms.

Prices are for dolls with excellent quality bisque, bodies that are French and have a straight wrist, nicely dressed and no damage.

8" on five-piece body - $825.00; 8" on jointed body - $975.00; 10" - $1,400.00; 12" - $1,800.00; 15" - $2,100.00; 18" - $2,500.00; 20" - $2,900.00; 23" - $3,200.00; 26" - $3,600.00. Bru Look: 16" - $2,000.00; 20" - $3,300.00.

14" Belton-type marked "111-6." Original wig, set eyes and on jointed body with straight wrists. Courtesy Sylvia Bryant. 14" - $1,900.00.

20" Belton-type with pink wash over eyes, open/closed mouth with space between lips, large paperweight eyes and on French jointed body with straight wrists. Courtesy Barbara Earnshaw-Cain. 20" - $2,900.00.

22" Belton-type with pale bisque, pink wash over eyes, open/closed mouth with space between, large paperweight eyes, and on early French body with straight wrist. Courtesy Barbara Earnshaw-Cain. 22" - $3,100.00.

Charles M. Bergmann made dolls from 1889 at both Walterhausen and Friedrichroda, Germany. Many of the Bergmann heads were made by other compaines for him, such as Simon & Halbig, Kestner, Armand Marseilles and others.

Marks:

C.M. BERGMANN

S. & H
C.M. BERGMANN
Walterhausen
Germany

Child: 1880's into early 1900's. On fully jointed composition bodies and open mouth. 18" - $475.00; 21" - $575.00; 24" - $625.00; 27" - $800.00; 30" - $1,000.00; 34" - $1,300.00; 40" - $2,400.00.

Character Baby: 1909 and after. Socket head on five bent limb baby body. Open mouth. 12" - $475.00; 16" - $625.00; 20" $750.00.

Mold # 612 Baby: Open/closed mouth. 16" - $1,000.00; 20" - $1,600.00.

Lady Doll: Adult-style body with long thin arms and legs. "Flapper-style" doll. 14" - $975.00; 17" - $1,700.00; 21"- $2,200.00.

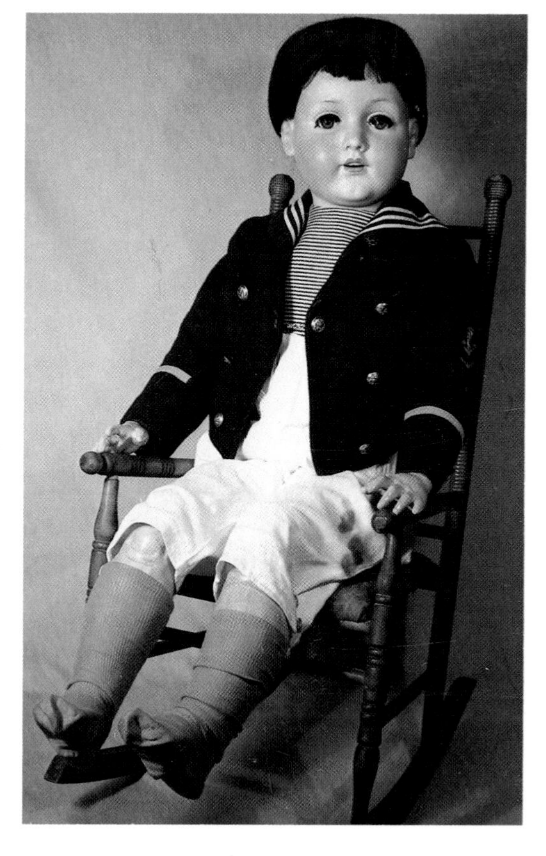

This 41" doll is marked "C.M. Bergmann, Walterhausen Germany 1916." Sleep eyes, open mouth with four teeth and on fully jointed composition body. Courtesy Frasher Doll Auctions. 41" - $2,500.00.

B.F.

The French dolls marked "B.F." were made by Ferte (Bébé Ferte), and some collectors refer to them as Bébé Française by Jumeau. They are now being attributed to Danel & Cie who also used the Bébé Française trademark. They have closed mouths and are on jointed French bodies with most having a straight wrist.

Marks:

B 6 F

Child: *12" - $2,400.00; 18" - $3,900.00; 20" - $4,200.00; 24" - $4,600.00; 27" - $4,900.00.

**All original in trunk or box: 15" - $4,800.00.*

B.L.

25" marked "B 11 L." Closed mouth and on French jointed body. Courtesy Frasher Doll Auctions. 25" -$4,900.00.

11½" marked "B 2 L." Closed mouth, pierced ears and on French jointed body. These dolls have been called "Bebe Louve" and now it is suspected that they are actually "Bebe Lefebvre," Alexandre Lefebvre made dolls from 1890 and by 1922 was part of S.F.B.J. 12" - $2,500.00.

Black or brown dolls can have fired-in color or be painted bisque, composition, cloth, papier mache′ and other materials. They can range from very black to a light tan and also be a "dolly" face or have Negroid features. The quality of these dolls differ greatly and prices are based on this quality. Both the French and German made these dolls. Prices are for undamaged, nicely dressed and clean dolls.

Alabama: See Cloth Doll section.

All Bisque: Glass eyes, one-piece body and head. 4-5" - $400.00.

All Bisque: Glass eyes, swivel head. 4-5" - $800.00.

All Bisque: Painted eyes, one-piece body and head. 5" - $200.00. Swivel head: 5" - $400.00.

A.M. 341 or 351: 12" - $425.00; 14" - $585.00; 18" - $1,000.00.

A.M. 390: 15" - $550.00, 18" - $675.00; 23" - $900.00.

A.M. 390n: 16" - $575.00; 21" - $750.00.

14" marked "1368 Germany S&H Simon & Halbig." Very black bisque, open mouth with four teeth. Courtesy Frasher Doll Auctions. 14" - $5,400.00.

A.M. 518, 362, 396, 513: 16"- $725.00; 20" - $975.00.

A.M. 451, 458 (Indians): 10" - $325.00; 13" - $465.00.

A.M. 971, 992, 995 Baby or Toddler: 10" - $285.00; 14" - $585.00; 18" - $875.00.

A.M 1894, 1897, 1914: 14" - $750.00; 17" - $950.00.

Baby Grumpy: Made by Effanbee. 12" - $285.00; 14-15" - $425.00. Craze, dirty: 12" - $100.00; 14" - $200.00.

Bahr & Proschild #277: Open mouth. 11-12" - $650.00; 14" - $750.00; 17" - $965.00.

Bruckner: See Cloth Section.

Bru Jne: 17" - $30,000.00 up; 22" - $44,000.00 up.

Bru, Circle Dot or Brevette: 17" - $33,000.00 up.

Bubbles: Made by Effanbee. 16" - $400.00; 20" - $650.00. Craze, dirty: 16" - $150.00; 20" - $225.00.

Bye-Lo: 13" - $2,800.00.

Candy Kid: 12" - $325.00. Craze, dirty: 12" - $125.00.

Celluloid: All cellulid (more for glass eyes.) 16" - $325.00; 19" - $700.00. Celluloid shoulder head, kid body (more for glass eyes): 16" - $250.00; 19" - $400.00.

Chase: 24" - $6,200.00; 28" - $6,900.00.

Cloth: See cloth section.

Composition: Made in Germany. 14" - $550.00; 18" - $675.00; 22" - $850.00; 26" - $1,100.00.

E.D.: Open mouth: 18" - $2,000.00; 24" - $2,600.00.

French, Unmarked: Closed mouth, bisque head: 14" - $3,200.00; 18" - $4,400.00. Painted bisque: 14" - $950.00; 18" - $1,200.00.

French, Unmarked: Open mouth, bisque head: 12" - $650.00; 16" - $1,300.00; 21" - $1,900.00. Painted bisque: 16" - $600.00; 21" - $850.00.

18" French Black character doll incised "8." Set eyes, molded eyelids, open mouth with very full lips and four teeth. French jointed body. Has old and may be original clothes and hat. Courtesy Frasher Doll Auctions. 18" - $5,600.00 up.

Left: 13½" unmarked "Kaiser Baby" by Kammer and Reinhardt. Solid dome, closed mouth, five-piece bent limb baby body. Right: 9½" marked "S&H 739." Jointed body, mouth has slightly parted lips, four tiny teeth, straight wrists. Courtesy Frasher Doll Auctions. 13½" - $800.00. 9½" S&H - $550.00.

Frozen Charlotte or Charlie: 3" - $65.00; 6" - $85.00; 8" - $100.00. Jointed shoulder: 3" - $95.00; 6" - $125.00.

German, Unmarked: Closed mouth, bisque head: 6½" - $300.00; 9" - $500.00; 14" - $850.00; 18" - $1,400.00. Painted bisque: 14" - $325.00; 20" - $575.00.

German, Open Mouth: Bisque head: 12" - $325.00; 16" - $550.00; 19" - $950.00. Painted bisque: 16" - $325.00; 19" - $550.00.

Heinrich Handwreck: Open mouth. 16" - $750.00; 20" - $950.00; 24" - $1,400.00.

Hanna: Made by Schoenau & Hoffmeister. 8" - $425.00; 12" - $650.00; 16" - $1,000.00.

Heubach, Gebruder Mold #7668: Wide smile mouth. 12" - $2,200.00; 14" - $2,600.00.

Heubach, Gebruder #7658, 7671: 8" - $1,000.00; 12" - $1,700.00; 14" - $2,000.00, 17" - $2,600.00.

Heubach, Gebruder: (Sunburst mark) Boy, eyes to side. 11" - $1,800.00.

Heubach Koppelsdorf Mold #320, 339: 9" - $350.00; 12" - $475.00; 16" - $675.00; 20" - $900.00; 22" - $1,200.00.

Heubach Koppelsdorf Mold #399: Allow more for toddler. 9" - $475.00; 12" - $550.00; 16" - $700.00. Celluloid: 12" - $250.00; 18" - $550.00.

Heubach Koppelsdorf Mold #300, 414: 12" - $625.00; 16" - $1,000.00; 18" - $1,400.00.

Heubach Koppelsdorf Mold #418: (Grin.) 10-11" - $700.00; 16" - $1,200.00.

Heubach Koppelsdorf Mold #463: 10" - $500.00; 14" - $825.00.

Heubach Koppelsdorf Mold #444, 451: 10" - $500.00; 14" - $825.00.

Heubach Koppelsdorf Mold #452: 9" - $325.00; 12" - $500.00.

Heubach Koppelsdorf Mold #458: 12" - $500.00; 16" - $700.00.

Heubach Koppelsdorf Mold #1900: 13" - $450.00; 16" $650.00.

Hottentot: (Kewpie) All bisque. 5" - $500.00 up. Maché: 8" - $150.00.

Kestner #134: 13-14" - $950.00.

Kestner #245, 237: Hilda. 12-13" - $3,800.00; 15" - $4,500.00; 17" - $5,400.00.

Kestner: Child, no mold number. 10" - $475.00; 14" - $600.00. Five-piece body: 10" - $325.00.

Jumeau: Open mouth. 12" - $1,900.00; 16" - $2,600.00; 21" - $3,200.00.

Jumeau: Closed mouth. 12" - $4,000.00; 16" - $4,800.00; 21" - $6,200.00.

Jumeau: Marked "E.J." 12" - $6,000.00; 16" - $7,200.00.

K Star R: Child, no mold number. 14" - $600.00.

K Star R #100: 12" - $800.00; 16" - $1,600.00; 18" - $2,200.00.

K Star R #101: 16" - $5,200.00.

K Star R #116, 116a: 16" - $3,000.00; 18" - $3,400.00.

K Star R #126: Baby. 11-12" - $750.00; 18" - $1,200.00.

23" marked "390 A. 7M." Set eyes, open mouth with four teeth and on fully jointed composition body. Holds a German bisque head Marotte toy. Open mouth, bisque head marked "13/0." Plays music as doll revolves. Original. Courtesy Frasher Doll Auctions. 23" - $900.00. Toy - $450.00.

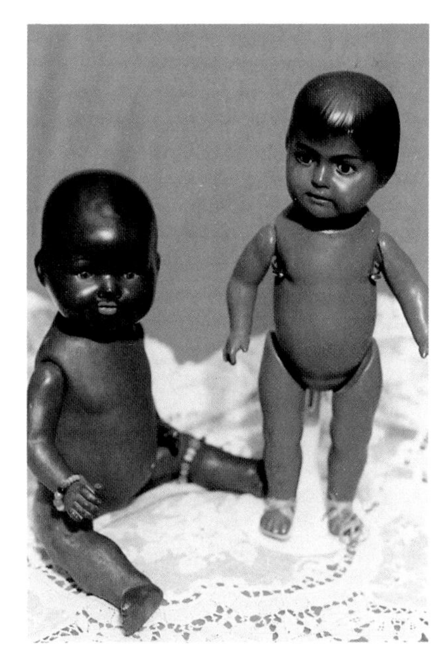

Left: 11" bisque head marked "A.M. Germany 351." Open mouth with two lower teeth, bent limb baby body.
Right: 10" marked "Heubach Koppelsdorf 451." Molded hair, open mouth, two tiny lower teeth and on five-piece child body. Courtesy Frasher Doll Auctions. 11" A.M. - $425.00. 10" #451 - $450.00.

Kewpie: Composition. 12" - $300.00. Toddler, 12" - $650.00; 16" - $975.00.

Papier Maché: Negroid features: 14" - $675.00. Others: 14" - $300.00; 24" - $500.00.

Paris Be'be': 16" - $4,500.00.

Recknagel: Marked "R.A." May have mold #138. 14" - $900.00; 20" - $1,900.00.

Schoenau & Hoffmeister #1909: 14" - $575.00; 17" - $675.00.

Scowling Indian: 10" - $325.00; 13" - $465.00.

Scootles: Composition: 15" - $725.00 up. Vinyl: 14" - $225.00; 19" - $400.00; 27" - $585.00.

Simon & Halbig #739: 24" - $4,000.00.

Simon & Halbig #939: Closed mouth: 17" - $3,000.00; 20" - $4,200.00. Open mouth: 17" - $1,700.00.

Simon & Halbig #949: Closed mouth: 17" - $2,400.00; 20" - $3,000.00. Open mouth: 17" - $1,400.00.

Simon & Halbig #1039, 1079: Open mouth: 14" - $650.00; 17" - $1,000.00.

Simon & Halbig #1248: Open mouth. 14" - $750.00.

Simon & Halbig #1358: 14" - $5,000.00; 17" - $6,200.00.

Simon & Halbig #1368: 14" - $5,600.00.

S.F.B.J. #301 or 60: Open mouth. 15" - $600.00; 17" - $850.00.

S.F.B.J. #235: Open/closed mouth. 14" - $2,500.00.

S.F.B.J. 34-29: Open mouth. 21" - $5,200.00 up.

Sarg, Tony: Mammy Doll. Composition/cloth. 18" - $575.00.

Steiner, Jules: Open mouth. "A" series: 14" - $2,800.00; 17" - $4,700.00.

Steiner, Jules: Closed mouth. "A" series: 15" - $5,000.00; "C" series: 15" - $4,800.00.

Stockenette: Oil painted features. 18" - $2,800.00 up.

S & Q #251: 10" - $650.00; 14" - $850.00. **#252:** $1,900.00.

Unis #301 or 60: Open mouth. 15" - $550.00; 17" - $800.00.

Left: 14" brown composition character with open/closed mouth and two molded teeth, deep intaglio painted eyes. Cloth body and legs and composition lower arms. Unmarked. Right: 16" celluloid marked "France 40." Celluloid toddler body with jointed wrists. Courtesy Frasher Doll Auctions. 14" - $550.00. 16" - $375.00.

8" all original "war painted" Indians from the Seminole tribe of the lower Eastern States. The man's face is thinner than the woman's face. Unmarked. On five-piece bodies. Courtesy Barbara Earnshaw-Cain.
8" - $400.00 each.

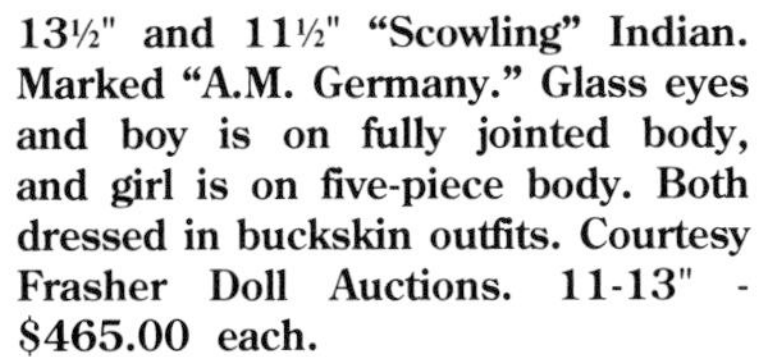

13½" and 11½" "Scowling" Indian. Marked "A.M. Germany." Glass eyes and boy is on fully jointed body, and girl is on five-piece body. Both dressed in buckskin outfits. Courtesy Frasher Doll Auctions. 11-13" - $465.00 each.

14" papier maché solid dome head with original wig, large lips, jointed body, painted features and has some original clothes, but no shoes. Unmarked. Courtesy Frasher Doll Auctions. 14" - $675.00.

13" unusual Bonnet doll with cloth body and stone bisque lower limbs. Nicely detailed face with molded hair and modeled on bonnet with flowers at side of head and has modeled shirt waist top with high ruffled neck. Courtesy Barbara Earnshaw-Cain. 13" - $675.00.

18" tall Bonnet doll with cloth body and stone bisque lower limbs. Has modeled shirt waist top with molded necklace and unusual tam-type hat on top of curls. Courtesy Barbara Earnshaw-Cain. 18" - $900.00.

13" tall Bonnet that is called "Butterfly" with the bonnet ties on chest painted gold. Cloth body with stone bisque lower limbs. Courtesy Barbara Earnshaw-Cain. 13" - $485.00.

The "Bonnie Babe" was designed by Georgene Averill in 1926 with the bisque heads being made by Alt, Beck & Gottschalck and the cloth bodies made by the K & K Toy Co. (NY). The dolls were distributed by George Borgfeldt. The doll can have cloth body and legs or can have composition arms and legs.

Marks: "Copr. by Georgene Averill/Germany/1005/3652" and sometimes "1368."

Bisque head, open, crooked smile mouth: 14" - $700.00; 23" - $1,500.00.

Celluloid head: 9" - $350.00; 15" - $600.00.

All Bisque: See the All Bisque section.

12½" tiny "Bonnie Babe" marked "Copr. by Georgene Averill 1003/3562 2/10 Germany." Flange bisque head with sleep eyes, painted hair, open mouth with lopsided smile and two lower teeth. Cloth body with celluloid hands. Original clothes. Courtesy Frasher Doll Auctions. 12" - $600.00.

BORGFELDT, GEORGE

George Borgfeldt imported, distributed and assembled dolls in New York, and the dolls that he carried or had made ranged from bisque to composition. He had many dolls made for him in Germany.

Marks: "G.B."

Child: Fully jointed composition body, open mouth. No damage and nicely dressed. 20" - $500.00; 25" - $675.00.

Baby: Five-piece bent limb baby body, open mouth. 20" - $825.00; 26" - $1,400.00.

Right: 27" character baby marked "G.B. Made in Germany for George Borgfeldt." Open mouth with molded tongue and two upper teeth. Five-piece bent limb baby body. Head circumference is 17½". Courtesy Frasher Doll Auctions. 27" - $1,500.00 up.

Left: 24" marked "G.B." Jointed body, open mouth and set eyes. Made in Germany for George Borgfeldt. Courtesy Frasher Doll Auctions. 24" - $650.00.

Boudoir dolls are also called "Flapper" dolls and were most popular during the 1920's and early 1930's, although they were made through the 1940's. Very rarely is one of these dolls marked with the maker or country of origin, but the majority were made in the United States, France and Italy.

The most desirable Boudoir dolls are the ones from France and Italy (Lenci, especially, see that section.) These dolls will have silk or cloth painted face mask, have an elaborate

Top Photo: 28" mask face with painted features, all cloth body and limbs. Arms and legs are gusseted so they can be posed. Mohair wig and original clothes. Courtesy Bonnie Stewart. 28" - $485.00.

Right Photo: 25" Smoking Flapper with composition head that is a shoulder head. Composition hands hold a Martini glass with olive. Painted features, mohair wig and original clothes. Marked "V-K-S Ind." Courtesy Ann Wencel. 25" - $350.00 up.

costume, and are of overall excellent quality.

The least expensive ones have a full or half-composition head, some with glass eyes, and the clothes will be stapled or glued to the body.

Boudoir Dolls: With excellent quality, finely painted features and excellent clothes. 28" - $485.00; 32" - $575.00.

Boudoir Dolls: With composition head, stapled or glued-on clothes. No damage, and original clothes. 28" - $125.00; 32" - $165.00.

Smoking Doll: All cloth: 25" - $550.00 up. All composition: 25" - $350.00; 28" - $425.00.

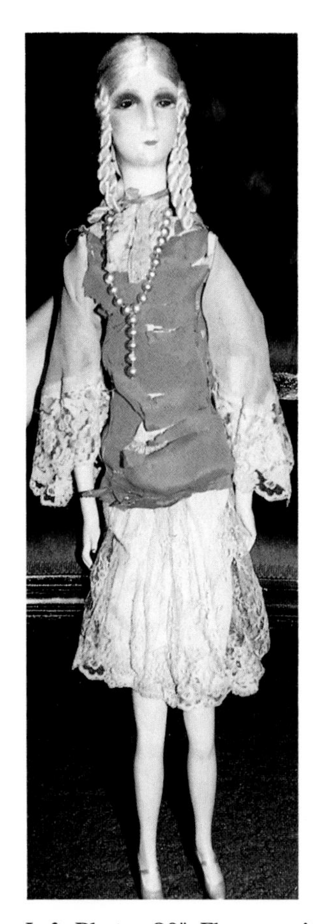

Left Photo: 30" Flapper with original clothing and beads. Silk oil painted face and silk thread hair. Arms and long legs are a plaster-style material with painted-on shoes. Probably made in France. Courtesy Bonnie Stewart. 30" - $500.00.

Right Photo: 21" Smoking Bed doll that is all original with mask face that is oil painted and has mohair wig. Rest is cloth. Original cigarette. Courtesy Bonnie Stewart. 21" - $475.00.

Bru dolls will be marked with the name Bru or Bru Jne, Bru Jne R. Some will have a circle and dot (⊙) or a half circle and dot (◠·). Some have paper labels - see below. Prices are for dolls with no damage at all, very clean, and beautifully dressed.

Marks:

Closed Mouth Dolls: *All kid body. Bisque lower arms. 16" - $9,000.00; 18" - $12,000.00; 21" - $18,000.00; 26" - $24,000.00.

Bru Jne*: Ca. 1880's. Kid over wood, wood legs, bisque lower arms. 12" - $20,000.00; 14" - $18,000.00; 16" - $20,000.00; 20" - $24,000.00; 22" - $26,000.00; 25" - $30,000.00 up; 28" - $36,000.00 up; 32" - $42,000.00 up.

Bru Jne: All wood body. 16" - $10,000.00; 18" - $14,000.00.

Circle Dot or Half Circle:** Ca. 1870's. 16" - $22,000.00; 19" - $25,000.00; 23" - $29,000.00; 26" - $32,000.00; 30" - $38,000.00.

Brevette:*** Ca. 1870's. 14" - $15,000.00; 17" - $20,000.00; 20" - $26,000.00.

Open Mouth Dolls: Bru Jne R. 1890's. Jointed composition body. First price for excellent quality bisque and second for poor quality bisque. 14" - $4,800.00, $3,200.00; 17" - $6,000.00, $4,000.00; 22" $7,200.00, $5,200.00; 25" - $8,200.00, $6,200.00; 28" - $9,000.00; $7,500.00.

Walker Body, Throws Kiss: 18" - $5,600.00; 22" - $6,400.00; 26" - $7,300.00.

Nursing Bru: 1878-1899. Operates by turning key in back of head. Early, excellent quality: 12" - $5,600.00; 15" - $7,800.00; 18" - $9,700.00. Not as good quality: 12" - $3,800.00; 15" - $5,400.00; 18" - $6,500.00. High color, late S.F.B.J. type: 12" - $1,900.00; 15" - $2,800.00; 18" $3,400.00.

Shoes: Marked "Bru Jne." 12" - $450.00; 17" - $650.00; 20" - $700.00.

** 11" all kid #O Bru and 11" Bru Jne at auction - $31,000.00.*

*** 11" - $21,000.00 at auction.*

**** 12" - $16,000.00 at auction.*

19" Bru Jne #3. Marked head and shoulder plate. Has kid over wood/wood walking body. Original wig and old costume. Courtesy Marlowe Cooper. 19" - $24,000.00.

Right: 13" marked "Bru Jne" on head and shoulder plate. May be original mohair wig. Bisque lower arms, wood lower legs. Original "Bébé Bru" sticker on front of body. Courtesy Frasher Doll Auctions. 13" - $17,000.00.

Left: 13" marked "Bru June 4" on head and shoulder plate. Bisque lower arms, kid over wood body and upper limbs and wood lower legs. Original factory clothes and wig. Has label on front of body "Bébé Bru." Courtesy Frasher Doll Auctions. 13" - $19,000.00.

23" marked "Bru Jne R 9." Open mouth with six teeth, French five-piece body, pierced ears. Courtesy Frasher Doll Auctions. 23" - $7,300.00.

The Bye-Lo baby was designed by Grace Storey Putnam, distributed by George Borgfeldt and the cloth bodies were made by K & K Toy Co. of NY. The bisque heads were made by Kestner, Alt & Gottschalck and others. The all bisque was made by Kestner. The dolls date from 1922. Celluloid or composition hands. Prices are for undamaged, clean and nicely dressed dolls.

Marks:

1923 by
Grace S. Putnam
Made in Germany
7372145

Copy. By
Grace S. Putnam

Bye-Lo Baby
Pat. Appl'd For

All measured by head circumference.

Bisque Head: 10" - $475.00; 12"- $600.00; 15" - $1,000.00; 18" - $1,600.00.

Smiling Mouth: Bisque - very rare. 14" - $4,800.00 up.

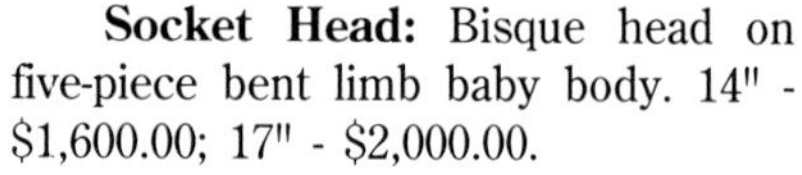

Socket Head: Bisque head on five-piece bent limb baby body. 14" - $1,600.00; 17" - $2,000.00.

Composition Head: 10" - $325.00; 12" - $400.00; 15" - $525.00.

Painted Bisque: With cloth body, composition hands. 10" - $275.00; 13" - $400.00; 15" - $600.00.

Wood: by Schoenhut. Cloth body, wooden hands. 13" - $1,800.00.

Celluloid: All celluloid: 6" - $200.00. Celluloid head/cloth body: 10" - $400.00.

All Bisque: See All Bisque section, Characters.

Vinyl Heads: Early 1950's. Cloth/stuffed limbs. Marked "Grace Storey Putman" on head. 16" - $300.00.

Honey Child: Bye-lo look-a-like made by Bayless Bros. & Co. in 1926. 16" - $300.00; 20" - $450.00.

Wax Bye-lo: Cloth or sateen body. 15-16" - $3,800.00.

Basket with blanket and extra clothes: Five babies in basket, bisque heads: 12" - $4,200.00 up. Composition heads: 12" - $3,000.00 up.

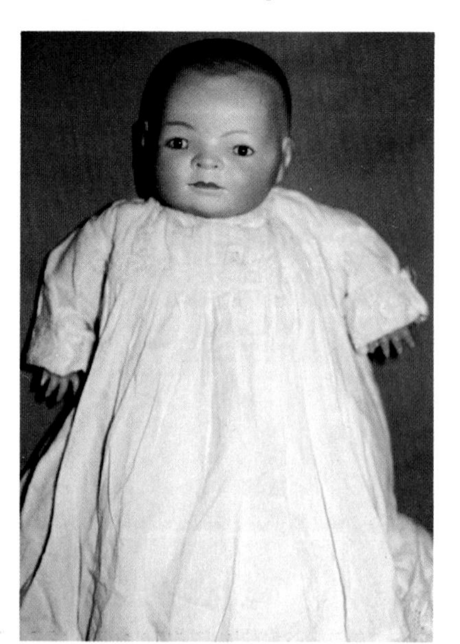

17" long with 14" head circumference marked "Copr. Grace S. Putnam Made in Germany." Bye-lo with bisque head, celluloid hands and frog-style cloth body. Body marked "Bye-Lo Baby. Pat. Appl'd for Grace Storey Putnam. Courtesy Frasher Doll Auctions. 17" - $1,000.00.

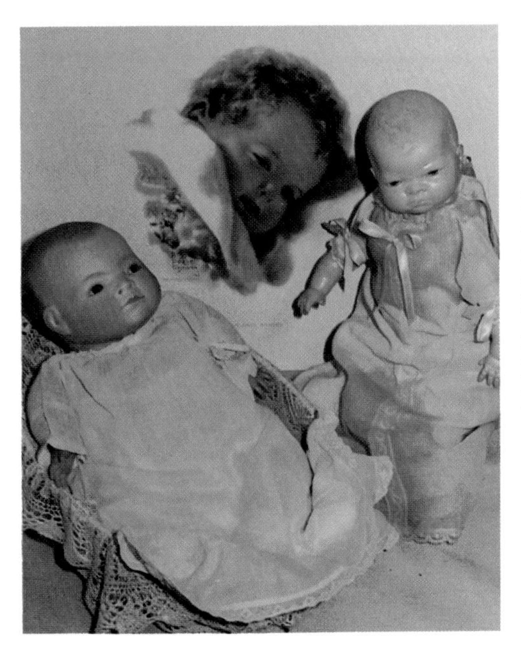

Left: 13" Bye-Lo with 12½" head circumference. Marked "Copr. Grace S. Putnam." Sleep eyes, cloth body. Right: 15" early vinyl head marked "Grace Storey Putnam." Has vinyl arms and legs, pink cloth body and painted blue eyes. Dress has cloth "Bye-Lo" label. Courtesy Frasher Doll Auctions. 13" - $650.00; 15" - $275.00.

CATTERFELDER PUPPENFABRIK

Catterfelder Puppenfabrik of Germany made dolls from 1902 until the late 1930's. The heads for their dolls were made by various German firms, including Kestner.

Marks:

CP
219
5

C P
201/40
Deponiert

Catterfelder
Puppenfabrik
45

Child: Ca. 1900's. Composition jointed body. Open mouth. Mold #264 or marked "C.P." 17" - $585.00; 23" - $785.00.

Character Child: 1910 or after. Composition jointed body, closed mouth and can be boy or girl, with character face. **Mold #207:** 15" - $3,600.00. **Mold #215:** 15" - $3,800.00. **Mold #219:** 16" - $3,400.00; 20" - $4,400.00.

Babies: 1909 or after. Wig or molded hair, five-piece bent limb baby body, glass or painted eyes.

Mold #262, 263: 15" - $575.00; 25" - $1,000.00.

Mold #200, 201: 16" - $600.00.

Mold #208, 209, etc.: 14" - $550.00; 18" - $700.00; 22" - $975.00; 26" - $1,200.00.

CATTERFELDER PUPPENFABRIK

Right: 19" marked "Catterfelder Puppenfabrik 264 2." Sleep eyes, open mouth and on fully jointed composition body. Left: 17" marked "Heubach Koppelsdorf 250. 2/9 Germany." Open mouth, sleep eyes and fully jointed composition body. Courtesy Frasher Doll Auctions. 19" - $675.00; 17" - $350.00.

CELLULOID DOLLS

Celluloid dolls date from the 1880's into the 1940's when they were made illegal in the United States because they burned or exploded if placed near an open flame or heat. Some of the makers were:

United States: Marks Bros., Irwin, Horsman, Averill, Parsons-Jackson, Celluloid Novelity Co., etc.

France: Societe Industrielle de Celluloid (Sisoine), Petitcolin (eagle symbol), Societe Nobel Francaise (SNF in diamond), Jumeau/Unis (1950's).

Germany: Rheinische Gummi and Celluloid Fabrik Co. (turtle mark), Minerva (Buschow & Beck) (helmet symbol), E. Maar & Sohn (3 M's mark), Adelheid Nogler Innsbruck Doll Co. (animal with spread wings and a fish tail, in square), Cellba (mermaid symbol).

21" celluloid shoulder head with glass eyes, open mouth, kid body with composition lower arms. Marked with turtle mark, Germany. 21" - $325.00.

Prices for perfect, undamaged dolls.

All Celluloid Baby: Painted eyes: 7" - $85.00; 10" - $145.00; 14" - $185.00; 16" - $200.00; 19" - $250.00; 22" - $325.00; 26" - $450.00. Glass inset eyes: 14" - $165.00; 16" - $275.00; 19" - $345.00; 22" - $400.00.

All Celluloid Dolls: (Germany) Jointed at neck, shoulders and hips. Painted eyes: 5" - $65.00; 9" - $95.00; 12" - $145.00; 16" - $225.00; 19" - $350.00. Jointed at neck and shoulders only: 5" - $25.00; 7" - $40.00; 9" - $60.00.

All Celluloid Dolls: Same as above, but with Glass Eyes: 12" - $200.00; 16" - $300.00. Jointed at neck and shoulders only: 12" - $150.00.

All Celluloid Dolls: Same as above, but marked France: 7" - $150.00; 9" - $200.00; 12" - $265.00; 19" - $425.00.

All Celluloid, Molded on Clothes: Jointed at shoulders only. 5" - $65.00; 7" - $85.00; 9" - $125.00.

All Celluloid - Black Dolls: See Black Doll section.

Celluloid Shoulder Head: Germany. Molded hair or wigged, painted eyes, open or closed mouth, kid or kidaleen bodies, cloth bodies and can have any material for arms. 14" - $165.00; 17" - $225.00; 20" - $300.00.

Celluloid Shoulder Head: Same as above, but with glass eyes: 14" - $200.00; 17" - $275.00; 20" - $385.00.

12" all celluloid, jointed neck, shoulder and hips. Painted hair and features with open/closed mouth and painted teeth. All original clothes. Marked "Japan" on back. Excellent quality and detail. Courtesy Jeanne Mauldin. 12" original - $75.00.

8" all celluloid Hitler's Youth Group doll in original uniform, painted hair in Hitler style and painted-on shoes and features. 8" - $150.00.

Standing doll: 18" all celluloid toddler marked "K*R 728 Germany 43/46." Open mouth with two upper teeth and has original wig and clothes. Small sitting doll: 12" bisque head marked "150," open/closed mouth and bent limb body. Cradle is folding and ca. 1910. Courtesy Frasher Doll Auctions. 18" - $650.00. 12" - $285.00. Cradle - $175.00 up.

Celluloid Socket Heads: (Germany.) Glass eyes (allow more for flirty eyes). Ball-jointed body or five-piece bodies. Open or closed mouths. 15" - $350.00; 18" - $500.00; 22" - $600.00; 25" - $725.00.

Heubach Koppelsdorf Mold #399: Brown or Black. See Black section.

Kruse, Kathe: All original. 14" - $400.00; 17" - $650.00.

Kammer & Reinhardt: (K star R) Mold #700: 14"- $525.00. **Mold #701:** 12" - $800.00. **Mold #714 or 715:** 15" - $750.00. **Mold #717:** 20" - $800.00; 25" - $1,400.00. **Mold #728:** 15" - $525.00; 19" - $700.00.

Konig & Wernicke: (K&W) Toddler: 14" - $400.00; 20" - $600.00.

Japan: 5" - $30.00; 8" - $45.00; 12" - $75.00; 16" - $145.00; 19" - $225.00; 22" - $300.00; 26" - $375.00.

All celluloid boy and girl that are all original. Ca. 1946-1950. Glass sleep eyes/lashes, glued-on wigs. Turtle mark. Courtesy Turn of Century Antiques. 12" - $175.00.

Chad Valley dolls usually will have a felt face and all-velvet body that is jointed at the neck, shoulders and hips. They can have painted or glass eyes and will have a mohair wig. First prices are for those in mint condition and second price for dolls that are dirty, worn or soiled and/or do not have original clothes.

Marks: "Hygenic Toys/Made in England by/Chad Valley Co. Ltd."

"The Chad Valley Hygenic Textile/Toys/Made in England."

Child With Painted Eyes: 9" - $150.00, $20.00; 12" - $325.00, $100.00; 16" - $500.00, $225.00; 18" - $650.00, $365.00.

Child With Glass Eyes: 14" - $550.00, $200.00; 16" - $700.00, $300.00; 18" - $845.00, $400.00.

Child Representing Royal Family: (Four in set: Princess Elizabeth, Princess Margaret Rose, Prince Edward, Princess Alexandria. All four have glass eyes.) Prince Edward as Duke of Kent: 15" - $1,700.00, $600.00; as Duke of Windsor: 15" - $1,700.00, $600.00. Others: 15" - $1,000.00 up, $450.00.

Long John Silver, Captain Blye: 20" - $2,600.00.

Golliwog: 16-17" - $200.00.

16" Chad Valley English "Bobby" (Policeman). All cloth with glass eyes, mohair wig, velvet body and all original with original tag. Courtesy Frasher Doll Auctions. 16" - $1,000.00.

Martha Jenks Chase of Pawtucket, Rhode Island began making dolls in 1893, and they are still being made my members of the family. They all have oil pinted features and are made of stockenette and cloth. They will be marked "Chase Stockenette" on left leg or under the left arm. There is a paper label (often gone) on the backs with a drawn head:

The older Chase dolls are jointed at the shoulders, hips, knees and elbows where the newer dolls are jointed at the shoulders and hips with straight arms and legs. Prices are for very clean dolls with only minor wear.

Older Dolls:

Babies: 16" - $600.00; 20" - $785.00; 24" - $925.00.

Child: 12" - $485.00; 16" - $1,000.00; 20" - $2,000.00 up.

Lady*: 16" - $1,800.00 up; 24" - $2,400.00; Life size: $2,600.00.

Man: 16" - $1,900.00 up; 24" - $2,600.00; Life size: $2,800.00.

Black: 24" - $6,200.00; 28" - $6,900.00.

Newer Dolls:

Babies: 14" - $185.00; 16" - $225.00.

Child, boy or girl: 14" - $200.00; 16" - $250.00.

** 14-16" Lady with Bun/Braids at auction - $2,600.00.*

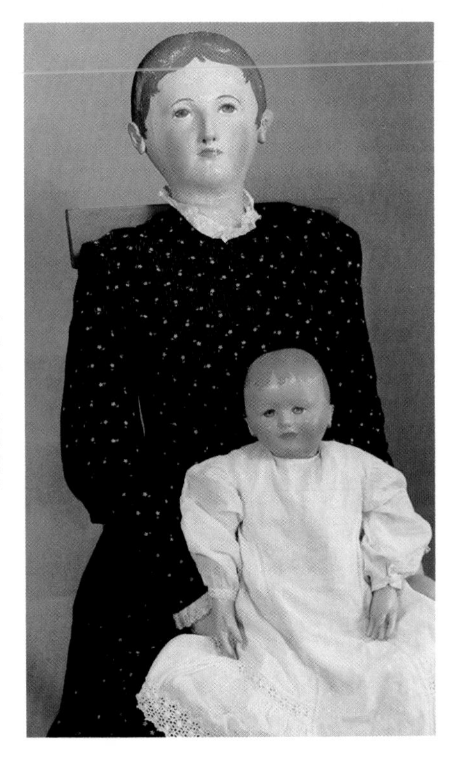

54" Martha Chase life-size lady. Head and body are stockenette, treated and painted in oils, open nostrils, jointed at shoulders, elbows, knees and hips. Baby is 24" and made of stockenette, treated and painted in oils and jointed same as lady. Courtesy Frasher Doll Auctions. 54" lady - $2,600.00; 24" baby - $925.00.

Almost all china heads were made in Germany between 1840 and the 1900's. Most have black hair, but blondes became popular by the 1880's and by 1900, one out of every three were blonde. China dolls can be on a cloth or kid body with leather or china limbs. Generally, these heads are unmarked, but a few will have a number and/or "Germany" on the back shoulder plate. Prices are for clean dolls with no cracks, chips, or repairs on a nice body and nicely dressed.

Adelina Patti: 1860's. Center part, roll curl from forehead to back on each side of head and "spit" curls at temples and above exposed ears. 14" - $325.00; 18" - $465.00; 22" - $625.00.

Bald Head/Biedermeir: Ca. 1840. Has bald head, some with top of head glazed black, takes wigs.

Excellent quality: 14" - $975.00; 20" - $1,500.00.

Medium quality: 16" - $475.00; 22" - $800.00.

Glass eyes: 24" - $2,800.00.

Bangs: Full across forehead, 1870's. Black hair: 16" - $300.00; 20" - $450.00; 26" - $750.00. Blondes: 16" - $325.00; 20" - $500.00; 26" - $800.00.

Brown eyes: Painted eyes, can be any hairstyle and date. 16" - $950.00; 20" - $1,450.00; 25" - $1,650.00.

Brown hair: Early hairdo with bun or long sausage curls around head. Center part and smooth around face. 16" - $3,000.00; 20" - $4,800.00.

Bun: China with bun, braided or rolled and pulled to back of head. Usually has pink luster tint. 1830's & 1840's. Cloth body, nicely dressed and undamaged. Prices depend upon rarity of hairdo and can run from $800.00 - 4,800.00.

Early Hairdo: 8" - $950.00; 16" - $1,800.00 - $1,500.00; 18" - $2,500.00 - $3,500.00; 21" - $3,500.00 - $4,800.00.

Right: 16" brown eye china with pink luster and flat top hairdo. Cloth body with leather hands. Left: 20" china with center part hairdo. Jointed kid body with bisque lower arms. Courtesy Frasher Doll Auctions. 16" - $950.00. 20" - $350.00.

Common Hairdo: Called "Lowbrow" or "Butterfly." Made from 1890, with most being made after 1900. Black or blonde hair. Wavy hairdo, center part with hair that comes down low on forehead. 8" - $85.00; 12" - $145.00; 16" - $200.00; 19" - $250.00; 23" - $300.00; 27" - $425.00.

Child: Swivel neck, china shoulder plate and may have lower torso and limbs made of china. 10" - $2,200.00; 12-13" - $2,600.00.

Child or Boy: Short black or blonde hairdo, curly with partly exposed ears. 14" - $300.00; 20" - $475.00.

Covered Wagon: 1840's - 1870's. Hair parted in middle with flat hairstyle and has sausage-shaped curls around head. 12" - $425.00; 16" - $575.00; 20" - $700.00; 24" - $850.00.

Curly Top: 1845 - 1860's. Ringlet curls that are loose and over entire head. 16" - $625.00; 20" - $750.00.

Dolly Madison: 1870's - 1880's. Loose curly hairdo with modeled ribbon and bow in center of the top of the head. Few curls on forehead. 14" - $250.00; 18" - $475.00; 21" - $525.00; 24" - $585.00; 28" - $785.00.

Left: 16" beautiful signed Nurenburg china with grey hairdo, downcast molded lid eyes and long "Roman" nose. Cloth body with china very detailed limbs. Original clothes and marked on inside shoulder plate. Right: Close-up of Nurenburg marked china. Courtesy Barbara Earnshaw-Cain. 16" - $3,200.00.

Early Marked China (Nurenburg, Rudustat, etc.): 16" - $3,200.00 up; 18" - $3,800.00 up.

Flat Top: 1850 - 1870's. Black hair parted in middle, smooth on top with short curls around head. 14" - $225.00; 17" - $285.00; 20" - $300.00; 24" - $400.00; 26" - $525.00.

Glass eyes: Can have a variety of hairdos. 1840 - 1970's. 14" - $1,800.00; 18" - $2,800.00; 22" - $3,000.00; 26" - $3,400.00.

Highbrow: Like Covered Wagon, but has very high forehead, smooth on top with a center part, curls over ears and around base of neck, and has a very round face. 1860 - 1870's. 14" - $250.00; 20" - $400.00; 24" - $525.00.

Japanese: 1910 - 1920's. Can be marked or unmarked. Black or blonde and can have a "common" hairdo, or have much more adult face and hairdo. 14" - $145.00; 17" - $185.00.

Kling: Number and bell. 16" - $450.00; 20" - $550.00.

Man or Boy: Excellent quality, early date, side part hairdo. Brown hair. 14" - $1,200.00; 16" - $2,600.00; 20" - $3,400.00.

Man or Boy: Glass eyes. 14" - $1,400.00; 17" - $2,900.00; 20" - $3,600.00.

Open Mouth: Common hairdo. 14" - $600.00; 18" - $900.00.

Pet Names: 1905, same as "Common" hairdo with molded shirtwaist with the name on front: "Agnes, Bertha, Daisy, Dorothy, Edith, Esther, Ethel, Florence, Helen, Mabel, Marion, Pauline. 8" - $125.00; 12" - $185.00;

16" - $250.00; 19" - $325.00; 23" - $400.00; 27" - $500.00.

Pierced Ears: Can have a variety of hairstyles (ordinary hairstyle, flat top, curly, covered wagon, etc.) 14" - $550.00; 18" - $800.00.

Pierced Ears: Rare hairstyles. 14" - $900.00; 18" - $1,300.00.

Snood, Combs: Applied hair decoration. 14" - $550.00; 17" - $800.00. Grapes in hairdo: 19" - $1,600.00.

Spill Curls: With or without headband. Many individual curls across forehead and over shoulders. Forehead curls continued to above ears. 14" - $400.00; 18" - $625.00; 22" - $725.00.

Swivel neck: 12" - $2,600.00.

Whistle: Has whistle holes in head. 14" - $600.00; 18" - $900.00.

Wood Body: Peg wooden body, wood or china lower limbs, china head with early unusual hairdo. Fine quality and in excellent condition. 9" - $2,600.00. Later hairdo (such as "covered wagon"): 9" - $1,600.00.

Wood Body: Articulated with slim hips, china lower arms. 1840 - 1850's. 12" - $1,400.00. Same with "covered wagon" hairdo: 7" - $950.00; 12" - $1,200.00; 15" - $1,500.00.

Right: 16½" bald china head with old cloth body and china lower arms. Left: 14½" marked "1014#" and made by Kling of Germany. Fully exposed ears and can be a boy or girl. Cloth body with china limbs. Courtesy Frasher Doll Auctions. 16½" - $1,250.00. 14½" - $400.00.

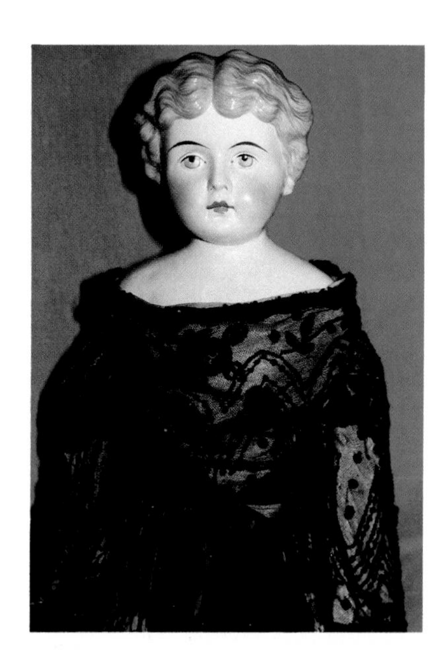

36" large china made by Kling of Germany and marked "180 Germany" with a "K" in a bell. Cloth body and china limbs. Courtesy Frasher Doll Auctions. 36" - $1,400.00.

29" "Spill Curl" china with molded head band, cloth body with china limbs. Courtesy Turn of Century Antiques. 29" - $975.00.

Right: 19" china head lady on old cloth body with slender waist and china limbs.
Left: 20" German bisque marked "7½" and most likely made by Kestner. Closed mouth, shoulder head on kid body with bisque lower arms. Courtesy Frasher Doll Auctions. 19" - $800.00. 20" - $595.00.

Prices are for clean dolls with only minor scuffs or soil.

Alabama Indestructible Doll: All cloth with head molded and painted in oils, painted hair, shoes and stockings. Marked on torso or leg "Pat. Nov. 9, 1912. Ella Smith Doll Co." or "Mrs. S.S. Smith/Manufacturer and dealer/ The Alabama Indestructible Doll/ Roanoke, Ala./Patented Sept. 26, 1905 (or 1907)."

Child: 18" - $2,400.00; 22" - $3,000.00.

Baby: 18" - $2,200.00.

Black Child: 18" - $2,900.00; 23" - $3,400.00.

Black Baby: 18" - $2,600.00.

Art Fabric Mills: See Printed Cloth Dolls.

Babyland: Made by E.I. Horsman from 1904 to 1920. Marked on torso or bottom of foot. Oil painted features, photographic features or printed features. With or without wig. All cloth, jointed at shoulders and hips. First price for extra clean, original dolls; second price for dolls in fair condition that show wear and have slight soil.

Oil Painted Features: 12" - $850.00, $400.00; 16" - $1,000.00, $500.00; 24" - $1,700.00, $800.00; 30" - $2,000.00, $950.00.

Black Oil Painted Features: 12" - $900.00, $450.00; 18" - $1,400.00, $600.00; 26" - $2,000.00 up, $800.00.

Photographic Face: 15" - $750.00, $350.00.

Black Photographic Face: 15" - $950.00, $450.00.

Printed: 16" - $500.00, $225.00; 24" - $675.00, $450.00; 30" - $1,200.00, $600.00.

Black printed: 16" - $700.00, $275.00; 24" - $1,000.00, $450.00.

Beecher: 1893 - 1910. Stuffed stockenette, painted eyes, needle sculptured features. Originated by Julia Jones Beecher of Elmira, N.Y., wife of Congregational Church pastor. Dolls made by sewing circle of church and all proceeds used for missionary work, so dolls can also be referred to as "Missionary Babies." Have looped wool hair. Extra clean: 16" - $1,600.00; 23" - $2,900.00. Slight soil and wear: 16" - $900.00; 23" - $1,600.00. Black: 16" - $2,000.00.

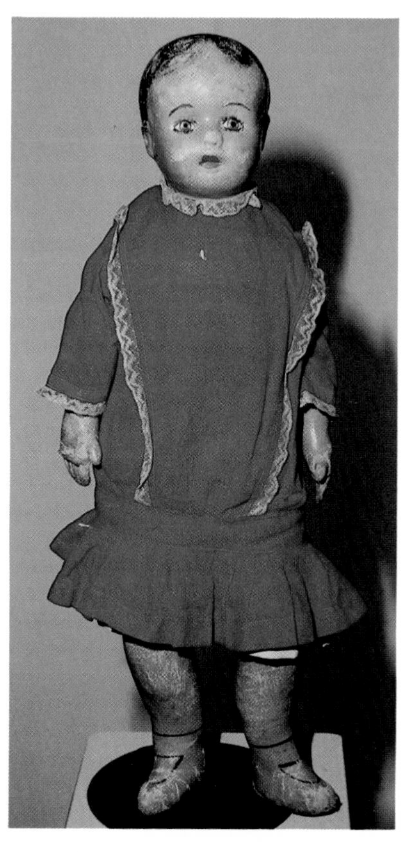

24" Alabama Baby. Marked with the Ella Smith Doll Co., patent stamped in red on the torso. All cloth, painted in oils, tab jointed shoulders and hips, painted limbs with outlined shoes, stitched in fingers and free standing thumb. Maybe original dress. Courtesy Barbara Earnshaw-Cain. 24" - $3,200.00.

Columbian Doll: Ca. 1890's. Sizes 15" - 29". Stamped "Columbian Doll/Manufactured by/Emma E. Adams/Oswego Centre/ N.Y." After 1905-1906, the mark was "The Columbian Doll/ Manufactured by/ Marietta Adams Ruttan/Oswego, NY." All cloth with painted features and flesh-painted hands and feet. Stitched fingers and toes. Extra clean: 19" - $4,100.00. Fair, with slight scuffs or soil: 19" - $2,000.00; Columbian type: 19" - $1,000.00, $400.00.

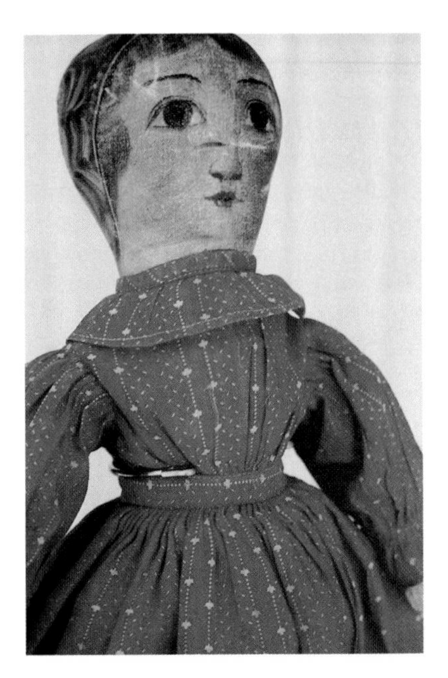

17" Columbian-type doll made of muslin, oil painted face stiffened with sizing, and head made in three pieces. ~~Five fingers indicated by stitching,~~ stitched jointed hips and knees, pointed toes with sewn-on black fine stockings. Original dress. Ca. 1900. Unmarked. Courtesy Margaret Mandel. 17" - $1,700.00.

Comic Characters: Extra clean: 14" - $400.00-475.00 up. Soil and wear: 14" - $175.00-225.00 up.

Drayton, Grace: Dolly Dingle. 1923 by Averill Mfg. Co. Cloth with printed features, marked on torso. 11" - $425.00; 14" - $565.00. **Chocolate Drop:** 1923 by Averill. Brown cloth with printed features and three tuffs of yarn hair. 11" - $395.00; 14" - $475.00. **Hug Me Tight:** By Colonial Toy Mfg. Co. in 1916. One-piece printed cloth with boy standing behind girl: 11" - $265.00; 14" - $325.00. **Peek-A-Boo:** Made by Horsman in 1913-1915. All cloth with printed features: 12" - $265.00.

Fangel, Maud Toursey: All cloth, printed features. Can have printed cloth body or plain without "undies clothes." Mitt-style hands with free-formed thumbs. Child: 10" - $400.00; 16" - $750.00. Baby: 12" - $465.00; 16" - $850.00.

Farnell's Alpha Toys: Marked with label on foot "Farnell's Alpha Toys/Made in England." **Child:** 14" - $425.00; 16" - $500.00. **Baby:** 12" - $300.00; 16" - $500.00. **King George VI:** 16" - $1,000.00. **Palace Guard/ Beefeater:** 16" - $675.00.

Georgene Novelities: See Averill, Georgene section.

Kamkins: Made by Louise Kampes. 1928 - 1934. Marked on head or foot, also has paper heart-shaped label on chest. All cloth with molded face mask and painted features, wigs, boy or girl. Extra clean: 19" - $1,300.00; 24" - $1,900.00. Slight wear/soil: 19" - $650.00; 24" - $800.00.

Kewpie Cuddles: See Kewpie section.

Lenci: See Lenci section.

Liberty of London Royal Dolls: Marked with cloth or paper tag. Flesh-colored cloth faces with stitched and painted features. All cloth bodies. 1939 Royal Portrait dolls are 10" and include Queen Mary, King George VI, Queen Victoria and Queen Elizabeth.

Extra clean: 10" - $200.00. Slight wear/soil: 10" - $85.00. Other Historical or Coronation figures - Extra clean: 10" - $200.00. Slight wear/soil: 10" - $85.00.

Kruse, Kathe: See Kruse section.

Madame Hendron: See Averill section.

Mammy Style Black Dolls: All cloth with painted or sewn features. Ca. 1910 - 1920's. 14" - $300.00; 17" - $375.00 up. Ca. 1930's: 14" - $175.00.

Missionary Babies: See Beecher in this section.

Mollye: See Mollye in Modern section.

Mother's Congress Doll: Patented Nov. 1900. All cloth, printed features and hair. Mitt-style hands without formed thumbs. Designed and made by Madge Mead. Marked with cloth label "Mother's Congress Doll/Children's Favorite/Philadelphia, Pa./Pat. Nov. 6, 1900." Extra clean: 17" - $900.00 up; 24" - $1,100.00 up. Slight soil: 17" - $400.00; 24" - $500.00.

Philadelphia Baby: Also called "Sheppard Doll" as made by J.B. Sheppard in late 1890's and early 1900's. Stockenette covered body with painted cloth arms and legs. Head is modeled and painted cloth. Extra clean: 22" - $2,700.00. Slight soil and wear: 22" - $900.00 - $1,000.00. Very worn: 22" - $500.00.

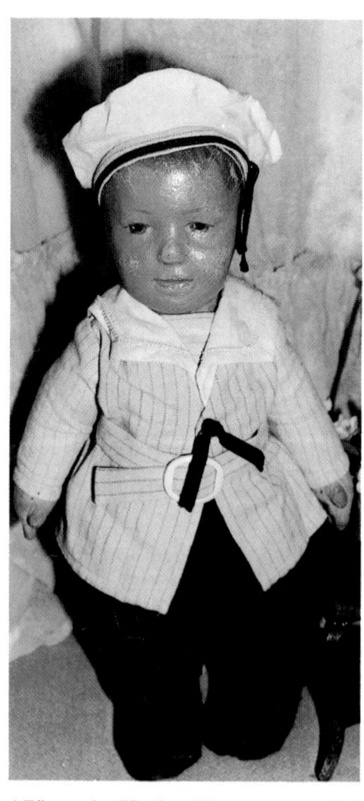

15" early Kathe Kruse-type doll with molded muslin head. Oil painted features, wide hips, jointed at shoulders and hips and separate sewn thumbs. Courtesy Frasher Doll Auctions. 15" - $900.00.

13" all cloth "Mammy" type made in a sitting position. Hand embroidered features; red and blue dotted cotton shoes sewn on. Untrimmed cheesecloth petticoat and undies. Earrings, necklace and bracelet made of seedbeads. Courtesy Genie Jinright. 13" - $285.00.

Poir, Eugenie: 1920's, made in New York and France. All-cloth body with felt face and limbs or can be all felt. Painted features, majority of eyes are painted to the side, mohair wig. Stitched four fingers together with free-standing thumb. Unmarked except for paper label. Extra clean: 17" - $700.00; 23" - $950.00. Slight soil and wear: 17" - $400.00; 23" - $500.00. Photographic faces: (also see Babyland in this section) - Extra clean: 17" - $800.00. Slight soil and wear: 17" - $400.00.

Printed Cloth Dolls: All cloth with features and/or underwear/clothes printed. These dolls are cut and sew types **Rastus, Cream of Wheat:** 18" - $185.00. **Aunt Jemima:** Set of four dolls. $100.00 each; **Printed on underwear (Dolly Dear, Merry Marie, etc.)** - Cut: 6" - $90.00; 15" - $190.00; 18" - $225.00. Uncut: 6" - $125.00; 15" - $225.00; 18" - $300.00. **Boys and girls with printed outer clothes** - Cut: 6" - $100.00; 15" - $175.00; 18" - $245.00. Uncut: 6" - $125.00; 15" - $245.00; 18" - $300.00. **Black boy or girl:** 18" - $425.00. **George and Martha Washington:** 1901 by Art Fabric - Cut: $425.00, set of four; Uncut: $800.00, set of four. **St. Nicholas/Santa Claus:** Marked "Pat. Dec. 28, 1886. Made by E.S. Peck, NY." One arm stuffed with toys and other arm holds American flag. Cut: 15" - $275.00. Uncut: 15" - $425.00

Raynal: Made in France by Edouard Raynal. 1920's. Cloth body and limbs (sometimes has celluloid hands), felt mask face with painted features. Eyes painted to side. Marked on soles of shoes or will have necklace imprinted "Raynal." Original clothes generally are felt, but can have combination felt/organdy or just organdy. Extra clean: 19" - $725.00. Slight soil and wear: 19" - $475.00.

Russian: 1920-1930's. All cloth with stockenette hands and head. Molded face mask with painted features. Dressed in regional costumes. Marked "Made in Soviet Union." Extra clean: 12" - $95.00, 16" - $175.00. Slight soil and wear: 12" - $40.00; 16" - $95.00. **Tea Cozies:** Doll from waist up and has full skirt that is hollow to be placed over pot to keep contents warm. 16" - $135.00; 20" - $200.00.

Rollinson Dolls: Molded cloth with painted features, head and limbs. Molded hair or wig. Designed by Gertrude F. Rollinson, made by Utley Doll Co. Marked with a stamp of doll in a diamond and printed around border "Rollinson Doll Holyoke, Ma." Molded hair, extra clean: 18" - $1,000.00 up. Molded hair slight soil and wear: 18" - $450.00. Wigged by Rollinson - Extra

12" all cloth with painted features, yarn hair and plastic/celluloid eyes. Clothes made on doll except felt coat. Tag "Dean's Childsplay Toys Ltd. Rye, Sussex. Made in England." Name of doll is "Goliwog." Courtesy Sandra Cummins. 12" - $200.00.

clean: 18" - $1,200.00 up. Wigged - Slight soil and wear: 18" - $600.00.

Smith, Mrs. S.S.: See Alabama in this section.

Steiff: See Steiff section.

WPA: See WPA section.

Walker, Izannah: Made in 1870's and 1880's. Modeled head with oil painted features. Ears are applied. Cloth body and limbs. Hands and feet are stitched and can have painted on boots. Marked "Patented Nov. 4, 1873." Brushstroke or corkscrew curls around face over ears. Fair condition: 18" - $12,000.00. Very good condition: 18" - $24,000.00. Two vertical curls in front of ears. Fair condition: 18"- $10,000.00; 24" - $14,000.00. Very good condition: 18" - $19,000.00; 24" - $26,000.00.

13" Bruckner Rag Doll, ca. 1901. All cloth with stiffened face mask, printed features. Cloth body and all original clothes. 21" bisque head doll marked "Heinrich Handwerch/Simon & Halbig." Open mouth and on jointed body. Courtesy Frasher Doll Auctions. 13" - $285.00. 21" - $600.00.

Most German makers made composition-headed dolls as well as bisque and other materials. Composition dolls were made in Germany before World War 1, but the majority were made in the 1920's and 1930's. They can be all composition or have a composition head with cloth body and limbs. Prices are for excellent quality and condition.

Child Doll: All composition with wig, sleep/flirty eyes, open or closed mouth and jointed composition body. Unmarked or just have numbers. 14" - $250.00; 18" - $300.00; 22" - $385.00; 25" - $550.00.

Child: Same as above, but with name of company (or initials): 14" - $285.00; 18" - $425.00; 22" - $500.00; 25" - $625.00.

Baby: All composition with open mouth. 16" - $225.00; 19" - $350.00; 24" - $500.00. Toddler: 18" - $325.00; 24" - $450.00.

Baby: Composition head and limbs with cloth body, open mouth, sleep eyes. 14" - $145.00; 18" - $275.00; 25" - $375.00.

Painted Eyes: Child: 14" - $100.00; 18" - $165.00. Baby: 16" - $125.00; 24" - $300.00.

Shoulder Head: Composition shoulder head, glass eyes, wig, open or closed mouth, cloth or kidaleen body with composition arms (full arms or lower arms only with cloth upper arms), and lower legs. May have barefeet or modeled boots. Prices for dolls in extra clean condition and nicely

Rear: 22½" German all composition marked "A.S. Germany 530/6K." Sleep eyes, open mouth with two upper teeth. Front: 22" baby marked "A.M. Germany 352." Sleep eyes, open smiling mouth, cloth body and composition lower arms and legs. Head is bisque. Courtesy Frasher Doll Auctions. 22½"- $385.00. A.M. - $800.00.

dressed. Unmarked.

Excellent Quality: Extremely fine modeling. 15" - $345.00; 21" - $475.00.

Average Quality: May resemble a china head doll. 12" - $165.00; 16" - $225.00; 20" - $265.00; 24" - $325.00.

Painted Hair: 10" - $185.00; 14" - $225.00; 18" - $325.00.

Swivel Neck: On composition shoulder plate. 16" - $500.00; 20" - $675.00.

Oriental: 14" - $400.00.

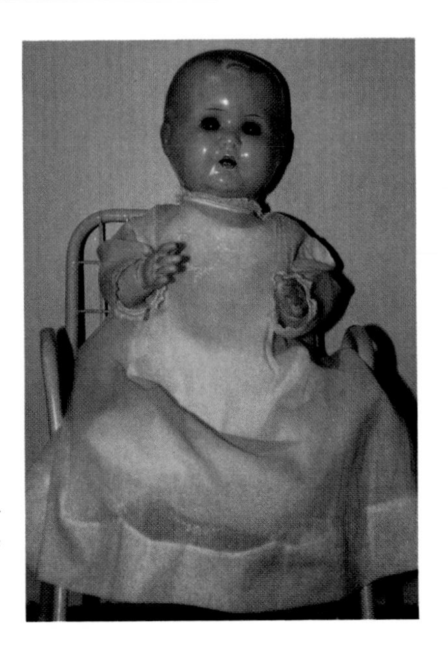

25" all composition marked "Germany" on head. Sleep eyes, open mouth with two lower teeth. On bent limb baby body with jointed wrists. Courtesy Jeannie Mauldin. 25" - $500.00.

Rear: German all composition marked "201 3½." Sleep eyes/ lashes and open mouth. Front: 12½" bisque head by Armand Marseille with mold number 351. Open mouth, cloth body with celluloid hands. Courtesy Frasher Doll Auctions. 16" "201" - $345.00. 12" "351" - $365.00.

Many French and German dolls bear the mark "DEP" as part of their mold marks, but the dolls referred to here are marked *only with the* DEP *and a size number.* They are on French bodies with some bearing a Jumeau sticker. The early 1880's DEP dolls have fine quality bisque and artist workmanship, and the later dolls of the 1890's and into the 1900's generally have fine bisque, but the color will be higher, and they will have painted lashes below the eyes with most having hair eyelashes over the eyes. The early dolls will have outlined lips where the later ones will not. Prices are for clean, undamaged and nicely dressed dolls.

Marks:

DEP
10

Open Mouth: 14" - $800.00; 18" - $1,125.00; 25" - $1,900.00; 30" - $2,400.00; 34" - $2,900.00.

Closed Mouth: 14" - $1,400.00; 18" - $2,400.00; 25" - $3,000.00; 30" - $3,400.00; 34" - $3,800.00.

Walking, Kissing, Open Mouth: 14" - $950.00; 18" - $1,300.00; 22" - $1,600.00; 26" - $2,000.00.

33" marked "DEP." Sleep eyes, hair lashes and painted lower lashes, open mouth and on French jointed body. Original clothing and in original box marked "Eden BéBé Articulado." Has very pale and excellent bisque. Courtesy Frasher Doll Auctions. 33" - $2,900.00.

28" marked "Tété" in red and incised "DEP 12." Open mouth, sleep eyes and on French jointed body. Courtesy Arthur Bouliette. 28" - $2,200.00.

20" marked "DEP 10" on head. Body has "Jumeau Bebe Diplome d'Honneur" oval sticker. Sleep eyes with hair lashes, open mouth and holding a German doll toy with bisque head marked "907." Glass set eyes, open mouth, wood handle and doll squeaks (may have been a music box) as it is twirled. Courtesy Frasher Doll Auctions. 20" doll - $1,300.00. Toy - $325.00 up.

DOLL HOUSE DOLLS

Doll House Man or Lady: With molded hair/wig and painted eyes. 6-7" - $150.00 - $165.00.

Man or Woman with Glass Eyes/Wigs: 6-7" - $325.00 - $400.00.

Man or Woman with Molded Hair, Glass Eyes: 6-7" - $385.00.

Grandparents, Old People, or Molded-on Hats: 6-7" - $225.00.

Military Men, Original: 6-7" - $585.00 up.

Black Man or Women: Molded hair, all original. 6-7" - $400.00.

Swivel Neck: Wig or molded hair. 6-7" - $800.00.

7" Bride and Groom Doll House dolls that are all bisque. He has a mustache and both are all original. Courtesy Arthur Bouliette. 7" man - $225.00. 7" lady - $165.00.

Cuno & Otto Dressel operated in Sonneberg, Thuringia, Germany and were sons of the founder. Although the firm was in business in 1700, they are not listed as dollmakers until 1873. They produced dolls with bisque heads, composition over wax, and can be on cloth, kid, or jointed composition body. Some of their heads were made for them by other German firms, such as Simon & Halbig, Heubach, etc. They registered the trademark for "Jutta" in 1906 and by 1911 were also making celluloid dolls. Prices are for undamaged, clean and nicely dressed dolls.

Marks:

C.O.D.

C.O.D 49 D.E.P.
Made in Germany

Babies: Marked "C.O.D." but without the word "Jutta." 14" - $425.00; 18" - $565.00; 24" - $785.00.

Child: On jointed composition body, with open mouth. 15" - $325.00; 18" - $395.00; 25" - $550.00; 30" - $800.00; 34" - $1,100.00; 38" - $1,400.00.

Child: On kid, jointed body, open mouth. 14" - $285.00; 18" - $350.00; 24" - $475.00.

Jutta: 1910-1922. **Baby:** Open mouth and five-piece bent limb body. 14" - $550.00; 17" - $675.00; 20" - $725.00; 24" - $1,200.00; 26" - $1,400.00.

Toddler Body: 14" - $750.00; 17" - $850.00; 20" - $1,100.00; 24" - $1,400.00; 26" - $1,800.00.

Child: Marked with "Jutta" or with S&H #1914, #1348, #1349, etc.: 14" - $550.00; 18" - $600.00; 24" - $775.00; 27" - $950.00; 32" - $1,400.00.

Lady Doll: 1920's with adult face, closed mouth and on five-piece composition body with thin limbs and high heel feet. Mark #1469. 14" - $3,200.00; 16" - $4,200.00.

Left: 12" Kammer and Reinhardt baby with mold number 115/A. Sleep eyes, closed mouth and on baby body. Right: 14" character girl by Cuno & Otto Dressel. Incised "A3." Painted eyes, closed pouty mouth and on fully jointed body. Courtesy Frasher Doll Auctions. 12" - $2,000.00. 14" - $2,800.00.

Character Dolls: 1909 and after. Closed mouth, painted eyes, molded hair or wig. 12" - $1,400.00; 14" - $2,400.00; 17" - $2,800.00.

Character Dolls: Same as above, but with glass eyes. 14" - $2,700.00; 17" - $3,000.00; 22" - $3,300.00.

Composition: Shoulder head of 1870's, glass or painted eyes, molded hair or wig and on cloth body with composition limbs with molded-on boots. Will be marked with Holz-Masse:

With wig: 14" - $300.00; 17" - $385.00; 24" - $525.00. Molded hair: 17" - $365.00; 24" - $450.00.

Portrait Dolls: 1896. Such as Uncle Sam, Farmer, Admiral Dewey, Old Rip, Witch, etc. Portrait bisque head, glass eyes, composition body. Some will be marked with a "D" or "S." Heads made for Dressel by Simon & Halbig. Prices for clean, undamaged and originally dressed. **Military dolls:** 14" - $2,000.00; 20" - $3,000.00. **Old Rip or Witch:** 12" - $1,500.00; 15" - $1,800.00. **Uncle Sam:** 14" - $1,700.00; 20" - $2,900.00; 24" - $3,800.00 up.

Above Photo:
Right: 38" marked "15½ Cuno & Otto Dressel Germany." Open mouth, sleep eyes and on fully jointed body. Left: 42" marked "Heinrich Handwerck Simon & Halbig." Sleep eyes and open mouth. On fully jointed body. Courtesy Frasher Doll Auctions. 38" - $1,400.00. 42" - $3,200.00.

Left Photo:
15" character "Admiral Dewey" with very life-like face with modeled-on mustache, glass eyes and on five-piece body. All original clothes. Grey molded hair under cap. Painted-on boots. Courtesy Barbara Earnshaw-Cain. 15" - $2,000.00.

22" Cuno and Otto Dressel doll marked:
"Made in Germany. 1912.4."

Jointed body, sleep eyes and open mouth. Courtesy Frasher Doll Auctions.
22" - $600.00.

E.D. BÉBÉ

E. Denamur of Paris made dolls from 1885 to 1898. The E.D. marked dolls seem to be accepted as being made by Denamur, but they could have been made by E. Dumont, Paris. Composition and wood jointed bodies. Prices are for excellent quality bisque, no damage and nicely dressed.

Marks:

21" marked "E.9D." Closed mouth, glass eyes, pierced ears and on French jointed body with straight wrists. Courtesy Frasher Doll Auctions. 21" - $3,300.00.

E.D. BÉBÉ

Closed Mouth: 14" - $2,500.00; 18" - $2,900.00; 22" - $3,400.00; 25" - $3,800.00; 29" - $4,600.00.

Open Mouth: 16" - $1,600.00; 20" - $2,200.00; 25" - $2,400.00.

Black: Open mouth. 18" - $2,200.00; 24" - $2,800.00.

15½" marked "E. 5 D. Depose." Paperweight glass eyes, open mouth with four teeth and on French jointed body. Courtesy Frasher Doll Auctions. Also shown is rare size 11" all bisque Kestner marked "150. 4." Jointed shoulders and hips, sleep eyes and open mouth. 15" - $1,500.00. 11" - $1,100.00.

EDEN BÉBÉ

Fleischmann & Bloedel of Bavaria, Furth and Oaris founded in 1873 and were making dolls in Paris by 1890, then became a part of S.F.B.J. in 1899. Dolls have composition jointed bodies and can have open or closed mouths. Prices are for dolls with excellent color and quality bisque, no damage and nicely dressed.

Marks:

EDEN BÉBÉ PARIS

Closed Mouth: Pale bisque. 15" - $2,400.00; 18" - $2,800.00; 22" - $3,200.00; 26" - $3,800.00.

Closed Mouth: High color bisque. 15" - $1,600.00; 18" - $2,000.00; 22" - $2,200.00; 26" - $2,600.00.

Open Mouth: 15" - $1,500.00; 18" - $2,200.00; 22" - $2,700.00; 26" - $3,000.00.

Walking Kissing Doll: Jointed body with walker mechanism, head turns and one arm throws a kiss. Heads by Simon & Halbig using mold #1039 (and others). Bodie's assembled by Fleischmann & Bloedel. Price for perfect, working doll. 21" - $1,200.00 up.

18" marked "Eden Be'be' 1." Closed mouth and pierced ears. Jointed French body and looks very much like an F.G. marked doll. Courtesy Frasher Doll Auctions. 18" - $2,800.00.

22" marked "Eden Be'be' Paris 9 Depose." Excellent quality bisque, large glass eyes, open mouth and on French jointed composition body. Courtesy Frasher Doll Auctions. 22" - $2,700.00.

ELLIS, JOEL

Joel Ellis made dolls in Springfield, Vermont in 1873 and 1874 under the name Co-operative Manufacturing Co. All wood jointed body have tenon and mortise joints (not jointing of legs to torso, arms are jointed in same manner). The hands and feet are made of pewter and has molded hair and painted features.

Doll in fair condition: Does not need to be dressed. 12" - $465.00. Excellent condition: 12" - $900.00; 15" - $1,100.00; 18" - $1,800.00.

Springfield Wooden Doll: It must be noted that dolls similar to the Joel Ellis ones were made in Springfield, Vt. also by Joint Doll Co. and D.M. Smith & Co. They are very much like the Joel Ellis except when standing the knee joint will be flush with the method of jointing not showing. The hips are cut out with the leg tops cut to fit the opening, and the detail of the hands are not as well done.

14" Joel Ellis wooden doll with mortise and tenon jointing, molded hair, painted features. Metal hands and feet. Courtesy Frasher Doll Auctions. 14" - $1,000.00.

FASHION DOLL, FRENCH

These "adult" style dolls were made by a number of French firms from about 1860 into 1930's. Many will be marked only with a number or have a stamp on the body, although some of the stamps/labels may be the store they were sold from and not the maker. The most available fashion doll seems to be marked F.G. dolls. Price are for dolls in perfect condition with no cracks, chips, or repairs and in beautiful old or newer clothes made of appropriate age materials.

Articulated Wood*: Or blown kid bodies and limbs. Some have bisque lower arms. 16" - $3,200.00; 20" - $4,200.00.

Articulated: With bisque lower legs and arms with excellent modeling detail. 16" - $4,200.00 up; 20" - $5,000.00 up.

Marked "Bru": (Also see Smiling Mona Lisa in this section.) Kid body, fully jointed wood arms. 16" - $14,000.00 up.

Marked "Huret": Bisque or china glazed shoulderhead, kid body with bisque lower arms. Painted eyes:

16" - $8,000.00 up; 20" - $14,000.00 up. Glass eyes: 16" - $9,000.00 up; 20" - $15,000.00 up. Wood body: 16" - $8,600.00 up; 20" - $16,000.00 up.

Huret Child: 18" - $22,000.00.

Marked "Rohmer": Bisque or china glazed shoulder head (can be jointed). Kid body with bisque lower arms (or china). Glass eyes: 16" - $7,000.00; 20" - $14,500.00; Painted eyes: 16" - $6,000.00; 20" - $13,000.00. Wood body: 16" - $8,000.00; 20" - $15,500.00.

Marked "Jumeau" **: Will have number on head and stamped body. Portrait-style head: 14" - $4,200.00; 18" - $6,500.00; 24" - $7,200.00; 28" - $9,000.00. Wood body: 18" - $9,000.00 up; 24" - $12,000.00 up.

Marked "F.G.": All kid body, one-piece shoulder and head, glass eyes. 14" - $1,300.00; 17" - $1,800.00; 21" - $2,300.00. Painted eyes: 12" - $1,000.00; 14" - $1,200.00.

Marked "F.G.": All kid body (or bisque lower arms), swivel head on bisque shoulder plate. 14" - $1,600.00; 17" - $2,300.00; 21" - $2,900.00.

Marked "F.G.": Gesland cloth-covered body with bisque lower arms and legs. 14" - $2,600.00; 17" - $3,300.00; 21" - $3,800.00; 25" - $4,400.00.

Marked "F.G.": Gesland cloth-covered body with composition or papier maché lower arms and legs. 14" - $2,400.00; 17" - $3,600.00; 21" - $4,000.00.

18" Fashion doll that is unmarked. Early almost white bisque swivel head on bisque shoulder plate. Kid fashion body with stitched fingers. May be original clothes and wig. Courtesy Frasher Doll Auctions. 18" - $3,000.00.

10" bisque shoulder head young lady. Solid dome head, closed mouth, painted eyes with molded eyelids. Cloth body with bisque limbs, painted-on shoes and hose. Original dress and wig; hat added. Courtesy Frasher Doll Auctions. 10" - $1,300.00.

Smiling "Mona Lisa": Now being referred to as being made by Bru. Kid body with leather lower arms, stitched fingers or bisque lower arms. Marked with letter (example: E, B, D, etc.) 13" - $2,600.00; 17" - $3,900.00; 21" - $4,500.00; 28" - $6,000.00; 34" - $12,000.00.

Unmarked with Numbers Only: With one-piece head and shoulder. Extremely fine quality bisque, undamaged. 12" - $1,400.00; 16" - $2,400.00; 20" - $2,900.00 up.

Unmarked with numbers only: Swivel neck with bisque shoulder plate. Extremely fine quality bisque and undamaged. 14" - $3,000.00; 18" - $4,200.00; 22" - $5,000.00.

Unmarked: Medium to fair quality. One-piece head and shoulder: 12" - $700.00; 16" - $950.00-1,400.00. Swivel head on bisque shoulder plate: 14" - $1,000.00; 18" - $1,600.00 up.

Marked E.B. (E. Barrois): Glass eyes: 15" - $3,000.00. Painted eyes: 17" - $3,200.00; 20" - $3,800.00.

**17" with trousseau - $7,900.00 at auction.*

*** 20" - $6,700.00 at auction; 27" - $15,000.00 at auction.*

22" Fashion marked "6" on head. Swivel head on fully articulated wood body with joints at mid upper thigh and arms and also jointed at wrists. Maybe original costume. Courtesy Frasher Doll Auctions. 22" - $4,400.00.

22" marked "F.G." on head and shoulder plate. Swivel head, kid body and stitched fingers. Original costume. Courtesy Frasher Doll Auction. 22" - $3,200.00.

15" marked "Bru Fashion" with all kid body, bisque shoulder plate and bisque socket head, cobalt outlined glass eyes and outlined lips. Original wig and costume of two-piece walking dress that is navy and brown. Courtesy Barbara Earnshaw-Cain. 15" - $14,000.00 up.

19" Portrait Jumeau incised "5." Swivel head on bisque shoulder plate, kid body with bisque lower arms. Courtesy Frasher Doll Auctions. 19" - $6,700.00.

F. Gaultier (earlier spelled Gauthier) is the accepted maker of the F.G. marked dolls. These dolls are often found on the cloth covered or all composition bodies that are marked "Gesland." The Gesland firm was operated by two brothers with one of them having the initial "F" (1887-1900).

Marks:

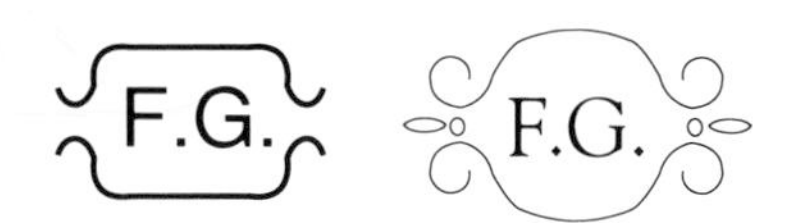

F. 8 G.

(block lettermark)

Child with Closed Mouth*: Excellent quality bisque, no damage and nicely dressed. 14" - $2,600.00; 16" - $2,900.00; 19" - $3,400.00; 22" - $3,700.00; 25" - $4,400.00.

Child with Closed Mouth: Same as above, but with high face color, no damage and nicely dressed. 14" - $1,800.00; 16" - $2,000.00; 19" - $2,400.00; 22" - $2,600.00; 25" - $3,700.00.

Child with Open Mouth: Excellent quality bisque, no damage and nicely dressed. 14" - $1,700.00; 16" - $2,000.00; 19" - $2,400.00; 22" - $2,800.00; 28" - $3,400.00.

Child with Open Mouth: With high face color, very dark lips, no damage and nicely dressed. 14" - $750.00; 16" - $900.00; 19" - $1,100.00; 22" - $1,600.00.

Marked "F.G. Fashion": See Fashion section.

Child on Marked Gesland Body: Bisque head on stockenette over wire frame body with composition limbs. Closed mouth: 16" - $4,200.00; 19" - $4,600.00; 25" - $5,200.00. Open mouth: 15" - $1,900.00; 18" - $3,000.00; 25" - $4,200.00.

Block Letter (so called) F.G. Child: Closed mouth, chunky composition body, excellent quality and condition. 16" - $3,600.00; 20" - $4,200.00; 25" - $5,200.00.

Block Letter (so called) F.G. Child: Closed mouth, bisque swivel head on bisque shoulder plate with gusseted kid body and bisque lower arms. 16" - $3,600.00; 20" - $4,200.00; 25" - $5,200.00.

** 25" - $6,750.00 at auction.*

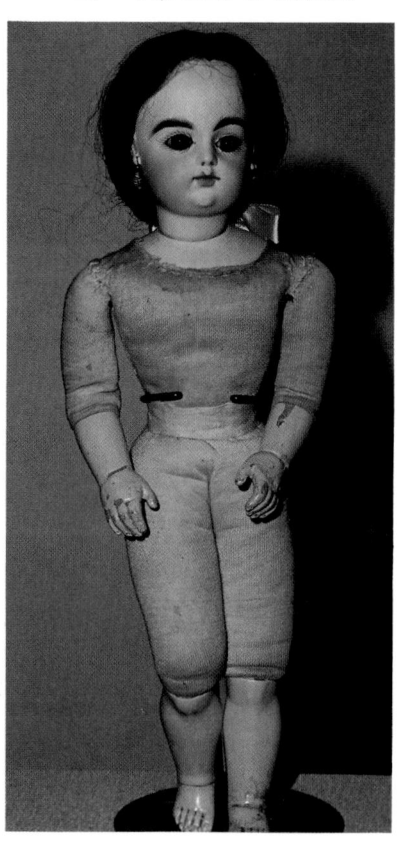

15" beautiful F.G. with closed mouth and paperweight glass eyes on Gesland body that is cloth covered and has composition lower limbs. Bisque socket head on bisque shoulder plate. Courtesy Barbara Earnshaw-Cain. 15" - $4,200.00.

20" marked "F.G." in scroll. Open mouth, pierced ears and on wood/composition body with red paper label marked "Fque De Bébés Gesland S.G.D.G." and Paris address. Courtesy Frasher Doll Auctions. 20" - $3,500.00.

31" body marked "Bébé Gesland," two rows of address, followed by "Paris." Head is incised "F.G." in scroll and number "11." Closed mouth, composition shoulder plate, lower arms and legs and has stockenette covered body. Courtesy Frasher Doll Auctions. 31" - $5,000.00.

14" Fortune Teller with head marked "F.G." Closed mouth and glass eyes. Bisque swivel head on bisque shoulder plate. Many cards are under skirt and have "fortunes" written on them. Body is kid. Courtesy Betty Shelly. 14" Fashion - $2,000.00. 23" open mouth - $2,600.00.

A variety of French doll makers produced unmarked dolls from 1880's into the 1920's. These dolls may only have a head size number or be marked "Paris" or "France." Many of the accepted French dolls that have a number are now being attributed to German makers and it will be questionable for some time.

Unmarked French BéBé: Closed or open/closed mouth, paperweight eyes, excellent quality bisque and artist painting on a French body. Prices are for clean, undamaged and nicely dressed dolls.

Early Desirable, Very French-style Face: 14" - $10,000.00; 18" - $16,000.00; 24" - $24,000.00.

Jumeau Style Face: 14" - $2,700.00; 18" - $3,000.00; 24" - $4,200.00.

Excellent Quality: 15" - $3,800.00; 22" - $5,000.00; 26" - $7,200.00.

14½" marked "136." Maker unknown. Closed mouth, pierced ears, Steiner composition jointed body with straight wrists and stamped "Le Petit Parisien Bébé Steiner." Courtesy Frasher Doll Auctions. 14½" - $2,400.00.

Medium Quality: May have poor painting and/or blotches to skin tones: 17" - $1,600.00; 22" - $2,000.00; 26" - $2,600.00.

Open Mouth: 1890's and later. Will be on French body. Excellent quality: 14" - $1,600.00; 17" - $1,900.00; 21" - $2,400.00; 24" - $3,000.00.

Open Mouth: 1920's with high face color and may have five-piece papier maché body. 16" - $750.00; 21" - $900.00; 25" - $1,100.00.

19" marked "136." Maker unknown. Resembles a "Long Face" Jumeau. Closed mouth, pierced ears, French jointed body and wears factory dress. Original wig. Courtesy Frasher Doll Auctions. 19" - $4,200.00. ($5,200.00 at auction in original clothes.)

13" marked "A/ and EF" with the rest unreadable. Closed mouth, pierced ears and is on a fully marked Schmitt body with crossed hammers in shield. Has straight wrists. Courtesy Frasher Doll Auctions. 13" - $2,700.00.

29" marked only "11" and may have been made by Jumeau or Stiener. Open mouth with six teeth, jointed composition body. Courtesy Frasher Doll Auctions. 29" - $3,400.00.

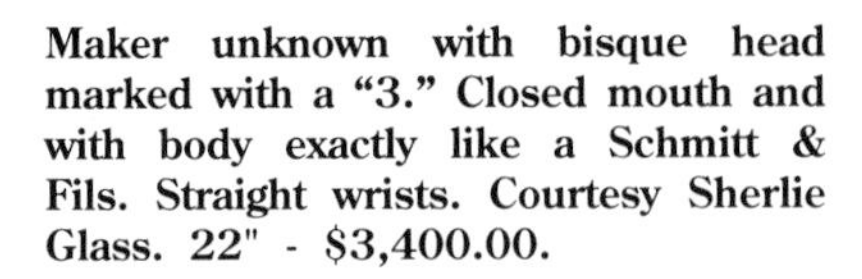

Maker unknown with bisque head marked with a "3." Closed mouth and with body exactly like a Schmitt & Fils. Straight wrists. Courtesy Sherlie Glass. 22" - $3,400.00.

Freundlich Novelty Company operated in New York in 1923. Most have a cardboard tag and the doll will be unmarked or may have the doll's name on the head, but no maker's name.

Baby Sandy: 1939 - 1942. All composition with molded hair, sleep or painted eyes. Marked "Baby Sandy" on head. Excellent condition with no cracks, craze or chips, original or appropriate clothes: 8" - $150.00; 11" - $200.00; 14" - $275.00; 19" - $500.00. With light crazing, but clean and may be redressed: 8" - $85.00; 11" - $95.00; 14" - $100.00; 19" - $200.00.

General Douglas MacArthur: Ca. 1942. Portrait doll of all composition, painted features and molded hat. Jointed shoulders and hips. Excellent condition and original. 18" - $275.00. Light craze, clothes dirty: 18" - $100.00.

Military Dolls: Ca. 1942 and on. All composition with painted features, molded-on hats and can be a woman or man (W.A.V.E, W.A.A.C., sailor, Marine, etc.) In excellent condition, original and no crazing: 15" - $185.00. Light craze and clothes in fair condition: 15" - $95.00.

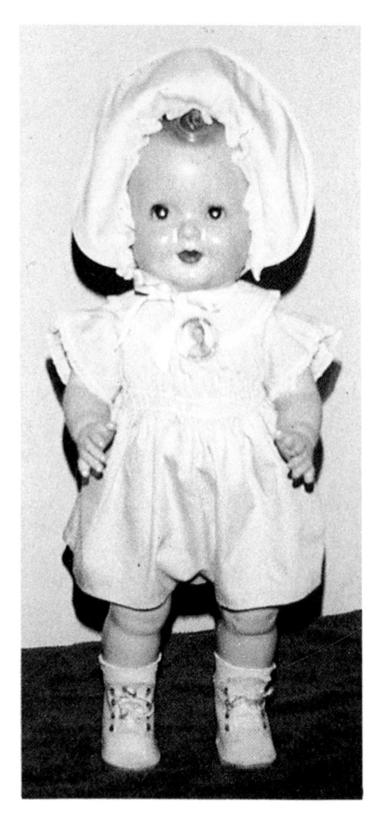

16" all composition and marked "Baby Sandy." Molded, painted hair, sleep eyes and open mouth and has all original clothes and pin. Courtesy Pamela Smith. 16" - $350.00.

Left: 16" "General Douglas MacArthur." All composition with molded cap, clothes has original tag "Freundlich Novelty Co. 1942." 16" - $250.00.
Right: 12" Liberty Boy. All composition with molded-on clothes. Felt hat missing. Made by Ideal in 1918. Courtesy Turn of Century Antiques. 12" - $175.00.

Frozen Charlotte and Charlie figures can be china, partly china (such as hair and boots), stone bisque or fine porcelain bisque. They can have molded hair, painted bald heads or take wigs. The majority have no joints with hands extended and legs separate (some are together) and unjointed. They generally come without clothes and they can have painted-on boots, shoes and socks or be barefooted.

It must be noted that in 1976 a large amount of the 15½-16" "Charlie" figures were reproduced in Germany and are excellent quality. It is almost impossible to tell these are reproductions.

Prices are for doll figures without any damage. More must be allowed for any with unusual hairdos, an early face or molded eyelids or molded-on clothes.

All China: Glazed with black or blonde hair, excellent quality of painting and unjointed. 1-2" - $50.00; 4-6" - $95.00; 8-10" - $250.00; 12" - $300.00. Bald head with wig: 7" - $195.00; 10" - $275.00. **Charlie:** Molded hair, flesh tones to neck and head. 13" - $350.00; 16" - $500.00; 18" - $700.00.

Untinted Bisque (Parian): Molded hair, unjointed. 4" - $140.00; 8" - $195.00.

Untinted Bisque: Molded hair, jointed at shoulders. 4" - $140.00; 8" - $300.00.

Stone Bisque: Unjointed, molded hair, medium to excellent quality of painting. 4" - $45.00; 8" - $65.00.

Black Charlotte or Charlie: Unjointed, no damage. 3" - $75.00; 6" - $100.00; 8" - $150.00. Jointed at shoulders: 3" - $100.00; 6" - $150.00.

Molded-on Clothes or Bonnet: Unjointed, no damage and medium to excellent quality. 6" - $400.00; 9" - $550.00 up.

Dressed: In original clothes. Unjointed Charlotte or Charlie. No damage and in overall excellent condition. 6" - $125.00; 8" - $165.00.

Jointed at Shoulder: Original clothes and no damage. 6" - $165.00; 8" - $260.00.

Molded-on, Painted Boots: Unjointed, no damage. 6" - $145.00; 9" - $285.00. Jointed at shoulders: 6" - $175.00; 9" - $325.00.

4½" "Frozen Charlotte." Bald head with wig, molded and painted white boots with gold. 5" all bisque marked "208" and made by Kestner. Open/closed mouth, molded teeth, molded shoes and socks. Courtesy Frasher Doll Auctions. 4½" - $135.00. 5" - $285.00.

Center: 15½" "Frozen Charlie" with china glaze and deep pink luster to neck, painted features and hair. Left: 27" marked "S&C." German doll on fully jointed body, open mouth and sleep eyes. Right: 26" French marked "AL & C Limoges Favorite." Open mouth and on French full jointed body. Courtesy Frasher Doll Auctions. 15½" Charlie - $500.00. 27" S&C - $850.00. 26" Limoges - $750.00 up.

FULPER

Fulper Pottery Co. of Flemington, N.J. made dolls from 1918-1921. They made children and babies and used composition and kid bodies.

Marks:

Child: Fair to medium quality bisque head painting. No damage, nicely dressed. Composition body, open mouth: 14" - $400.00; 16" - $500.00; 20" - $600.00. Kid body, open mouth: 14" - $350.00; 16" - $425.00; 20" - $525.00.

Child: Poor quality (white chalky look, may have crooked mouth and be poorly painted.) Composition body: 16" - $350.00; 21" - $450.00. Kid body: 16" - $200.00; 21" - $365.00.

Baby: Bent limb body. Fair to medium quality bisque, open mouth, no damage and dressed well. Good artist work on features. 18" - $600.00; 25" - $950.00.

Toddler: Same as baby but has toddler jointed or straight leg body. 18" - $700.00; 25" - $1,100.00.

Baby: Poor quality bisque and painting. 18" - $250.00; 25" - $475.00.

Toddler: Poor quality bisque and painting. 18" - $365.00; 25" - $700.00.

25" Fulper that has fully marked head, open mouth and set glass eyes. Feathered eyebrows and above average bisque for a Fulper. On fully jointed composition body. Courtesy Sylvia Bryant. 25" - $695.00.

GANS & SEYFORTH

23½" marked "G & S Germany 6 Seyforth." Open mouth and on fully jointed body. Sitting: 22" doll by Cuno & Otto Dressel. Mold number 1912. Open mouth and on fully jointed body. Courtesy Frasher Doll Auctions. 23½" - $525.00. 22" - $445.00.

Dolls with the "G.S." or "G & S" were made by Gans & Seyforth of Germany who made dolls from 1909 into the 1930's. Some dolls will be marked with the full name.

Child: Open mouth, composition body. Good quality bisque, no damage and nicely dressed. 16" - $325.00; 20" - $475.00; 22" - $500.00; 26" - $700.00.

Baby: Bent limb baby body, in perfect condition and nicely dressed. 18" - $550.00; 23" - $700.00. (Add more for toddler body.)

Some of these unmarked dolls will have a mold number and/or a head size number and some may have the mark "Germany."

Closed Mouth Child: 1880-1890's. Composition jointed body, no damage and nicely dressed. 12" - $1,200.00; 16" - $1,600.00; 21" - $2,200.00; 25" - $2,700.00.

Closed Mouth Child: On kid body (or cloth). May have slight turned head, bisque lower arms. 12" - $600.00; 16" - $850.00; 21" - $1,050.00; 25" - $1,200.00.

Open Mouth Child: Late 1880's to 1900. Excellent pale bisque, jointed composition body. Glass eyes, no damage and nicely dressed. 16" - $475.00; 21" - $600.00; 25" - $750.00; 29" - $1,200.00.

Open Mouth Child: Same as above, but on kid body with bisque lower arms. 16" - $375.00; 21" - $500.00; 25" - $650.00; 29" - $800.00.

Open Mouth Child: 1900 to 1920's. With very "dolly" type face. Overall excellent condition, composition jointed body. 16" - $365.00; 21" - $525.00.

Open Mouth Child: Same as above, but with kid body and bisque lower arms. 16" - $325.00; 21" - $465.00.

Bonnet or Hatted: Bisque head with modeled-on bonnet or hat, molded hair and painted features. Cloth body with bisque limbs. No damage and nicely dressed. Dates from about 1880's into 1920's.

Bisque: 12" - $400.00 up; 15" - $575.00 up.

Stone Bisque: Whitish and more porous than bisque. 12" - $265.00; 15" - $475.00.

Glass Eyes: Excellent overall quality. 18" - $2,900.00; 24" - $3,900.00.

All Bisque: See "All Bisque - German" section.

Molded Hair: See that section.

28" incised "18 103." Most likely German, but may be French. Sleep eyes, closed mouth and is on a French composition jointed body. Holds a marotte made by Simon & Halbig marked "S&H 1010 DEP." Open mouth, wood handle, and body holds music box and when twirled, it plays. Courtesy Frasher Doll Auctions. 28" - $6,000.00 up; S&H - $625.00.

Infants: Bisque head, molded/painted hair, cloth body with composition or celluloid hands, glass eyes. No damage. 12" - $385.00; 17" - $625.00.

Babies: Solid dome or wigged, glass eyes, five-piece baby body, open mouth, nicely dressed and no damage. (Allow more for closed or open/closed mouth or very unusual face.) 13" - $475.00; 16" - $525.00; 20" - $650.00.

Babies: Same as above, but with painted eyes. 13" - $425.00; 16" - $475.00; 20" - $575.00.

Tiny Unmarked Doll: Head is bisque of good quality on five-piece papier maché or composition body, glass

11" multi-faced probably made by Carl Bergner of Germany. Has three faces, one asleep, one smiling, and one crying. Papier maché hood/bonnet and head is rotated from top. Composition jointed body with straight wrists. Courtesy Frasher Doll Auctions. 11" - $1,000.00 up.

eyes, open mouth. No damage. 6" - $245.00; 8½" - $300.00; 10" - $395.00.

Tiny Doll: Same as above, but on full jointed composition body. 6" - $275.00; 8½" - $400.00; 10" - $475.00.

Tiny Doll: Closed mouth, jointed body. 6" - $325.00; 8½" - $450.00. Five-piece body: 6" - $275.00; 8½" - $375.00.

Character Child: Unidentified, closed mouth, very character face, may have wig or solid dome, glass eyes, closed or open/closed mouth. Excellent quality bisque, no damage and nicely dressed. 17" - $2,600.00 up.

Character: Closed mouth, mold numbers 111, 128, 134, and others of this quality. 21" - $8,000.00 up.

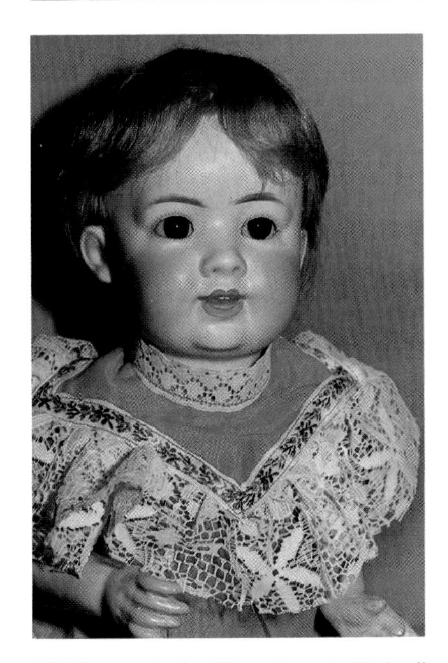

13½" marked "My Sweet Baby." Socket head on five-piece bent limb baby body, open/closed mouth with molded tongue and two teeth, sleep eyes. Courtesy Frasher Doll Auctions. 13½" - $475.00. 16" - $600.00. 20" - $750.00. 24" - $1,100.00.

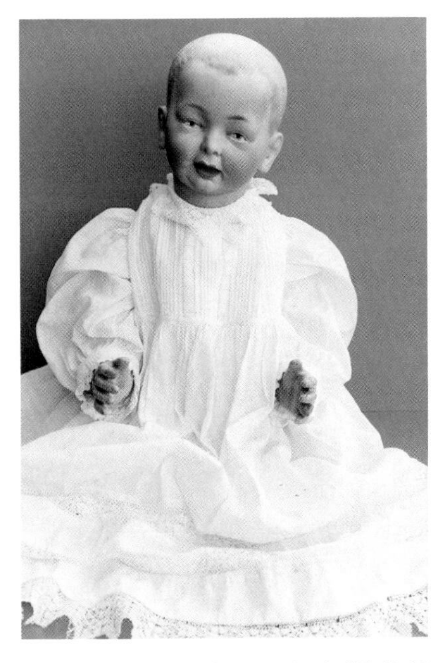

21" Character baby marked "F 3 B Germany." Brush stroked hair, painted eyes and open/closed mouth. Five-piece bent limb baby body. Most likely made by Fritz Bierschenk about 1910. Courtesy Frasher Doll Auctions. 21" - $850.00.

8" Character baby marked "A 2/0 R." Molded hair, sleep eyes, open/closed smiling mouth, flange neck on cloth bent limb baby body and celluloid hands. Courtesy Frasher Doll Auctions. 8" - $325.00.

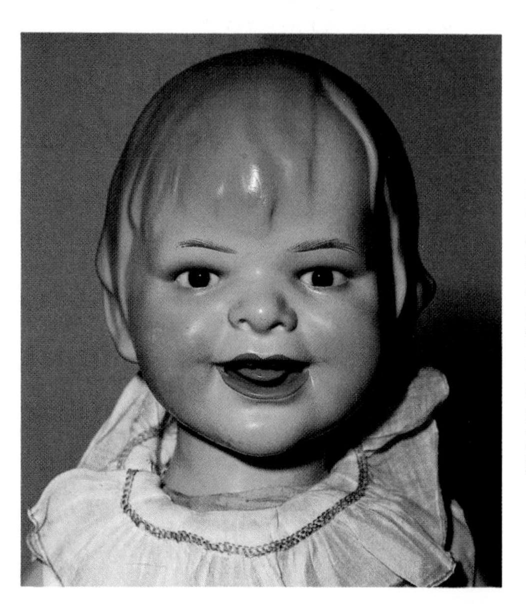

19½" rare "Gladdie" with excellent face coloring, glass eyes and most unusual mouth modeling. She has open/closed mouth with very detailed tongue and teeth rest on the tongue. The mouth is actually open more than the regular "Gladdie" dolls. Cloth body with composition limbs. Courtesy Barbara Earnshaw-Cain.
20" - $2,000.00.

17" "Gladdie" marked "Gladdie Copr. By Helene W. Jensen." Ceramic-style material, painted head with open/closed mouth, painted teeth, glass eyes. Cloth body with composition limbs. Shown with 18" Black doll marked "S&H 949" with open mouth and on jointed composition body. 17" ceramic head - $1,000.00 up. 17" bisque head - $3,600.00 up. 18" - S&H - $1,400.00.

The Goebel factory has been operating since 1879 and is located in Oeslau, Germany. The interwoven W.G. mark has been used since 1879. William Goebel inherited the factory from his father, Granz Detley Goebel. About 1900, the factory only made dolls, dolls heads and porcelain figures. They worked in both bisque and china glazed items.

Marks:

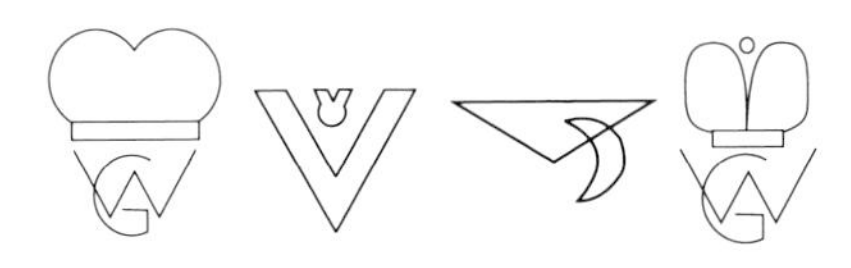

Child: 1895 and later. Open mouth, composition body, sleep or set eyes with head in perfect condition, dressed and ready to display. 6" - $195.00; 16"- $375.00; 20" - $475.00; 24" - $595.00.

Character: After 1910. Molded hair that can be in various styles, with or without molded flowers or ribbons, painted features and on five-piece papier maché body. No damage and nicely dressed. 6" - $350.00; 8" - $450.00.

Character Baby: After 1909. Open mouth, sleep eyes and on five-piece bent limb baby body. No damage and nicely dressed. 14" - $465.00; 17" - $600.00; 21" - $700.00; 25" - $950.00.

Molded-on Bonnet: Closed mouth, five-piece papier maché body, painted features and may have various molded-on hats or bonnets and painted hair. 6" - $350.00; 8" - $475.00.

23" baby marked with Goebel trademark plus "W" over "G/B5-11 Germany." Open mouth and on five-piece bent limb baby body. 11½" baby on five-piece bent limb body and head marked "150." Attributed to Hertal, Schwab & Co. 23" - $785.00. 11½" - $450.00.

Bisque head with glass or set eyes to the side, closed smiling mouth, impish or watermelon-style mouth, original composition or papier maché body. Molded hair or wigged. 1911 and after. Not damaged in any way and nicely dressed.

All Bisque: See All Bisque section.

Armand Marseille: #200: 11" - $2,800.00. **#210:** 8" - $2,200.00. **#223:** 6" - $800.00; 8" - $1,000.00. **#241:** 12" - $2,800.00. **#248:** 6" - $900.00. **#252:** 9½-10" - $795.00. **#253:** 6½" - $750.00; 8" - $900.00; 10" - $1,100.00; 16" - $2,800.00. **#254:** 8" - $950.00. **#255 -#310:** (Just Me) fired-in color: 7-8" - $1,200.00; 12" - $1,500.00. **#310** with painted bisque: 7-8" - $700.00; 12"- $1,000.00. **#320:** 8" - $1,200.00. **#323** fired-in color: 6½" - $650.00; 8" - $850.00; 12-14" - $1,600.00. On baby body: 12" - $1,200.00. Painted bisque: 8" - $500.00; 12" - $775.00. **#325:** 8" - $750.00.

B.P. (Bahr & Proschild) #686: 12" - $2,400.00. Baby: 12" - $1,200.00.

Demalcol: 8" - $600.00; 11" - $750.00; 14" - $900.00.

Hertel Schwab: See that section.

Heubach Einco: 14" - $7,000.00 up.

Heubach (marked in square): 8" - $950.00; 12" - $1,800.00. **#9573:** 10" - $1,800.00. **#11173:** 8" - $1,500.00 up.

Heubach Koppelsdorf: #318: 9" - $1,400.00; 14" - $2,200.00. **#319:** 12" - $1,300.00. **#417:** 12" - $1,000.00.

Kestner: #165 (This number now attributed to Hertel & Schwab): 16" - $5,500.00. **#172-173** (Attributed to Hertel & Schwab): 16" - $6,400.00. **#221:** 12" - $4,000.00; 16" - $6,000.00; 18" - $6,800.00.

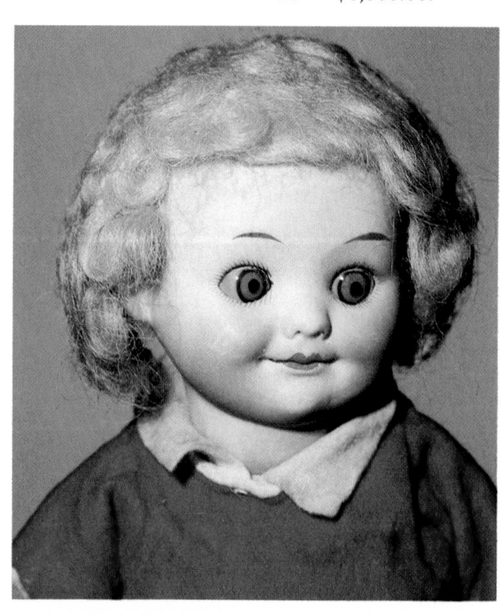

11" Armand Marseille googly incised "323." Side glance large glass eyes that are sleep eyes, closed "watermelon" mouth and all original with red/white check short pants, white shoes and socks. Original wig and on five-piece body. Courtesy Barbara Earnshaw-Cain. 11" original - $1,600.00.

15" composition head googly with very large glass eyes, cloth body and legs with composition lower arms. Maker unknown. 12" Teddy bear of gold mohair, straw-filled head and limbs. Velveteen nose and pads. Courtesy Turn of Century Antiques. 15" - $1,200.00.

Kammer & Reinhardt (K star R): 8" on five-piece body: $2,600.00. **#131:** 12" - $5,600.00; 15" - $7,200.00.

Oscar Hitt: 15" - $7,800.00 up.

P.M. (Otto Reinecke): #950: 8" - $1,300.00; 12" - $2,400.00.

S.F.B.J.: #245: 9" on five-piece body - $1,600.00. 9" on fully jointed body: 12" - $2,800.00; 14-15" - $5,800.00.

Steiner, Herm: 8" - $825.00; 12" - $975.00.

Composition Face: Very round composition face mask or all composition head with wig, glass eyes to side and closed impish watermelon-style mouth. Body is stuffed felt. In original clothes and all in excellent condition. 6½" - $425.00; 10" - $650.00; 12" - $875.00; 16" - $1,200.00; 20" - $1,700.00. Fair condition, cracks or crazing, nicely redressed: 6½" - $175.00; 10" - $300.00; 12" - $425.00; 16" - $550.00; 20" - $700.00.

Painted Eyes: Composition or papier maché body with painted-on shoes and socks. Bisque head with eyes painted to side, closed smile mouth and molded hair. Not damaged and nicely dressed (such as A.M. 320, Goebel, R.A., Heubach, etc.): 8" - $400.00; 12" - $650.00.

Disc Eyes: Bisque socket head or shoulder head with molded hair (can have molded hat-cap), closed mouth and inset celluloid disc in large googly eyes. 10" - $650.00; 12-13" - $875.00; 16" - $1,200.00; 20" - $1,700.00.

Molded-on Hat: Marked "Elite." 12" - $2,600.00.

6" all bisque googly by Kestner with mold number 217. Sleep eyes to side, closed smiling mouth. Jointed at shoulders and hips with painted-on shoes and socks. Original with original dome trunk with lift-out tray. 5 outfits, undies, comb mirror and parasol. Courtesy Frasher Doll Auctions. 6" in trunk - $2,400.00 up.

15½" S.F.B.J. 245 googly and so marked. Bisque head with original wig and clothes. Sleep eyes, closed mouth, and jointed French body. Very rare. Also shown, 8" all original marked "A 323 M" with sleep eyes, closed mouth, and five-piece body. Courtesy Barbara Earnshaw-Cain. 15½" "245" - $5,800.00 up. 8" - $850.00. Painted bisque - $500.00.

8½" Googly by Gebruder Heubach marked "9578 3/0" and "Heubach" in a square. Sleep eyes and on five-piece body. Shown also is an 11" Black doll marked "SFBJ Paris" and made from a Jumeau mold. Open mouth and on jointed French body. Courtesy Frasher Doll Auctions. 8½" - $1,200.00 up. 11" S.F.B.J. - $550.00.

Ludwig Greiner of Philadelphia, PA made dolls from 1858 into the 1800's. The heads are made of papier maché, and they can be found on various bodies, can be all cloth (many homemade), many have leather arms or can be found on Lacmann bodies that have stitched joints at the hips and the knees and are very wide at the hip line. The Lacmann bodies will be marked "J. Lacmann's Patent March 24th, 1874" in an oval. The Greiner heads will be marked "Greiner's Patent Doll Heads/Pat. Mar. 30, '58." Also "Greiner's/Improved/Patent Heads/ Pat. Mar. 30, '58." The later heads are marked "Greiner's Patent Doll Heads/ Pat. Mar. 30, '58. Ext. '72."

Greiner Doll: Can have black or blonde molded hair, blue or brown painted eyes and be on a nice homemade cloth body with cloth arms or a commerical cloth body with leather arms. Dressed for the period and clean, with head in near perfect condition with no paint chips and not repainted.

With '58 Label: 18" - $975.00; 22" - $1,300.00; 25" - $1,500.00; 28" - $1,750.00; 31" - $2,100.00; 35" - $2,500.00; 38" - $3,200.00. With chips and flakes or repainted: 18" - $400.00; 25" - $700.00; 31" - $1,000.00; 38" - $1,600.00.

With '72 Label: 18" - $650.00; 22" - $950.00; 25" - $1,150.00; 28" - $1,300.00; 31" - $1,500.00; 35" - $1,800.00; 38" - $2,100.00. With chips and flakes or repainted: 18" - $350.00; 25" - $425.00; 28" - $600.00.

Glass Eyes: 20" - $2,000.00; 25" - $2,600.00. With chips and flakes or repainted: 20" - $725.00; 25" - $975.00.

Left: 32" Greiner papier maché with paper label "Pat. Mar. 30 '58, Ext. '72." Painted eyes, cloth body with sewn-on boots and is stamped "J. Lacmann's Patent March 24th, 1874." Center: 29" pre-Greiner papier maché, glass eyes, cloth body with leather arms. Right: 21" Griener with the '58 label. Glass eyes doll has a repainted head. Courtesy Frasher Doll Auctions. 32" - $1,600.00. 29" - $2,400.00. 21" repainted- $700.00; if mint - $1,300.00.

23½" bisque head on jointed body, open mouth with five teeth, original wig and redressed in old material. Marked "G & S/Germany/6." Made by Guttman & Schiffnie, who made dolls from 1897 into 1930's. Child with open mouth: 16" - $400.00; 22-23" - $650.00; 26-27" - $900.00.

Henri and Grange Guimonneau and Cie were the makers of the rare French dolls marked "H.G. and Paris." They were in business from 1879 to 1885 and these dolls are very hard to locate to add to a collection. The H.G. marked dolls came on kid or composition bodies and they made closed, open/closed and open mouthed dolls.

H.G. (incised on head): With open/closed or closed mouth. 16" - $7,500.00; 20" - $12,000.00; 25"- $16,000.00. Open mouth: 16" - $2,800.00; 20" - $5,400.00; 25" - $7,000.00.

24½" very rare marked "H.G. 11." Open/closed mouth. May be original wig and costume. Made by Henri & Grange Guimonneau and Cie of Paris, who produced dolls from 1879 to 1885. Perfect condition and no damage. 25" - $16,000.00.

HALF DOLLS (PINCUSHIONS)

Half dolls can be made of any material including bisque, papier maché and composition. Not all half dolls were used as pin cushions. They were also used for powder box tops, brushes, tea cozies, etc. Most date from 1900 into the 1930's, and the majority were made in Germany, but many were made in Japan. Generally they will be marked with "Germany" or "Japan." Some have numbers and others may have the marks of companies such as William Goebel W or Dressel, Kister & Co.

The most desirable are the large ones, or any size for that matter, that have both arms molded away from the body, or are jointed at the shoulder.

Arms/Hands: Completely away from figure. China or bisque: 5" - $300.00 up; 8" - $425.00 up; 12" - $900.00 up.

Arms Extended: But hands attached to figure. China or bisque: 3" - $60.00; 5" - $70.00; 8" - $95.00. Papier maché or composition: 4½" - $20.00;

6½" - $65.00.

Common Figures: With arms and hands attached. China: 3" - $25.00; 5" - $35.00; 8" - $50.00. Papier maché or composition: 3" - $15.00; 5" - $22.00.

Jointed Shoulders: China or bisque: 5" - $95.00; 8" - $110.00; 12" - $145.00. Papier maché: 4" - $28.00; 7" - $70.00. Wax over papier maché: 4" - $38.00; 7" - $90.00.

Children or Men: 3" - $40.00; 5" - $65.00; 7" - $95.00. Jointed shoulders: 3" - $60.00; 5" - $90.00; 7" - $145.00.

Japan marked: 3" - $15.00; 5" - $28.00; 7" - $45.00.

Very outstanding half figure with both arms away from body and she holds a letter, has a high hairdo with "court appearance" feather plumes, but a downcast look to the face modeling. Marked "Dressel, Kister." Courtesy Barbara Earnshaw-Cain. 5" - $500.00.

5" tall half figure with both arms modeled away from body, excellent face detail and has very high pale brown hairdo. Very small busted for these figures. Courtesy Barbara Earnshaw-Cain. 5" - $375.00.

Large half figure with grey hair and applied porcelain flowers and leaves in hair and hand. Both arms are modeled away from figure and has excellent quality of face detail. Made by Dressel, Kister. Courtesy Barbara Earnshaw-Cain. 5" - $485.00.

Beautiful large 5" half doll of the 1920's. Extremely fine artist detail and has folded hands away from body. Courtesy Barbara Earnshaw-Cain. 5" - $575.00.

Most unusual Dressel, Kister half doll pincushion with both arms modeled away from body and with one arm outstretched and the other is cupped on hip. Has modeled cap, dark hair and very detailed face. Courtesy Barbara Earnshaw-Cain. 5" - $750.00.

5½" tall half doll pincushion with long, wide base that is a tea cozy. Both arms and hands are modeled away from the body. Marked with the Dressel, Kister mark, Germany. Courtesy Barbara Earnshaw-Cain. 5½" - $425.00.

Large half doll that has an older lady's face, blonde hair with comb band and has large bust. Both hands and arms modeled away from body and she holds a rose. Courtesy Barbara Earnshaw-Cain. 5" - $450.00.

PHOTO, NEXT PAGE:

Half figure that is 5" tall, has wide base and arms modeled away from body. She holds a flower with applied leaves and has modeled bow in hair with applied flower and leaves. Modeled dress and light brown hair. Courtesy Barbara Earnshaw-Cain. 5" - $375.00.

Heinrich Handwerck began making dolls and doll bodies in 1876 at Gotha, Germany. Majority of their heads were made by Simon & Halbig. In 1897 they patented, in Germany, a ball jointed body #100297 and some of their bodies will be marked with this number.

Mold numbers include: 12x, 19, 23, 69, 79, 89, 99, 100, 109, 118, 119, 124, 125, 139, 152, 189, 199, 1001, 1200, 1290.

Sample mold marks:

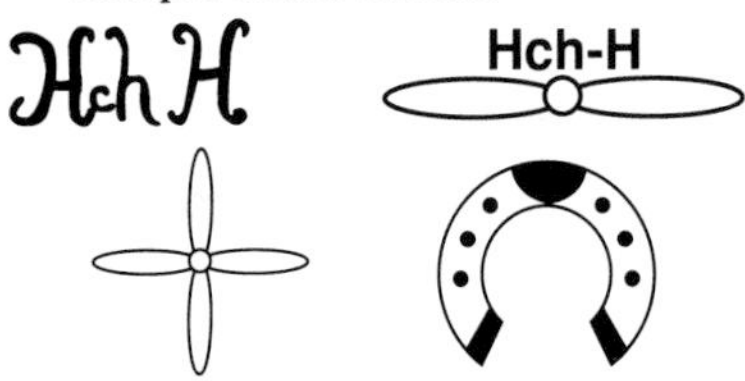

Child: After 1885. Open mouth, sleep or set eyes, on ball-jointed body. Bisque head with no cracks, chips or hairlines, good wig and nicely dressed. 16" - $485.00; 19" - $565.00; 23" - $675.00; 25" - $775.00; 27" - $1,000.00; 30" - $1,200.00; 33" - $1,600.00; 36" - $1,900.00; 40" - $2,800.00; 42" - $3,200.00.

Kid Body: Bisque shoulder head, open mouth. All in good condition and nicely dressed. 16" - $375.00; 19" - $450.00; 25" - $625.00; 27" - $850.00.

Closed Mouth: Marked with company name and sometimes with Simon & Halbig. May have mold numbers 79 or 89. 12" - $1,300.00; 19" - $2,000.00; 25" - $2,600.00.

18" marked "HCH," horseshoe mark/ 5/9H. Shoulder head on kid body with bisque lower arms. Open mouth and set eyes. Courtesy Frasher Doll Auctions. 18" - $425.00.

35" marked "Heinrich Handwerck S&H #7." Jointed body, open mouth and body is marked "Heinrich Handwerck." Courtesy Arthur Boutiette. 35" - $1,900.00.

Max Handwerck started making dolls in 1900 and his factory was located at Walterhausen, Germany. In 1901, he registered "Bébé Elite" with the heads made by William Goebel. The dolls from this firm are marked with the full name, but a few are marked with "M.H."

Child: Bisque head, open mouth, sleep or set eyes, on fully jointed composition body, no damage and nicely dressed. **Mold #287, etc.:** 16" - $400.00; 20" - $475.00; 24" - $625.00; 28" - $800.00; 32" - $1,200.00; 36" - $1,500.00; 40" - $2,200.00.

Bébé Elite: Bisque heads with no cracks or chips, sleep or set eyes, open mouth. Can have a flange neck on cloth body with composition limbs or be on a bent leg composition baby body. Upper teeth and smile: 17" - $475.00; 21" - $675.00. Socket head on fully jointed body: 17" - $585.00; 21" - $800.00.

30" marked "Max Handwerck S&H/Germany." Jointed body, open mouth and sleep eyes. Courtesy Frasher Doll Auctions. 30" - $1,100.00.

Hertal, Schwab & Co. have been recognized as the maker of many dolls that were attributed to other companies all these years (by the German authors Jurgen and Marianne Cieslik.) There does not seem to be a "common denominator" to Hertal, Swhwab line of dolls and can include any style.

Babies: Bisque head, molded hair or wig, open or open/closed mouth, sleep or painted eyes, bent limb baby body. No damage and all in good condition.

Mold numbers: 130, 142, 150, 151, 152: 12" - $450.00; 16" - $575.00; 20" - $675.00; 24" - $875.00.

Child: Bisque head, painted or sleep eyes, closed mouth, jointed composition body, no damage and nicely dressed. **#134, 141, 149:** 16" - $5,400.00; 20" - $8,000.00. **#154 with Closed Mouth:** 18" - $2,500.00; 22" - $2,900.00. Open Mouth: 20" - $1,300.00. **#169:** 20" - $3,600.00. Toddler: $4,200.00.

All Bisque: One-piece body and head, glass eyes, closed or open mouth. All in perfect condition. **Prize Baby (mold #208):** 5" - $275.00; 7" - $385.00; 8" - $550.00. Swivel Neck: 6" - $475.00; 8" - $725.00.

Googly: Wig or molded hair. Large, side glance sleep or set eyes. Closed mouth, no damage and nicely dressed. **#163:** 12" - $3,200.00; 16" - $5,600.00. **#165*:** 12" - $3,200.00; 16" - $5,500.00; **#172, 173:** 12" - $4,000.00; 15" - $6,000.00.

** At auction, 22" - $10,200.00; 11½" - $3,650.00.*

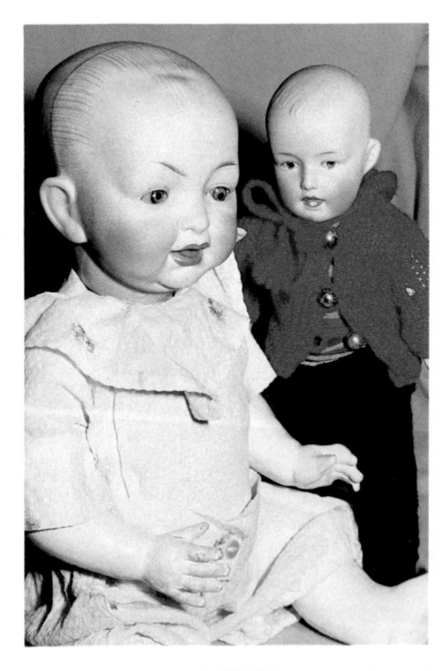

Left: 14" marked "142" and attributed to Hertal Schwab. Has always been an acceptable Kestner. Open/closed mouth and on five-piece bent limb baby body. Right: 10" by Gebruder Heubach marked "G.H. dep 2/0 08 Germany 7129." Shoulder head on kid body, intaglio eyes and open/closed mouth. Courtesy Frasher Doll Auctions. 14" - $500.00; 10" - $475.00.

18" marked "152 Made in Germany." Open mouth and on five-piece bent limb baby body. This doll is now being attributed to Hertal Schwab instead of Kestner. Courtesy Frasher Doll Auctions. 18" - $625.00.

The Heubach Brothers (Gebruder) made dolls from 1863 into the 1930's at Lichte, Thur, Germany. They started producing character dolls in 1910. Heubach dolls can reflect almost every mood and are often found on rather crude, poor quality bodies, and many are small dolls.

Marks:

Character Dolls: Bisque head, open/closed or closed mouth, painted eyes (allow more for glass eyes), on kid, papier maché or jointed composition bodies. Molded hair or wig. No damage and nicely dressed. **#5636:** Laughing child, intaglio painted eyes. 12" - $1,000.00. Glass eyes: 12" - $1,600.00. **#5689:** Open mouth, smiling. 16" - $1,700.00; 18" - $2,000.00; 28" - $4,200.00. **#5730 (Santa):** 14" - $2,300.00; 17" - $2,700.00; 32" - $3,400.00. **#5777, #9355 (Dolly Dimples):** Ball-jointed body. 16" - $1,700.00; 22" - $2,800.00; 24" - $3,000.00. **#6692:** Shoulder head, smiling, intaglio eyes. 15" - $850.00. **#6736, #6894:** Laughing, wide open/closed mouth, molded lower teeth. 10-12" - $900.00; 16" - $1,800.00. **#6896:** Pouty, jointed body. 19" - $1,100.00. **#6969, #6970, #7246, #8017, #8420:** Pouty boy or girl, jointed body, painted eyes. 12" - $1,000.00; 16" - $1,900.00; 20" - $2,300.00. Toddler: 20" - $2,500.00. Glass eyes: 14" - $2,400.00; 17" - $2,800.00; 20" - $3,100.00. Toddler, glass eyes: 20" - $3,500.00. **#7172, #7550:** 14" - $1,400.00. **#7448:** Open/closed mouth, eyes half shut. 14" - $2,600.00. **#7602:** Painted eyes and hair, long face pouty, closed mouth. 16" - $2,800.00; 20" - $3,200.00 up. Glass eyes: 14" - $3,400.00; 20" - $3,600.00 up. **#7604:** Laughing, jointed body, intaglio eyes. 12" - $600.00. Baby: 14" - $750.00. **#7616:** Open/closed mouth with molded tongue. Socket or shoulder head. Glass eyes: 12" - $1,400.00; 15" - $1,900.00. **#7622:**

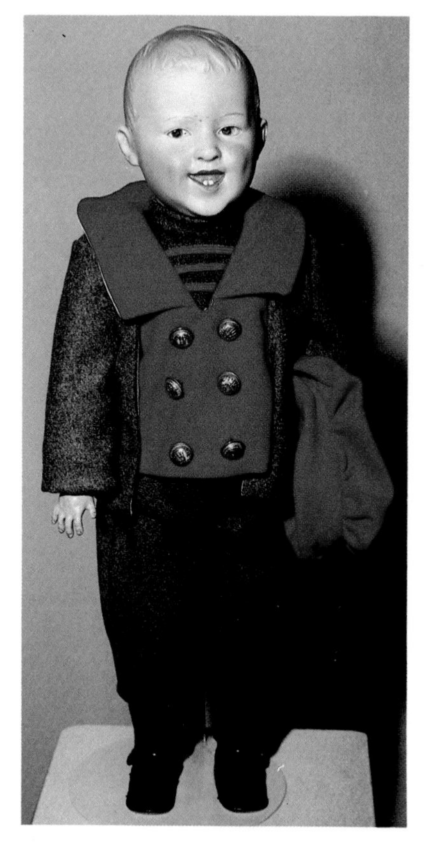

19½" marked Heubach mold number 6894. Intaglio eyes and wide open/closed laughing mouth with two lower teeth. On fully jointed body. Large detailed ears. Courtesy Barbara Earnshaw-Cain. 19½" - $2,600.00.

Molded hair, intaglio eyes, closed mouth and light cheek dimples. 12" - $675.00; 16" - $1,100.00. **#7623:** Molded hair, intaglio eyes, open/closed mouth, molded tongue, on bent limb baby body. 12" - $750.00; 16" - $1,200.00. Jointed body: 16" - $1,600.00. **#7634:** Crying, squinting eyes. 14" - $1,100.00. **#7636:** 10" - $750.00. **#7644:** Laughing, socket or shoulder head, intaglio eyes. 14" - $750.00. **#7679:** Whistler, socket head. 14" - $1,200.00. **#7701:** Pouty, intaglio eyes. 18" - $1,800.00. **#7711:** Open mouth, jointed body. 12" - $400.00; 16" - $600.00; 20" - $800.00; 24" - $1,100.00. **#7768, #7788:** "Couquette," tilted head, molded hair and can have ribbon modeled into hairdo. 12" - $975.00; 14" - $1,100.00; 17" - $1,800.00. **#7849:** Closed mouth, intaglio eyes. 12" - $675.00. **#7852 or #119:** Braids coiled around ear (molded), intaglio eyes. 16" - $2,500.00 up. **#7925, #7926:** Adult, painted eyes: 16" - $3,000.00. Glass eyes: 16" - $4,200.00. **#7977, #7877:** "Stuart Baby," molded baby bonnet. Painted eyes: 12" - $1,200.00; 14" - $1,600.00; 16" - $1,900.00. Glass eyes: 12" - $1,600.00; 14" - $1,900.00; 16" - $2,100.00. **#8191:** Smiling openly, jointed body. 12" - $900.00; 14" - $1,100.00; 17" - $1,400.00. **#8192:** Open/closed smiling mouth with tongue molded between teeth. 15" - $1,200.00; 22" - $2,300.00. Open mouth: 14" - $600.00; 17" - $1,000.00.

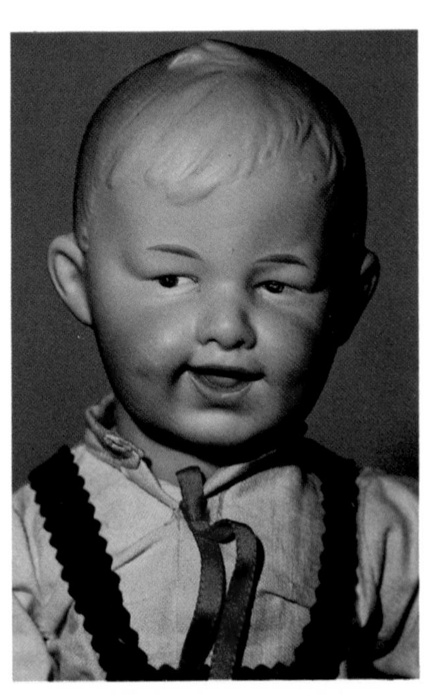

15½" boy marked with "Heubach" in square and no mold number. Open/closed mouth with modeled tongue, side glancing intaglio eyes and protruding ears. On fully jointed toddler body. All original and he also has a chain and pipe attached to suspenders. Courtesy Barbara Earnshaw-Cain. 15½" - $2,800.00.

22" marked "Heubach" in square. Sleep eyes, smiling open/closed mouth with two molded teeth resting on tongue and is on toddler jointed body. Courtesy Frasher Doll Auctions. 22" - $3,700.00 up.

#8420: Pouty, painted eyes. 14" - $550.00; 17" - $750.00. Glass eyes: 14" - $750.00; 17" - $900.00. **#8469:** Wide open/closed laughing mouth, glass eyes. 11" - $2,600.00; 14" - $3,200.00. **#8590:** Pouty, intaglio eyes. 14" - $650.00. **#8596:** Smile, intaglio eyes. 14" - $650.00. **#8774:** "Whistling Jim," eyes to side and mouth modeled as if whistling. 12" - $1,000.00; 16" - $1,400.00. **#9355:** Shoulder head. 16" - $900.00; 22" - $1,600.00. **#10586, #10633:** Child with open mouth, jointed body. 16" - $525.00; 20" - $725.00; 25" - $1,000.00. **#10532:** Open mouth, jointed body. 12" - $485.00; 16" - $750.00; 18" - $1,000.00; 22" - $1,400.00. **#11173:** Glass eyes, five-piece body, pursed closed mouth with large indented cheeks. Called "Tiss-Me." 8" - $1,500.00 up.

Child with Dolly-type Face (non-character): Open mouth, glass sleep or set eyes, jointed body, bisque head with no damage and nicely dressed. 16" - $525.00; 19" - $775.00; 24" - $900.00.

** #7745, 16" - $5,400.00 at auction.*

10½" incised "Heubach 8459" that is all original and has glass eyes, open/closed mouth with two lower teeth and very character modeling. On fully jointed body. Courtesy Barbara Earnshaw-Cain. 10½" - $2,200.00.

12" Heubach Twins with mold number 8192. Both have open/closed mouths with two upper teeth. All original and on five-piece bodies. Courtesy Barbara Earnshaw-Cain. 12" - $900.00 each.

Googly: Marked with a Heubach mark. Glass eyes: 8" - $950.00; 12" - $1,800.00.

Indian Portrait: Man or woman. 13-14" - $3,200.00 up.

Babies or Infants: Bisque head, wig or molded hair, sleep or intaglio eyes, open/closed pouty-type mouths. **Mold #6894, #6898, #7602:** 6" - $265.00; 8" - $400.00; 10" - $425.00; 14" - $550.00; 18" - $800.00; 22" - $950.00; 25" - $1,300.00; 28" - $1,600.00.

10" marked "Heubach 350" on flapper body with knee joints high on legs, slim limbs and one-piece arms. In basket with wardrobe. Sleep eyes and open mouth. Courtesy Barbara Earnshaw-Cain. 10" doll only - $500.00; 10" with trunk, original - $1,750.00.

Ernst Heubach began making dolls in 1887 in Koppelsdorf, Germany and the marks of this firm can be the initials "E.H." or the dolls can be marked with the full name Heubach Koppelsdorf, or:

Some mold numbers from this company: 27X, 87, 99, 230, 235, 236, 237, 238, 242, 250, 251, 262, 271, 273, 275, 277, 283, 300, 302, 312, 317, 320, 321, 330, 338, 339, 340, 342, 349, 350, 367, 399, 407, 410, 417, 438, 444, 450, 452, 458, 616, 1310, 1900, 1901, 1906, 1909, 2504, 2671, 2757, 3027, 3412, 3423, 3427, 7118, 32144.

Child: After 1888. Jointed body, open mouth, sleep or set eyes. No damage and nicely dressed. 8" - $175.00; 10" - $195.00; 14" - $285.00; 20" - $425.00; 24" - $500.00; 30" - $900.00; 34" - $1,000.00; 38" - $1,400.00.

Child: On kid body with bisque lower arms, bisque shoulder head, some turned head, open mouth. No damage and nicely dressed. 14" - $185.00; 20" - $295.00; 24" - $385.00; 30" - $800.00.

Child: Painted bisque. 8" - $125.00; 12" - $185.00.

Babies: 1910 and after. On five-piece bent limb baby body, open mouth with some having wobbly tongue and pierced nostrils. Sleep eyes. No damage and nicely dressed. 6" - $265.00;

Left: 19" marked "Heubach Koppelsdorf" on kid body with bisque shoulder head and lower arms. Open mouth and sleep eyes. Right: 24" German turned head with open mouth. Maker unknown. Kid body with bisque lower arms. Courtesy Frasher Doll Auctions. 19" - $295.00. 24" - $550.00.

Left: Marked "Heubach Koppelsdorf 320." Socket head on jointed body. Open mouth and sleep eyes. Right 24½" marked "G.B." Open mouth and on jointed body. Courtesy Frasher Doll Auctions. 24" "320" - $600.00. 24½" "G.B." - $625.00.

9" - $300.00; 12" - $385.00; 16" - $475.00; 20" - $565.00; 26" - $900.00.

Baby on Toddler Body: Same as above, but on a toddler body. 14" - $550.00; 16" - $600.00; 20" - $700.00; 26" - $1,000.00.

Baby, Painted Bisque: Baby, 12" - $245.00; 16" - $350.00. Toddler, 12" - $295.00.

Infant: 1925 and after. Molded or painted hair, sleep eyes, closed mouth, flange neck bisque head on cloth body with composition or celluloid hands. No damage and nicely dressed. **#338, #340:** 12" - $600.00; 14" - $825.00. **#339, #349, #350:** 12" - $585.00; 14" - $785.00. **#399** (White only): 12" - $325.00.

Infant: Same as above but with fired-in tan or brown color. 12" - $500.00; 14" - $650.00.

#452: Tan/brown fired-in color bisque head with same color toddler body, open mouth, painted hair. Earings. No damage and originally dressed or redressed nicely. 12" - $525.00.

Black or Dark Brown: #320, #339, #399: Painted bisque head, on five-piece baby body or toddler cut body. Sleep eyes, painted hair or wig. No damage and very minimum amount of paint pulls (chips) on back of head and none on face. 12" - $475.00; 16" - $650.00; 20" - $850.00; 22" - $1,100.00.

Character Child: 1910 on. Molded hair, painted eyes and open/closed mouth. No damage. **#262, #330 and others:** 12" - $465.00; 16" - $800.00.

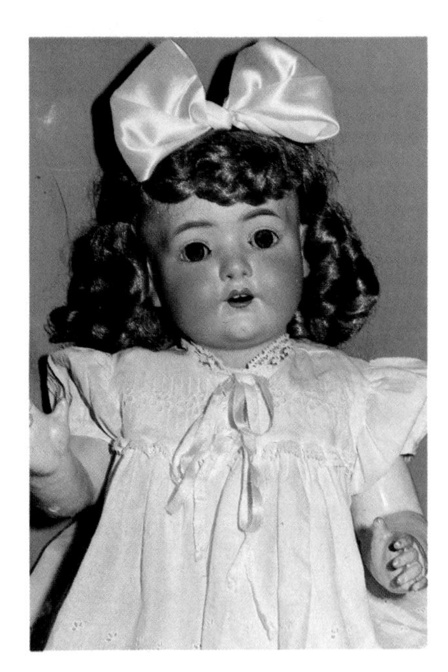

22" marked "Heubach Koppelsdorf 320.8." Open mouth with two upper teeth, five-piece bent limb baby body. Courtesy Frasher Doll Auctions. 22" - $600.00.

24" marked "Heubach Koppelsdorf 342 Germany." On bent limb baby body, open mouth with two upper teeth. Courtesy Frasher Doll Auctions. 24" - $600.00.

Jullien marked dolls were made in Paris, France from 1875 to 1904. The heads will be marked Jullien and a size number. In 1892, Jullien advertised "L'Universal" and the label can be found on some of his doll bodies.

Child: Closed mouth, paperweight eyes, French jointed body of composition, papier maché with some having wooden parts. Undamaged bisque head and all in excellent condition. 18" - $4,000.00; 20" - $4,400.00; 24" - $4,800.00; 28" - $5,300.00.

Child: Same as above, but with open mouth. 18" - $2,000.00; 20" - $2,300.00; 24" - $2,700.00; 28" - $3,000.00.

22" incised "Jullien 8." Open mouth, French jointed body with straight wrists. Wears old factory dress and has old mohair wig. Courtesy Frasher Doll Auctions. 22" - $2,500.00.

19" marked "J 6 J." Closed mouth and on French jointed body. Courtesy Frasher Doll Auctions. 19" - $4,200.00.

Tete Jumeau* : 1879-1899 and later. Marked with red stamp on head and oval sticker on body. Closed mouth, paperweight eyes, jointed body with full joints or jointed with straight wrists. Pierced ears with larger sizes having applied ears. No damage at all to bisque head, undamaged French body, dressed and ready to place into collection. 10" - $3,600.00 up; 12" - $3,000.00; 14" - $3,300.00; 16" - $3,800.00; 19" - $4,200.00; 21" - $4,800.00; 23" - $5,300.00; 25" - $5,500.00; 28" - $6,400.00; 30" - $7,000.00.

Tete Jumeau on Adult Body: 19-20" - $5,900.00.

Tete Jumeau: Same as above, but with open mouth. 10" - $995.00; 14" - $1,800.00; 16" - $2,300.00; 19" - $2,500.00; 21" - $2,700.00; 23" - $3,200.00; 25" - $3,500.00; 28" - $3,900.00; 30" - $4,100.00.

1907 Jumeau: Incised 1907, sometimes has the Tete Jumeau stamp. Sleep or set eyes, open mouth, jointed French body. No damage, nicely dressed. 14" - $1,400.00; 17" - $2,300.00; 20" - $2,600.00; 25" - $3,200.00; 28" - $3,600.00; 32" - $4,000.00.

E.J. Child:** Ca. early 1880's. Head incised "Depose/E.J." Paperweight eyes, closed mouth, jointed body with straight wrist (unjointed at wrist). Larger dolls will have applied ears. No damage to head or body and nicely dressed in excellent quality clothes. 10" - $5,200.00 up; 14" - $5,700.00; 16" - $6,200.00; 19" - $6,600.00; 21" - $7,200.00; 25" - $10,000.00.

17½" stamped "Depose Tete Jumeau 7." Open mouth with six teeth. Jointed body marked "Bebe Jumeau Bte. S.G.D.G. Depose." Has Mama/Papa pull strings in torso with cryer box. Courtesy Frasher Doll Auctions. 18" - $2,400.00.

19½" marked "Depose Tete Jumeau 8" and incised "8." Closed mouth and on jointed body marked "Bébé Jumeau Bte S.D.G.D. Depose." Courtesy Frasher Doll Auctions. 19½" - $6,400.00.

E.J./A Child*:** 25" - $18,000.00 up.

Depose Jumeau: (Incised) 1880. Head will be incised "Depose Jumeau" and body should have Jumeau sticker. Closed mouth, paperweight eyes and on jointed body with straight wrists, although a few may have jointed wrists. No damage at all and nicely dressed. 10" - $4,200.00; 15" - $5,600.00; 18" - $6,200.00; 22" - $7,200.00; 25" - $8,000.00.

Long Face (Triste Jumeau): 1870's. Closed mouth, applied ears, paperweight eyes and stright wrists on Jumeau marked body. Head is generally marked with a size number. No damage to head or body, nicely dressed. 20-21" - $23,000.00 up; 25-26"- $23,000.00 up; 29-30" - $26,000.00 up.

16½" marked "Depose E. 7 J." (incised). Closed mouth, Jumeau body with straight wrists and marked "Jumeau Medialle D' or Paris." Wears original clothes and shoes. Courtesy Frasher Doll Auctions. 16½" - $6,300.00.

Portrait Jumeau**:** 1870's. Closed mouth, usually large almond-shaped eyes and jointed Jumeau body. Head marked with size number only and body has the Jumeau sticker or stamp. 12" - $4,600.00; 16" - $5,800.00; 20" - $7,400.00; 24" - $8,600.00.

Phonograph Jumeau***:** Bisque head with open mouth. Phonograph in body. No damage, working and nicely dressed. 20" - $7,200.00; 25" - $9,000.00.

Wire Eye (Flirty) Jumeau: Lever in back of head operates eyes. Open mouth, jointed body with straight wrists: 20" - $6,200.00; 24" - $7,000.00.

Celluloid Head: Incised Jumeau. 14" - $650.00.

Mold Number 200 Series: *Very character faces* and marked Jumeau.

28" "Long Face" Jumeau incised "13." Closed mouth and on jointed body marked "Jumeau Medialle D' or Paris." Courtesy Frasher Doll Auctions. 28" - $23,000.00.

Closed mouth. No damage to bisque or body. 19" - $2,5000.00.

Mold Number 200 Series: Open mouths. 14" - $5,200.00 up; 20" - $10,000.00.

S.F.B.J. or Unis: Marked along with Jumeau. Open mouth, no damage to head and on French body. 16" - $1,200.00; 20" - $1,700.00. Closed mouth: 16" - $2,200.00; 20" - $2,800.00.

Two-Faced Jumeau: Has two different faces on same head, one crying and one smiling. Open/closed mouths, jointed body. No damage and nicely dressed. 14" - $10,000.00 up.

Fashion: See Fashion section.

Mold 221: Ca. 1930's. Small dolls (10") will have a paper label "Jumeau." Adult style bisque head on five-piece body with painted-on shoes. Closed mouth and set glass eyes. Dressed in original ornate gown. No damage and clean. 10" - $950.00.

Mold 306: Jumeau made after formation of Unis and mark will be "Unis/France" in oval and "71" on one side and "149" on other, followed by "306/Jumeau/1939/Paris." Called "Princess Elizabeth." Closed mouth, flirty or paperweight eyes. Jointed French body. No damage and nicely dressed. 20" - $1,900.00; 30" - $2,900.00.

** Size "O", 9" - $25,000.00 at auction.*

*** E.J. Child: 25" - $18,000.00 at auction.*

**** E.J./A: 26" - $18,500.00; 25" child - $22,000.00 at auction.*

***** Portrait: 10" - $6,600.00 at auction.*

****** Phonograph (original in box): 25" - $23,000.00 at auction.*

11½" Jumeau called "The Screamer" that is incised "Depose Jumeau 3," glass eyes and wide open/closed mouth. On French jointed body. Courtesy Frasher Doll Auctions. 11½" - $4,600.00.

20½" marked "E. 10 J." Closed mouth with Jumeau jointed body with straight wrists. Body marked "Jumeau Medaille D' or Paris." Courtesy Frasher Doll Auctions. 20½" - $6,700.00.

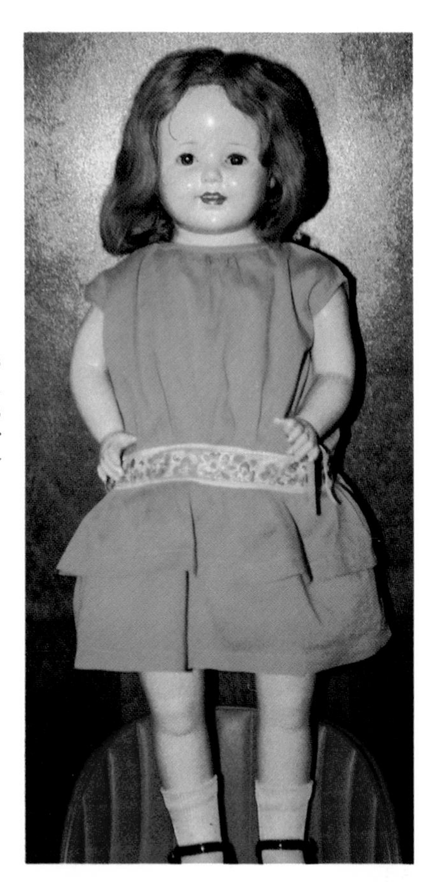

28" composition shoulder head and limbs with cloth body. Tin sleep eyes, open mouth with four upper teeth, dimples and human hair wig. Marked on shoulder plate "K&K Toy Co. Inc." Courtesy Jeannie Mauldin. 28" - $400.00.

19½" marked "K&K 45. Made in Germany." Made by one of the German makers for K&K Toy Co. of New York City. 1915 and 1920's. Open mouth, shoulder head on cloth body with composition arms and legs. Courtesy Frasher Doll Auctions. 19½" - $500.00. 22" - $625.00.

Kammer and Reinhardt dolls generally have the Simon and Halbig name or initials incised along with their own name or mark, as Simon & Halbig made most of their heads. They were located in Thur, Germany at Walterhausen and began in 1895, although their first models were not on the market until 1896. The trademark for this company was registered in 1895.

Marks:

Character Boy or Girl: Closed or open/closed mouth, on jointed body or five-piece body. No damage and nicely dressed. **#101:** 8" on five-piece body - $1,400.00; 8" on fully jointed body - $1,600.00; 14" - $2,400.00; 17" - $3,400.00; 21" - $4,300.00. Glass eyes: 16" - $4,800.00; 21" - $7,000.00. **#102:** Extremely rare. 12" - $16,000.00; 14" - $19,000.00. Glass eyes: 16" - $21,500.00; 20" - $24,500.00 up; **#103 or #104:** Extremely rare. 17" - $52,000.00 up. **#105*:** Extremely rare. Open/closed mouth and much modeling around intaglio eyes. 20" - $62,000.00. **#106:** Extremely rare. Full round face, pursed closed full lips, intaglio eyes to side and much chin modeling. 20" - $48,000.00 up. **#107**:** Pursed, pouty

22" incised "K star R 117." Most unusual because she has red eyebrows that match the color of her original red wig. Closed mouth and on fully jointed body. Courtesy Barbara Earnshaw-Cain. 22" - $5,400.00.

24" marked "K * R 114." Called "Gretchen." Painted eyes, closed mouth and on fully jointed body. Courtesy Frasher Doll Auctions. 24" - $7,200.00.

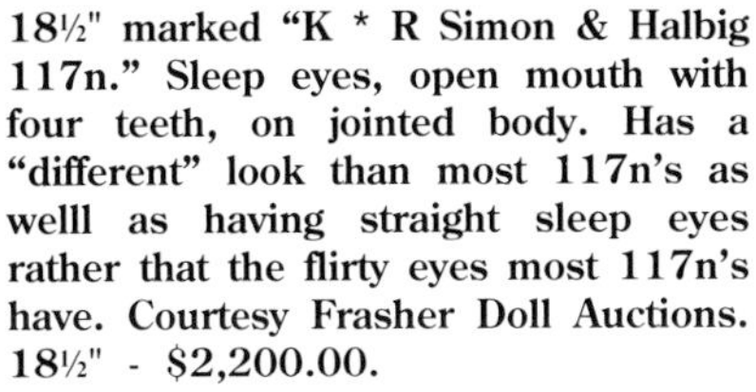

18½" marked "K * R Simon & Halbig 117n." Sleep eyes, open mouth with four teeth, on jointed body. Has a "different" look than most 117n's as welll as having straight sleep eyes rather that the flirty eyes most 117n's have. Courtesy Frasher Doll Auctions. 18½" - $2,200.00.

mouth, intaglio eyes. 15" - $16,000.00; 21" - $23,000.00. Glass eyes: 20" - $28,000.00. **#109:** Very rare. 14" - $14,000.00; 19" - $20,000.00. Glass eyes: 20" - $26,000.00. **#112, #112X, #112A:** Very rare. 14" - $9,500.00; 19" - $12,000.00; 22" - $17,000.00. Glass eyes: 16" - $14,000.00; 22" - $24,000.00. **#114***:** 8" - $1,600.00; 11" - $3,000.00; 14" - $3,600.00; 18" - $5,600.00. Glass eyes: 18" - $7,000.00; 23" - $9,500.00. **#117****:** Closed mouth. 14" - $3,600.00; 16" - $4,000.00; 18" - $4,600.00; 24" - $6,400.00; 28" - $7,200.00. **#117A:** Closed mouth. 16" - $4,300.00; 20" - $5,200.00; 24" - $7,000.00; 28" - $8,600.00. **#117n:** Open mouth, flirty eyes (Take off

25" marked "K * R 14." Open mouth with four teeth, sleep eyes and on jointed body. Hair lashes. Courtesy Frasher Doll Auctions. 25" - $1,100.00.

$200.00 for just sleep eyes): 16" - $1,600.00; 20" - $2,200.00; 26" - $2,600.00; 32" - $3,500.00. **#123, #124 (Max & Moritz):** 17" - $18,000.00 up each. **#127:** Molded hair, open/closed mouth. Toddler or jointed body: 16" - $1,800.00; 20" - $2,400.00. Baby: see that section.

** #105: $169,576.00 at auction (includes buyers premium.)*

*** #107: 12" - $17,000.00 at auction.*

**** #114: Original in box, glass eyes- $8,200.00 at auction.*

*****#117: 25" - $7,750.00 at auction.*

Character Babies: Open/closed mouth or closed mouth on five-piece bent limb baby body, solid dome or wigged. No damage and nicely dressed.

#100: Called "Kaiser Baby." Intaglio eyes, open/closed mouth. 10" -

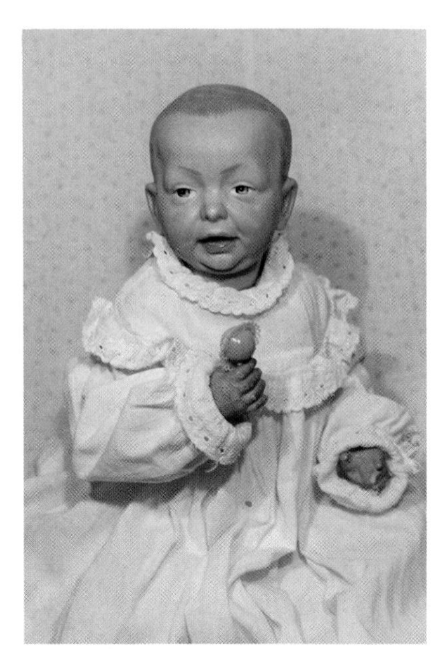

15" marked "K * R 100" and called "Kaiser Baby." Open/closed mouth, intaglio eyes and on five-piece bent limb baby body. Courtesy Frasher Doll Auctions. 15" - $725.00.

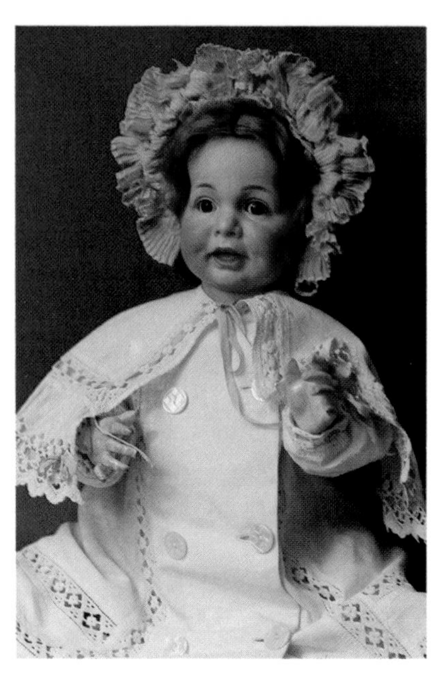

24" marked "K * R Simon & Halbig 116/A." Has 16" head circumference. On five-piece bent limb baby body. Open/closed mouth, sleep eyes. Courtesy Frasher Doll Auction. 24" - $6,200.00.

$500.00; 16" - $725.00; 18" - $1,000.00. Glass eyes: 16" - $2,000.00; 18" - $2,600.00. Black: 16" - $1,400.00; 18" - $2,000.00. **#115, #115a:** 15" - $3,300.00; 18" - $4,600.00; 22" - $4,900.00. Toddler: 15" - $3,800.00; 18" - $5,000.00; 22" - $5,400.00; 26" - $6,200.00. **#116, #116a:** 15" - $2,400.00; 18" - $3,200.00; 22" - $4,000.00. **Toddler*:** 15" - $2,700.00; 18" - $3,500.00; 22" - $4,600.00. Open Mouth: 15" - $1,600.00; 18" - $2,000.00. **#119**:** 25" - $6,400.00 up. **#127:** 12" - $1,000.00; 16" - $1,500.00; 20" - $1,900.00. Toddler: 13" - $1,300.00; 24" - $2,200.00. Child: 14" - $1,300.00; 25" - $2,200.00.

Babies with Open Mouth: Sleep eyes on five-piece bent limb baby body. Wigs, may have tremble tongues or "mama" cryer in body. No damage and nicely dressed. Allow more for flirty eyes. **#121:** 14" - $750.00; 18" - $1,000.00; 22" - $1,400.00. Toddler: 14"- $1,000.00; 18" - $1,400.00; 22" - $1,700.00. **#122, #128:** 15" - $850.00; 18" - $1,200.00; 22" - $1,600.00. Toddler: 15" - $1,300.00; 18" - $1,700.00. **#126:** 12" - $525.00; 15" - $750.00; 20"- $950.00; 25" - $1,600.00; 31" - $2,400.00. Toddler: 8" - $600.00; 15" - $850.00; 20" - $1,300.00; 25" - $1,700.00; 31" - $2,400.00. **#118a:** 16" - $1,800.00; 20" - $2,300.00. **#119:** 20" - $4,800.00. **#135:** 16" - $1,300.00; 20" - $2,100.00.

**#116a Toddler: 21" - $5,000.00 at auction.*

***Character Baby #119: 24" - $4,900.00 at auction.*

Child Dolls: 1895-1930's. Open mouth, sleep or set eyes and on fully jointed body. No damage and nicely dressed. Most often found mold numbers are: #400, #403, #109. Add more for flirty eyes. 8" - $485.00; 16" - $700.00; 18" - $800.00; 22" - $925.00; 26" - $1,300.00; 30" - $1,700.00; 33" - $2,000.00; 36" - $2,400.00; 38" - $2,800.00; 42" - $3,400.00. **#192:** Closed mouth, sleep eyes, fully jointed body. No damage. 15" - $1,400.00; 21"- $2,000.00. Open mouth: 7" - $465.00; 16" - $725.00; 22" - $950.00; 26" - $1,400.00.

Small Child Dolls: Open mouth, sleep eyes (some set) and on five-piece bodies. No damage. 5" - $350.00; 8" - $495.00. Jointed body: 8" - $500.00; 10" - $675.00.

Small Child Doll: Closed mouth: 6-7" - $485.00; 9-10" - $600.00.

Googly: See Googly section.

Celluloid: Babies will have kid, kidaleen or cloth bodies. Child will be on fully jointed body. Open mouth. Some mold numbers: #225, 255, 321, 406, 717, 826, 828, etc. Babies: 15" - $500.00; 20" - $700.00. Child: 16" - $600.00; 20" - $900.00.

Infant: Molded hair and glass eyes, open mouth and cloth body with composition hands. 14-15" - $1,500.00.

25" marked "K * R Simon & Halbig 126." Head made by Simon & Halbig for Kammer & Reinhardt. Open mouth, sleep eyes and on five-piece bent limb baby body. Courtesy Frasher Doll Auctions. 25" - $1,600.00.

Johanne Daniel Kestner's firm was founded in 1802, and his name was carried through the 1920's. The Kestner Company was one of the few that made entire dolls, both body and heads. In 1895, Kestner started using the trademark of the crown and streams.

Sample marks:

B MADE IN 6
GERMANY
J.D.K.
126

F GERMANY 11

J.D.K.
208
GERMANY

Child Doll: Ca. 1880. Closed mouth, some appear to be pouties, sleep or set eyes, jointed body with straight wrist. No damage and nicely dressed. **#X:** 14" - $2,400.00; 17" - $2,550.00; 20" - $2,800.00; 24" - $3,200.00. **#X1:** 14" - $2,600.00; 17" - $2,750.00; 20" - $3,000.00; 24" - $3,500.00. **#128x or 169:** 14" - $1,750.00; 17" - $2,300.00; 20" - $2,500.00; 24" - $2,950.00; 28" - $3,400.00.

Turned Shoulder Head: Ca. 1880's. Closed mouth. Set or sleep eyes, on kid body with bisque lower arms. No damage and nicely dressed. 17" - $900.00; 20" - $1,1000.00; 24" - $1,500.00. Open mouth: 17" - $525.00; 20" - $600.00; 24" - $700.00; 31" - $1,000.00.

Early Child: Square cut porcelain teeth, jointed body and marked with number and letter. 12" - $600.00; 16" - $1,100.00.

Character Child: 1910 and after. Closed mouth or open/closed unless noted. Glass or painted eyes, jointed body and no damage and nicely dressed. **#175, 176, 177, 178, 179, 180, 181, 182, 183, 184, 185, 187, 188, 190, 206, 208, 212:** These mold numbers can be found on the boxed set dolls that has one body and interchangable four heads. Boxed set with four heads: 11-12" - $8,500.00 up. Larger size with painted eyes, closed or open/closed mouth: 11-12" - $2,200.00; 16" - $3,200.00; 18-19" - $4,500.00. Glass eyes: 16" - $4,500.00; 18-19" - $5,500.00. **#220:** Child or toddler. 16" - $5,000.00; 20" - $7,200.00; 27" - $9,800.00. **#239:** Child or toddler (also see under "Babies"): 16" - $2,900.00; 20" - $3,900.00; 27" - $6,000.00. **#241:** Open mouth, glass eyes: 16" - $3,200.00; 20"- $4,700.00. **#249:** 20" - $1,800.00.

18" child doll marked "X1" and made by Kestner. Closed mouth, set eyes and very pale early bisque. On jointed body with straight wrists. Courtesy Barbara Earnshaw-Cain. 18" - $2,800.00.

28" early solid dome, closed mouth Kestner marked "123 12." Bisque shoulder head, kid body with bisque lower arms. Courtesy Frasher Doll Auctions. 28" - $3,000.00.

33" marked "Made in Germany 16½ 171." In original box and clothes with original wig. Box is marked Kestner and has the crown mark. Open mouth with four teeth. Courtesy Jeannie Mauldin. 33" - $2,900.00 (original in box).

Right Photo:
19" child doll marked "13." Early Kestner, closed mouth with upper lip slightly protruding, squared off on sides and red line between lips. On body marked "Jumeau Medaille D' or Paris." Courtesy Frasher Doll Auctions. 19" - $2,800.00.

Left: K star R "Marie" mold number 101. 13" tall with painted eyes, closed mouth and on fully jointed body. Right: 15" Kestner marked "182." Large painted eyes, closed mouth and on fully jointed body. Old clothes which may be original. The dog is 6½" Steiff, pre-1940. Courtesy Frasher Doll Auctions. 13" - $2,300.00. 15" - $3,100.00. Dog: $200.00 up.

Left: 20" "Gibson Girl' by Kestner with mold number 172. Bisque shoulder head, kid body with bisque lower arms. Sleep eyes and closed mouth. Right: 18" French Fashion marked: "B.4S." Bisque shoulder head, kid over wood lower legs, kid fashion body. Dog is a Fox Terrier on wheels, glass eyes and is 7" tall and 7½" long. Courtesy Frasher Doll Auctions. 20" - $3,900.00. 18" - $1,800.00 up. Dog - $600.00 up.

#260: Jointed or toddler body: 8" - $625.00; 12" - $825.00; 16" - $1,300.00; 20" - $1,800.00.

Child Doll: Late 1880's to 1930's. Open mouth on fully jointed body, sleep eyes, some set, with no damage and nicely dressed. **#129, 142, 144, 145, 146, 152, 156, 159, 160, 162, 164, 167, 168, 174, 196, 214, 215, etc.:** 12" - $345.00; 14" - $625.00; 17" - $650.00; 20" - $750.00; 26" - $975.00; 30" - $1,400.00; 36" - $2,000.00; 42" - $3,600.00. **#143:** Character face, open mouth. 8" - $600.00; 12" - $825.00; 17" - $975.00; 20" - $1,300.00. **#192:** 14" - $600.00; 17" - $625.00; 20" - $795.00.

Child Doll: "Dolly" face with open mouth, sleep or set eyes, bisque shoulder head on kid with bisque lower arms. No damage and nicely dressed. **#147, 148, 149, 166, 195, etc.** (Add more for fur eyebrows): 17" - $475.00; 20" - $550.00; 26" - $900.00; 30" - $1,200.00. **#154, #171:** Most often found mold numbers. "Daisy," jointed body, open mouth. 15" - $575.00; 18" - $775.00; 22" - $925.00; 27" - $1,300.00; 32" - $1,700.00; 40" - $2,600.00. Same mold numbers, but with swivel bisque head on bisque shoulder head. Open mouth: 18" -

$775.00; 22" - $975.00; 27" - $1,300.00. Same mold, numbers on kid body: 18" - $550.00; 22" - $650.00; 27" - $800.000.

Character Babies: 1910 and later. On bent limb baby bodies, sleep or set eyes, open mouth, can be wigged or have solid dome with painted hair. No damage and nicely dressed. **#121, 142, 150, 151, 152:** 12" - $450.00; 16" - $600.00; 20" - $700.00; 25" - $1,000.00. **#211, 226, 260:** 10" - $425.00; 12" - $485.00; 16" - $675.00; 20" - $975.00; 24" - $1,400.00. **#220:** (Add more for Toddler body) 16" - $4,000.00; 18" - $4,900.00. **#234, 235, 238:** 16" - $725.00; 20" - $900.00; 24" - $1,200.00. **#237, 245, 1070 (Hilda):** Wigged or solid dome. 12" - $2,500.00; 16" - $3,400.00; 20" - $4,600.00; 23" - $4,900.00. Kestner Toddler: 16" - $3,600.00; 20" - $4,200.00; 23" - $4,900.00. **#239:** 12" - $1,000.00; 16" - $2,800.00. **#247:** 16" - $2,000.00; 18" - $2,500.00; 21" - $3,000.00; 25" - $3,400.00. **#257:** 14" - $600.00; 18" - $825.00; 21" - $975.00; 25" - $1,600.00. **#262:** 16" - $675.00. **#257, 262 Toddler:** 21" - $1,400.00; 26" - $1,900.00.

J.D.K. Marked Baby: Solid dome, painted eyes and open mouth. 15" - $1,000.00; 20" - $1,800.00.

Adult Doll: #162. Sleep eyes, open mouth, adult jointed body (thin waist and molded breasts) with slender limbs. No damage and very nicely dressed. 16" - $1,500.00; 18-19" - $1,800.00; 22" - $2,200.00.

Adult #172: "Gibson Girl." Bisque shoulder head with closed mouth, kid body with bisque lower arms, glass eyes. No damage and beautifully dressed. 12" - $1,400.00; 17" - $2,900.00; 22" - $4,100.00.

16" marked "B Made in Germany 6/ 162." Open mouth, original wig. Adult formed body with this waist and modeled bust. Courtesy Frasher Doll Auctions. 16" - $1,500.00.

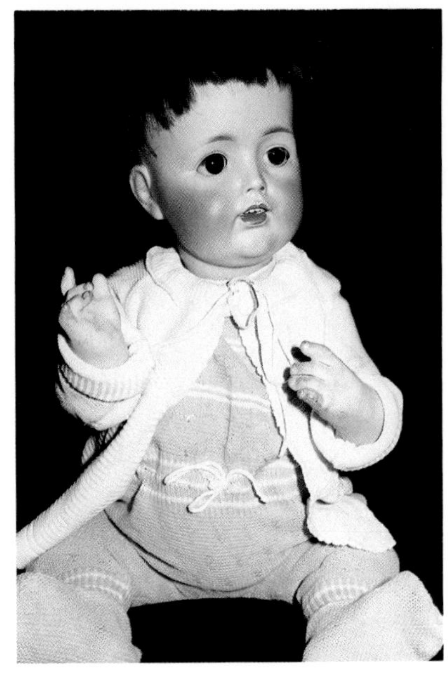

20" marked "Germany J.D.K. 260." Sleep eyes with hair lashes, open mouth and on five-piece bent limb baby body. Courtesy Frasher Doll Auctions. 20" - $975.00.

Oriental #243: Olive fired-in color to bisque. Matching color five-piece bent limb baby body (or jointed toddler-style body), wig, sleep or set eyes. No damage and dressed in oriental style. 14" - $4,600.00; 18" - $7,400.00. Child: Same as above, but on jointed Kestner olive-toned body. 16" - $4,900.00; 20" - $8,200.00. Molded hair baby: 18" - $6,500.00.

Small Dolls: Open mouth, five-piece bodies or jointed bodies, wigs, sleep or set eyes. No damage and nicely dressed. 7" - $350.00; 9" - $450.00. **#133:** 7-8" - $600.00. **#155:** 8" - $600.00.

27" character child by Kestner with mold number 143. Sleep eyes, open mouth with two upper teeth and on jointed body. Courtesy Frasher Doll Auctions. 27" - $2,400.00.

All prices are for dolls that have no chips, hairlines or breaks. (See Modern section for composition and vinyl Kewpies.) Designed by Rose O'Neill and marketed from 1913.

Labels:

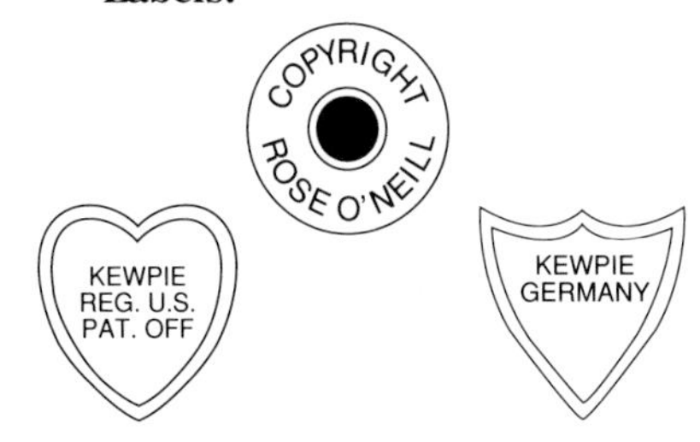

All Bisque: One-piece body and head, jointed shoulders only. Blue wings, painted features with eyes to one side. 1½" - $95.00; 2½" - $115.00; 4-5" - $145.00; 6" - $185.00; 7" - $250.00; 9" - $400.00; 12" - $1,300.00.

All Bisque: Jointed at hips and shoulders. 4" - $465.00; 9" - $850.00; 12" - $1,500.00.

Shoulder Head: Cloth body. 6" - $600.00.

Action Kewpie: Confederate Soldier: 6" - $775.00. Farmer: 4" - $485.00. Gardener: 4" - $485.00. Governor: 4" - $400.00. Groom with Bride: 4" - $465.00. Guitar Player: 3½" - $345.00. Holding Pen: 3" - $365.00. Holding cat: 4" - $425.00; Holding butterfly: 4" - $450.00. Hugging: 3½" - $225.00. On stomach: 4" - $425.00. Thinker: 4" - $465.00; 6" - $600.00. Traveler (tan or black suitcase): 3½" - $325.00. With broom: 4" - $465.00. With dog, Doodle: 3½" - $1,500.00. With helmet: 6" - $700.00. With outhouse: 2½" - $1,100.00. With Rabbit: 2½" - $365.00. With rose: 2" - $350.00. With Teddy Bear: 4" - $750.00. With turkey: 2" - $350.00. With umbrella and dog: 3½" - $1,200.00. Soldier: 4½" - $500.00.

Kewpie Soldier & Nurse: 6" - $1,800.00.

Kewpie In Basket With Flowers: 3½" - $600.00.

Kewpie With Drawstring Bag: 4½" - $575.00.

Buttonhole Kewpie: $165.00.

Kewpie Doodle Dog: 1½" - $675.00; 3" - $1,400.00.

Hottentot Black Kewpie: 3½" - $325.00; 5" - $465.00; 9" - $850.00.

Kewpie Perfume Bottle: 3½" - $475.00.

Pincushion Kewpie: 2½" - $285.00.

Celluloid Kewpies: 2" - $40.00; 5" - $85.00; 9" - $165.00. Black: 5" - $100.00. Jointed shoulders: 3" - $60.00; 5" - $95.00; 9" - $175.00; 12" - $250.00; 16" - $500.00; 22" - $700.00.

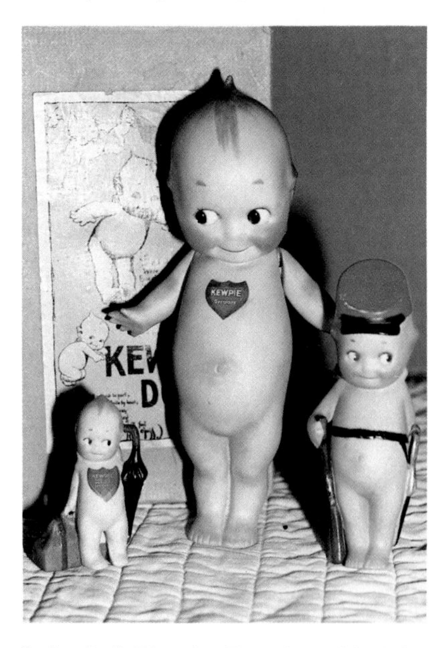

Left: 2½" Kewpie Traveler with label on chest. Satchel can be tan or dark brown. Center: 7½" Kewpie in original box with label on chest and signed "O'Neill" on foot. Right: 4½" Kewpie Confederate Soldier with molded-on cap, rifle and sword. Courtesy Frasher Doll Auctions. 2½" - $325.00. 7½" (in box) - $425.00. 4½" - $500.00.

Back row: 6" and 8½" Kewpies marked "O'Neill" on foot. Both are jointed at shoulders only. Sitting Kewpie has hand extended and holds a ladybug. Kewpie Huggers - the groom has painted-on black slippers and he has original black crepe paper tux and hat. Courtesy Frasher Doll Auctions. 6" (in box) - $295.00. 8½" - $425.00. Sitting: $425.00. Huggers: $225.00.

Cloth Body Kewpie: With bisque head, painted eyes. 12" - $2,200.00. Glass eyes: 12" - $3,000.00 up.

Glass Eye Kewpie: On chubby toddler, jointed. Bisque head. Marks: "Ges. Gesch./O'Neill J.D.K." 10" - $4,000.00; 12" - $4,500.00; 16" - $6,400.00; 20" - $8,200.00.

All Cloth: (Made by Kreuger) All one-piece with body forming clothes, mask face. Mint condition: 12" - $175.00; 16" - $300.00; 20" - $475.00; 25" - $900.00. Fair condition: 12" - $90.00; 16" - $125.00; 20" - $200.00; 25" - $350.00.

All Cloth: Same as above, but with original dress and bonnet. Mint condition: 12" - $250.00; 16" - $375.00; 20"- $600.00; 25" - $1,200.00. Fair condition, not original: 12" - $100.00; 16" - $150.00; 20" - $265.00; 25" - $275.00.

Kewpie Tin or Celluloid Talcum Container: Excellent condition: 7-8" - $195.00. Composition: See Modern section.

Kley & Hahn operated in Ohrdruf, Germany from 1895 to 1929. They made general dolls as well as babies and fine character dolls.

Marks:

K & H   K&H

Character Child: Boy or girl. Painted eyes (some with glass eyes), closed or open/closed mouth; on jointed body. No damage and nicely dressed. **#520:** Solid dome or cut pate: 16" - $3,400.00; 20" - $4,600.00; 24" - $5,000.00. **#523, 525, 526, 531, 536, 549, 552:** 16" - $3,400.00; 20" - $4,600.00; 24" - $5,000.00.

Same Mold Numbers on Toddler Bodies: 16" - $3,600.00; 20" - $4,600.00; 24" - $5,000.00.

Same Mold Numbers on Bent Limb Baby Body: 14" - $2,400.00; 17" - $3,500.00; 21" - $4,000.00; 25" - $4,600.00.

Same Mold Numbers with Glass Eyes: 14" - $3,000.00; 16" - $3,600.00; 20" - $5,000.00; 24" - $5,700.00.

Character Baby: Molded hair or wig, glass sleep eyes or painted eyes. Can have open or open/closed mouth. On bent limb baby body, no damage and nicely dressed. **#130, 132, 138, 142, 150, 151, 158, 160, 162, 167, 176, 199, 522, 531, 585,**

Left: 20" character Simon & Halbig with mold number 1279. Set eyes, open mouth and on fully jointed body. Right: 20" character Kley & Hahn mold number 549. Sleep eyes, closed mouth and on fully jointed body. Courtesy Frasher Doll Auctions. 20" S&H: $2,600.00. 20" K&H - $4,600.00.

Kley & Hahn girl marked "536/5/K & H." Intaglio painted eyes, open/closed mouth and on jointed body. Courtesy Beres Lindus, South Australia. 20" - $4,600.00.

680: 12" - $485.00; 16" - $585.00; 20" - $765.00; 24" - $1050.00.

Same Mold Numbers on Toddler Bodies: 14" - $625.00; 16" - $700.00; 18" - $775.00; 20" - $875.00; 24" - $1,200.00.

#548, #568: 16" - $750.00; 18" - $925.00; 21" - $1,200.00. Toddler: 20" - $1,400.00; 25" - $1,800.00.

#162 with Talker Mechanism in Head: 17" - $1,400.00; 23" - $2,400.00; 26" - $3,000.00.

#162 with Flirty Eyes and Clockworks in Head: 18" - $1,600.00; 25" - $3,200.00.

#680: 16" - $850.00. Toddler: 16" - $1,000.00.

#153, 154, 157, 169: Child, closed mouth: 16" - $2,900.00; 19" - $3,600.00. Open mouth: 16" - $1,100.00; 19" - $1,500.00.

#159 Two-faced Doll: 12" - $2,400.00; 16" - $3,100.00.

#166: With molded hair and open mouth. 17-18" - $1,400.00. Closed mouth: 18" - $2,500.00.

#119: Child, glass eyes, closed mouth. 20" - $4,400.00. Painted eyes: 20" - $3,000.00. Toddler: Glass eyes. 20" - $4,500.00. Painted eyes: 20" - $3,200.00.

Child Dolls: Walkure and/or 250 mold number. Sleep or set eyes, open mouth, jointed body. No damage and nicely dressed. 16" - $475.00; 20" - $600.00; 24" - $695.00; 28" - $875.00; 32" - $1,400.00.

23" marked "250 Walkure." Open mouth, set eyes and on fully jointed body. Courtesy Turn of Century Antiques. 23" - $695.00.

15" bisque doll by Kling marked "167-4." Turned shoulder head with closed mouth, set eyes, kid body with bisque lower arms. Courtesy Frasher Doll Auctions. Closed mouth: 15" - $500.00; 18" - $795.00; 23" - $975.00. Open mouth: 15" - $350.00; 18" - $475.00; 23" - $575.00.

KONIG & WERNICKE

39" marked "4711-105" and made by Koning & Wernicke. In Coleman's new encyclopedia (page 663), this model was made for George Borgfeldt and named "Mein Stolz" (My Pride). Open mouth and on fully jointed body. Sleep eyes with hair lashes. Courtesy Frasher doll Auctions. 15" - $425.00. 18" - $600.00. 21" - $725.00. 31" - $1,200.00. 35" - $1,600.00.

18½" marked "Made in Germany 98/9." Made by Konig & Wernicke. On five-piece toddler body, smiling open mouth with molded tongue, pierced nostrils. Courtesy Frasher Doll Auctions. 15" - $500.00; 18" - $650.00; 21" - $775.00. Flirty eyes: 18" - $725.00; 21" - $800.00.

KRUSE, KATHE

Kathe Kruse began making dolls in 1910. In 1916, she obtained a patent for a wire coil doll and in 1923, she registered a trademark of a double K with the first one reversed, along with the name Kathe Kruse. The first heads were designed after her own children and copies of babies from the Renaissance period. The dolls have a molded muslin head that are handpainted in oils and a jointed cloth body. These early dolls will be marked "Kathe Kruse" on the foot and sometimes with a "Germany" and number.

Early Marked Dolls: In excellent condition and with original clothes: 17" - $3,400.00; 20" - $3,700.00. In fair condition, not original: 17" - $1,100.00; 20" - $1,400.00.

1920's Dolls: Molded hair, hips are wide. In excellent condition and original: 17" - $1,200.00; 20" - $1,800.00. In fair condition, not original: 17" - $500.00; 20" - $900.00.

U.S. Zone: Germany 1945-1951 (Turtle mark.) 16" - $900.00.

Plastic Dolls: With glued-on wigs, sleep or painted eyes. Marked with turtle mark and number on head and on back "Modell/Kathe Kruse/" and number. 16" - $565.00.

Baby: Painted closed or open eyes. 1922. 20" - $3,400.00. Plastic head: 16" - $500.00.

Celluloid: 14" - $400.00; 17" - $650.00.

1975 to date: 10" - $235.00; 14" - $375.00; 19" - $465.00.

Left: 14½" Kathe Kruse. All cloth with molded muslin head, handpainted in oils. Right: 18" Kruse, ca. 1961. Hard plastic head with painted features, cloth body jointed at shoulder and hips and left foot signed "Kathe Kruse" and "Made in Germany US Zone Mar. 1961." Courtesy Frasher Doll Auctions. 14½" - $1,900.00. 18" - $750.00.

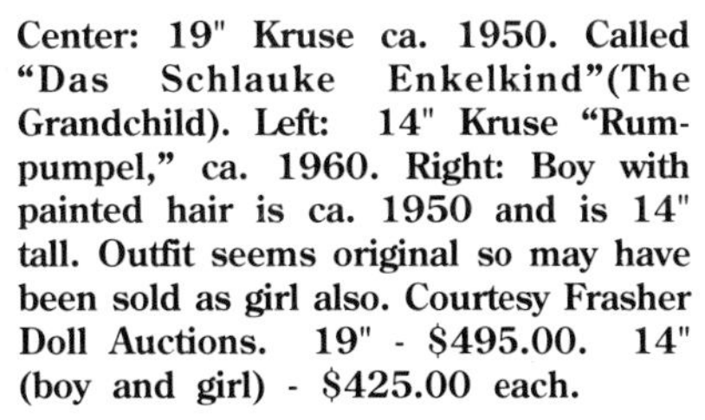

Center: 19" Kruse ca. 1950. Called "Das Schlauke Enkelkind"(The Grandchild). Left: 14" Kruse "Rumpumpel," ca. 1960. Right: Boy with painted hair is ca. 1950 and is 14" tall. Outfit seems original so may have been sold as girl also. Courtesy Frasher Doll Auctions. 19" - $495.00. 14" (boy and girl) - $425.00 each.

Baby: Kathe Kruse "Traumerchen" (Dreaming Baby). Plastic head with painted hair and lcosed eyes. Pink stockenette-covered body. Foot marked "Kathe Kruse Nov. 1985." 24" bisque head marked "S&H Halbig 9½." Sleep eyes, open mouth and jointed body. Courtesy Frasher Doll Auctions. Baby - $3,400.00. 24" - $745.00.

Kuhnlenz made dolls from 1884 to 1930 and was located in Kronach, Bavaria. Marks from this company include the "G.K." plus numbers such as 56-38, 44-26, 41-28, 56-18, 44-15, 38-27, 44-26, etc. Other marks now attributed to this firm are:

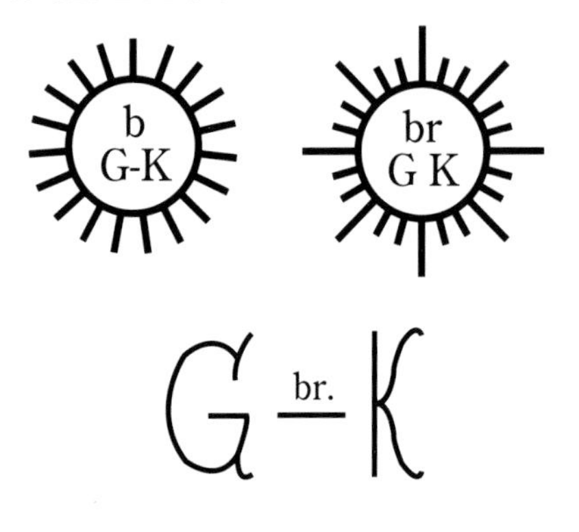

Child with Closed Mouth: Mold #31, 32. Bisque head in perfect condition, jointed body and nicely dressed. 14" - $900.00; 18" - $1,400.00; 22" - $1,800.00. **Mold #34:** Bru type. 17" - $2,600.00. **Mold #38:** Kid body, bisque shoulder head. 16" - $675.00; 23" - $950.00.

Child with Open Mouth: Mold #41, 44, 56. Bisque head in perfect condition, jointed body and nicely dressed. 14" - $575.00; 18" - $825.00; 22" - $1,000.00. **Mold #161, 165:** Bisque head in perfect condition, jointed body and nicely dressed. 16" - $425.00; 22" - $550.00.

Tiny Dolls: Bisque head in perfect condition, five-piece body with painted-on shoes and socks, open mouth. 8" - $195.00. Closed mouth: 8" - $650.00.

21" marked "G.K. 44-30." Made by Gebruder Kuhnlenz. Bisque head with set eyes, open mouth and fully jointed body. Courtesy Frasher Doll Auctions. 21" - $950.00.

A. Lanternier & Cie of Limoges, France made dolls from about the 1890's on into the 1930's. Before making dolls, they produced porcelain pieces as early as 1855. Their doll heads will be fully marked and some carry a name such as "Favorite, Lorraine, Cherie," etc. They generally are found on papier maché bodies but can be on fully jointed composition bodies. Dolls from this firm may have nearly excellent quality bisque to down right poor quality.

Marks:

AL & CIE
LIMOGES

FABRICATION
FRANCAISE

Right: 20" marked "Depose Francaise 'Favorite' No. 6/Ed Tasson AL & Cie. Limoge." Made by Lanternier. Open mouth and set eyes and has replaced early straight wrist body. Left: 20" "Laughing Jumeau" toddler marked "SFBJ 236 Paris." Courtesy Frasher Doll Auctions. 20" - $900.00. #236: $2,300.00.

Child: Open mouth, set eyes on jointed body. No damage and nicely dressed. Good quality bisque with pretty face. 16" - $800.00; 20" - $900.00; 23" - $1,000.00; 26" $1,500.00. Poor quality bisque with very high coloring or blotchy color bisque. 16" - $500.00; 20" - $575.00; 23" - $625.00; 26" - $750.00.

"Jumeau" Style Face: Has a striking Jumeau look. Good quality bisque: 20" - $1,000.00; 24" - $1,300.00. Poor quality bisque: 20" - $550.00; 24" - $650.00.

Character: Open/closed mouth with teeth, smiling fat face, glass eyes, on jointed body. No damage and nicely dressed. Marked "Toto." 16" - $750.00; 18" - $1,200.00; 22" - $1,500.00.

Lady: Adult-looking face, set eyes, open/closed or closed mouth. Jointed adult body. No damage and nicely dressed. 14" - $900.00; 17" - $1,350.00.

20" marked "Fabrication Francaise ALEC Limoges H 8." Open mouth, set eyes and on jointed Jumeau-style body. Has very Jumeau-style face. Courtesy Shirley Glass. 20" - $1,000.00.

Lenci dolls are all felt with a few having cloth torsos. They are jointed at neck, shoulder and hips. The original clothes will be felt or organdy or a combination of both. Features are oil painted and generally eyes are painted to the side. Size can range from 5" - 45". Marks: On cloth or paper label "Lenci Torino Made in Italy." "Lenci" may be written on bottom of foot or underneath one arm. *Mint or rare dolls will bring higher prices.*

Children: No moth holes, very little dirt, doll as near mint as possible and all in excellent condition. 14" - $825.00 up; 16" - $975.00 up; 18" - $1,000.00 up; 20" - $1,300.00 up. Dirty, original clothes in poor condition or redressed: 14" - $165.00; 16" - $225.00; 18" - $285.00; 20" - $325.00.

Tiny Dolls (Called Mascottes): In excellent condition: 5" - $175.00; 9-10" - $300.00. Dirty, redressed or original clothes in poor condition: 5" - $50.00; 9-10" - $95.00.

Ladies with Adult Faces: "Flapper" or "Boudoir" style with long limbs. In excellent condition: 24" - $1,800.00 up; 28" - $2,000.00 up. Dirty or in poor condition: 24" - $500.00; 28" - $800.00.

Clowns: Excellent condition: 18" - $1,500.00; 26½" - $2,000.00. Poor condition: 18" - $600.00; 26½" - $950.00.

Indians or Orientals: Excellent condition: 16" - $3,800.00. Dirty and poor condition: 16" - $1,000.00.

Golfer: Excellent, perfect condition: 16" - $2,100.00. Poor condition: 16" - $600.00.

Shirley Temple Type: Excellent condition: 30" - $2,600.00. Dirty and poor condition: 30" - $900.00.

Bali Dancer: Excellent condition: 22" - $2,400.00. Poor condition: 22" - $700.00.

Smoking Doll: In excellent condition, painted eyes: 25" - $2,000.00. Poor condition: 25" - $900.00.

Glass Eyes: Excellent condition: 16" - $2,500.00; 20" - $3,100.00. Poor condition: 16" - $700.00; 20" - $900.00.

"Surprise Eyes" Doll: Very round painted eyes and "O"-shaped mouth. 16" - $2,000.00; 20" - $2,600.00. With glass eyes that are flirty: 16" - $2,500.00; 20" - $3,100.00.

Boys: Side part hairdo. Excellent condition: 19" - $2,000.00 up; 24" - $2,600.00. Poor condition: 19" - $600.00; 24" - $800.00.

Babies: Excellent condition: 16" - $1,400.00 up; 20" - $2,000.00 up. Poor condition: 16" - $500.00; 20" - $900.00.

26" Lenci long-limbed lady marked "Lenci" on foot. Painted features, all felt and has felt and organdy costume. 17" Lenci girl from series 110. Ca. 1925. All felt doll; felt and organdy clothes. Tag on clothes - "Lenci Made in Italy." Courtesy Frasher Doll Auctions. 26" - $2,000.00; 17" - $985.00.

17" Lenci pouty character of the 1500 series. Marked "Lenci" on bottom of foot. 10" "Mascot" all cloth character by Lenci. Courtesy Frasher Doll Auctions. 17" - $985.00. 10" - $300.00.

27" Lenci (Lillian Gish face). Mohair wig, painted features, sawdust-filled cloth body and felt arms. The legs are long and cloth. Organdy and felt clothes. Courtesy Glorya Woods. 27" - $2,000.00.

15" Lenci marked on bottom of foot. All felt with painted features. Original taffeta dress with organdy sleeves, applied felt flowers on dress and trim at base of dress. Shoes are felt. Courtesy Frasher Doll Auctions. 15" - $950.00.

LIMBACH

Left: 14" Belton-type marked "117." French jointed body with straight wrists. Closed mouth. Right: 14¼" Limbach marked with cloverleaf 7. Open mouth with four teeth, on French jointed body with straight wrists. Limbach dolls were made mostly from 1893 into the 1920's. Marks: ☘

GERMANY

Courtesy Frasher Doll Auctions. Child: Open mouth: 14" - $350.00; 17" - $575.00; 23" - $675.00. 14" Belton - $1,900.00.

LORI

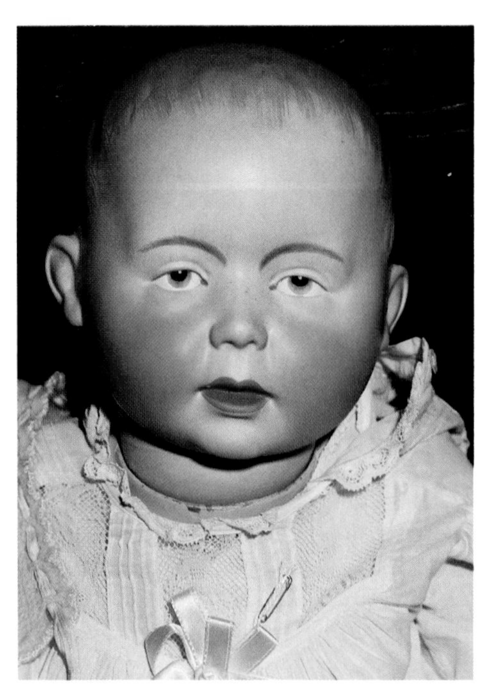

24" large "Lori" baby and marked as such with deep modeling around intaglio eyes. Wide open/closed mouth and socket head sets into body that is modeled up around neck. Five-piece bent limb baby body. Courtesy Barbara Earnshaw-Cain. 24" - $3,200.00.

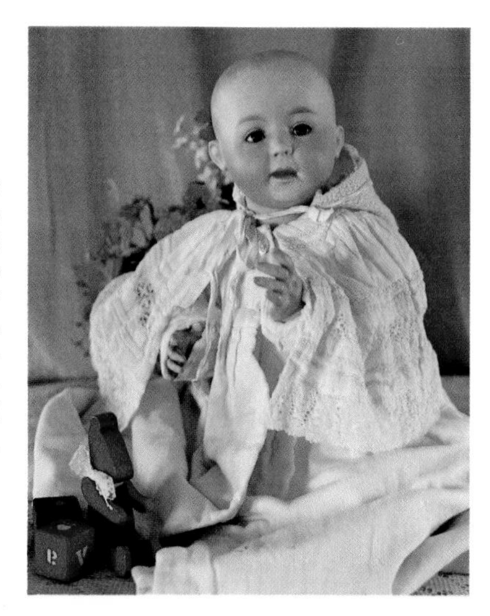

Large "Lori Baby," painted hair, sleep eyes and open/closed mouth. Five-piece bent limb baby body. Marks: "Lori" and stamped "Geschutz S & CO. Made by Swaine & Co. 1910." Courtesy Frasher Doll Auctions. 14" - $1,600.00; 20" - $2,500.00; 23" - $3,100.00; 26" - $3,800.00. Intaglio eyes: 20" - $2,000.00; 24" - $2,400.00. Flocked hair: 20" - $2,800.00; 25" - $3,900.00.

MASCOTTE

Mascotte Dolls were made by May Freres Cie. They operated from 1890 to 1897, then became part of Jules Steiner in 1898. This means the dolls were made from 1890 to about 1902, so the quality of the bisque can vary greatly, as well as the artist painting. Dolls will be marked "BÉBÉ MASCOTTE PARIS" and some incised with "M" and a number.

Child: Closed mouth and marked "Mascotte." Excellent condition and no damage. 16" - $4,000.00; 18" - $4,600.00; 20" - $5,000.00; 22" - $5,500.00; 24" - $5,800.00; 30" - $6,800.00.

Child: Same as above, but marked with "M" and a number. 16" - $3,600.00; 18" - $4,200.00; 20" - $4,600.00; 22" - $5,100.00; 24" - $5,400.00; 30" - $6,400.00.

15½" "Bébé Mascotte" incised "M 4." Closed mouth, paperweight eyes and French jointed body. Courtesy Frasher Doll Auctions. 15½" - $3,600.00.

A. Theroude mechanical walker patented in 1840 with papier maché head, bamboo teeth in open mouth and stands on three wheels (two large and one small), tin cart with mechanism attached to legs. 16" - $2,600.00.

Autoperipatetikos: Base is like clock works and has tin feet and when key wound, the doll walks. Heads can be china, untinted bisque or papier maché. Early China Head: 11" - $1,800.00. Untinted Bisque: 11" - $1,000.00. Papier maché: 11" - $900.00.

Hawkins, George walker with pewter hands and feet, wood torso. Hands modeled to push a carriage, which should be a Goodwin, patented in 1867-1868. Carriage has two large wheels and one small one in front. Molded hair and dolls head will be marked "X.L.C.R./Doll head/Pat. Sept. 8, 1868." (China heads may not be marked.) 11" - $2,000.00.

Jumeau: Raises and lowers both arms and head moves. Holds items such as a hankie and bottle, book and fan, etc. - one in each hand. Key wound music box is base. Closed mouth and marked "Jumeau." 15" - $3,700.00 up; 20" - $4,600.00 up. Same with Open Mouth: 15" - $2,400.00 up; 20" - $3,900.00 up.

Marked "Tete Jumeau Bte. S.G.D.G. 4." Overall is 19" tall. Boy that pours a drink, takes a long drink, then sticks his tongue out several times as if savoring the drink. Stands on music box and is key wound. Courtesy Frasher Doll Auctions. 20" - $5,200.00.

Vichy mechanical mother and child. Key wound with mother moving hand with bottle. Both dolls have glass eyes and closed mouths. Sitting on chair that holds music box that is operated by a pull cord. Wooden carved hands. Courtesy Shirlie Glass. $9,000.00.

Jumeau: Marked "Jumeau." Standing or sitting on key wound music box and doll plays an instrument. 14" - $3,800.00 up; 17" - $5,000.00 up.

Jumeau: Marked "Jumeau" walker with one-piece legs, arms jointed at elbows and she raises her arm to an open mouth to throw kisses as head turns. 16" - $1,900.00 up; 22" - $2,900.00 up.

Jumeau: Marked "Jumeau" and stands on three-wheel cart and when cart is pulled, doll's head turns from side to side and arms go up and down. 15" - $3,500.00 up; 18" - $4,000.00 up.

Paris Bébé, R.D., E.D marked dolls standing on key wound music box and has closed mouth. Holds items in hands and arms move and head nods or moves from side to side. 20" - $5,000.00 up.

Jumeau: 18-20" doll stands at piano built to scale and hands attached to keyboard with rods. Key wound piano. $20,000.00 up.

Steiner, Jules: Bisque head on composition upper and lower torso-chest, also lower legs and all the arms. Twill-covered sections between parts of body. Key wound, cries, moves head and kicks legs. Open mouth with two rows of teeth. 18" - $2,400.00; 23" - $3,000.00. Same as above, but Bisque Torso Sections: 18" - $6,000.00.

German Makers: One or two figures on music box, key wound, or pulling cart. Dolls have open mouths. Marked with name of maker: $1,400.00. 1960's, 1970's German-made reproductions of this style dolls: $300.00.

23" tall key-wound mechanical by Jules Steiner. Composition arms and legs. Cries, kicks, and moves head from side to side. Open mouth with two rows of teeth. All original clothes and wig. Courtesy Frasher Doll Auctions. 23" - $3,000.00.

13" bisque head marked "1078 S&H 5" (Simon*Halbig). Open mouth and hair lashes. Body and/or mechanism by French firm of Roullet & Decamps. Key wound, key marked "R.D." Courtesy Frasher Doll Auctions. 13" - $1,400.00.

MOLDED HAIR BISQUE

The molded hair bisque dolls are just like any other flesh-toned dolls, but instead of having a wig, they have molded hair, glass set eyes or finely painted and detailed eyes, and generally they will have a closed mouth. They almost always are a shoulder head with one-piece shoulder and head. They can be on a kid body or cloth with bisque lower arms, with some having compostion lower legs. These dolls are generally very pretty. Many molded hair dolls are being attributed to A.B.G. (Alt, Beck & Gottschalck) mold numbers 890, 1000, 1008, 1028, 1064, 1142, 1256, 1288, etc.

Child: 8" - $150.00; 12" - $250.00; 16" - $475.00; 19" - $700.00; 21" - $950.00; 24" - $1,200.00.

Boy: 16" - $600.00; 19" - $800.00; 21" - $1,000.00.

Decorated Shoulder Plate: With elaborate hairdo. 20" - $1,600.00.

Right: 15½" molded hair bisque with glass eyes, kid body with bisque lower arms. Left: 20" brown eye china of the Covered Wagon style. Has cloth body with china limbs. Courtesy Frasher Doll Auctions. 15½" - $525.00. 20" - $1,400.00.

MOSS, LEO

Leo Moss made dolls during the late 1800's and the early 1900's. He was a black man who lived in Macon, Georgia where he made his living as a handy man and dollmaker. This extremely talented man would be commissioned by a child's parents to create a doll and the results would be a doll that bore a striking resemblance to the child. Mr. Moss made both black and white dolls.

The Moss dolls have heads that are individually molded of papier maché, and the bodies were mainly purchased from a white toy supplier.

The dealer from whom Mr. Moss bought parts did not feel there was a market in the North and never purchased any from him, but a few were exported to Europe.

During the very early 1900's, a family tragedy, which we feel need not be published here, took place. Thereafter, Mr. Moss modeled a tear on the cheek of all his babies. He died in 1932 and unfortunately is buried in a pauper's grave without a headstone.

Child: 20" - $6,500.00; 25" - $7,600.00. With tear: 20" - $7,000.00; 25" - $7,800.00.

Baby: 20" - $6,500.00; 25" - $7,600.00; 30" - $8,200.00. With tear: 20" - $7,000.00; 25" - $7,800.00; 30" - $8,600.00.

Very large Leo Moss baby with glass eyes and closed smile mouth and 20" laughing open mouth, glass-eyed girl. Owner's name withheld by request. 30" baby - $8,600.00; 20" girl - $6,500.00.

MOTSCHMANN (SONNEBERG TÄUFLING)

Charles Motschmann has always been credited as the manufacturer of a certain style doll, but now his work is only being attributed to the making of the voice boxes in the dolls. Various German makers such as Heinrich Stier and others are being given the credit for making the dolls. They date from 1851 into the 1880's.

The early dolls were babies, children and Orientals. They have glass eyes, closed mouths, heads of papier maché, wax over papier maché or wax over composition. They can have lightly brush stroked painted hair or come with a wig. If the mouth is open, the doll will have bamboo teeth. The larger dolls will have arms and legs jointed at wrists and ankles. The torso (lower) body is composition or wooden, as are the arms and legs, except for the upper parts which will be twill-style cloth. The mid-section will also be cloth. If the doll is marked, it can be found on the upper cloth of the leg and will be stamped:

Baby: Motschmann marked or type. In extremely fine condition: 14" - $650.00; 17" - $775.00; 21" - $1,000.00; 25" - $1,500.00. In fair condition: 14" - $465.00; 17" - $545.00; 21" - $500.00; 25" - $700.00.

Child: In extremely fine condition: 16" - $700.00; 19" - $925.00; 24" - $1,400.00. In fair condition: 16" - $500.00; 19" - $650.00; 24" - $750.00.

11" Motschmann (Sonneberg Täufling) combination wood and composition limbs and shoulder head. Upper torso and upper parts of limbs are pink twill-like fabric (called floating joints). Molded hair and painted features. Courtesy Frasher Doll Auctions. 11" - $500.00.

MUNICH ART DOLL

19" composition Munich Art Doll designed by Marion Kaulitz. Marked "11" high on dome. Painted features, closed mouth and fully jointed body. 1908-1912. Courtesy Frasher Doll Auctions. 18-19" - $3,200.00.

Bisque dolls were made in Germany by various firms with fired-in Oriental color and on jointed yellowish tinted bodies. They could be a child or baby and most were made after 1900. All must be in excellent condition in Oriental clothes and no damage to head.

Armand Marseilles: Girl or boy marked only "A.M." 8" - $700.00; 12" - $950.00. Painted Bisque: 8" - $200.00.

#353 Baby: 14" - $1,400.00; 18" - $2,100.00. Painted Bisque: 14" - $600.00.

Bruno Schmidt (BSW) #220: Closed mouth. 16" - $3,400.00.

#500: 14" - $2,200.00; 18" - $3,200.00.

Kestner (J.D.K.) #243: Baby: 14" - $4,800.00; 18" - $6,800.00. Molded hair baby: 18" - $6,300.00. Child: 16" - $5,400.00; 20" - $8,600.00.

Schoenau & Hoffmeister: (S, PB in star H) #4900: 14" - $1,400.00; 18" - $1,800.00.

Simon & Halbig (S & H) #164: 16" - $2,400.00; 20" - $2,900.00.

#220: Solid dome or "Belton" type. Closed mouth. 18" - $3,700.00.

#1099, 1129, 1199: 16" - $2,600.00; 20" - $3,200.00.

#1329: 16" - $2,500.00; 20" - $3,000.00.

All Bisque: 7-8" - $1,100.00.

Unmarked: Open mouth: 16" - $1,400.00; 20" - $2,100.00. Closed mouth: 16" - $2,000.00; 20" - $3,000.00.

Nippon - Caucasian Dolls Made in Japan: 1918-1922. Most made dur-

Oriental bisque head marked "220." Pierced ears, closed mouth and on jointed body with straight wrist. This mold number can be a "Belton" type with concave top to head and two to three holes or can have a cut pate. Courtesy Frasher Doll Auctions. 18" - $3,000.00.

Left: 13" Oriental baby by Kestner marked "F Made in Germany 10/ J.D.K. 243." Bisque head with sleep eyes, open mouth with two upper teeth and on five-piece bent limb baby body. Right 13" Tete Jumeau with closed mouth and Jumeau marked body. Courtesy Frasher Doll Auctions. 13" Oriental - $5,000.00. 13" Jumeau - $3,300.00.

ing World War 1. These dolls can be near excellent quality to very poor quality. Morimura Brothers mark is (M✝B). Dolls marked FY were made by Yamato. Others will just be marked with NIPPON along with other marks such as "J.W.", etc.

Nippon Marked Baby: Good to excellent bisque, well painted, nice body and no damage. 11" - $265.00; 15" - $350.00; 19" - $575.00; 24" - $800.00. Poor quality: 11" - $100.00; 15" - $150.00; 19" - $250.00; 24" - $350.00.

Nippon Child: Good to excellent quality bisque, no damage and nicely dressed. 16" - $350.00; 20" - $575.00; 24" - $725.00. Poor quality: 16" - $150.00; 20" - $250.00; 24" - $350.00.

Baby: 15" marked "FY Nippon No. 76018." Solid dome with lightly painted hair, sleep eyes, pierced nostrils and five-piece bent limb baby body. 19" marked "K*R 46 Simon & Halbig." Made by Kammer and Reinhardt. Jointed body and open mouth. Courtesy Frasher Doll Auctions. 15" - $350.00. 19" - $675.00.

17½" marked "22 Morimura Bros." Socket head on bent limb five-piece baby body, set eyes, open mouth with two upper teeth. Courtesy Frasher Doll Auctions. 18" - $500.00.

Traditional Doll: Made in Japan. Papier maché swivel head on shoulder plate, cloth mid-section and upper arms and legs. Limbs and torso are papier maché, glass eyes, pierced nostrils. The early dolls will have jointed wrists and ankles and will be slightly sexed. **Early fine quality:** Original dress, 1890's. 15" - $350.00; 20" - $600.00; 27" - $1,100.00. **Early Boy:** With painted hair. 15" - $400.00; 20" - $750.00; 27" - $1,400.00. 1930's or later: 13" - $95.00; 16" - $145.00. **Lady:** All original and excellent quality. 1920's: 12" - $185.00; 16" - $300.00. Later Lady: 1940's-1950's. 12" - $100.00; 14" - $125.00. **Emperor or Empress in Sitting Position:** 1920's-1930's. 8" -

11" bisque head Oriental doll on jointed body, open mouth and set eyes. Original costume. Made by Schoenau & Hoffmeister. Courtesy Turn of Century Antiques. 11" - $1,100.00.

$175.00 up; 12" - $325.00 up. **Warrior:** Early 1920's. 12" - $350.00 up. On horse: 12" - $650.00 up.

Japanese Baby: With bisque head. Sleep eyes, closed mouth and all white bisque. Papier maché body: Original and in excellent condition. Late 1920's. 8" - $65.00; 12" - $165.00. Glass Eyes: 8" - $80.00; 12" - $175.00.

Japanese Baby: Head made of crushed oyster shells painted flesh color, papier maché body, glass eyes and original. 8" - $85.00; 12" - $145.00; 16" - $200.00; 19" - $300.00.

Oriental Dolls: All composition, jointed at shoulder and hips. Painted features, painted hair or can have bald head with braid of yarn down back with rest covered by cap, such as "Ling Ling" or "Ming Ming" made by Quan Quan Co. in 1930's. Painted-on shoes. 10" - $145.00.

Chinese Traditional Dolls: Man or woman. Composition-type material with cloth-wound bodies or can have wooden carved arms and feet. In traditional costume and in excellent condition. 9" - $300.00; 12" - $500.00.

Door of Hope Dolls: Wooden head, cloth bodies and most have carved hands. Chinese costume. Adult: 11" - $365.00. Child: 7" - $450.00. Mother and Baby: 11" - $500.00. Man: 11" - $400.00.

Back: 24" tall Japanese child, crushed oyster shell, painted over papier maché, inset glass eyes, holes in nostrils, toe separated to fit sandal. All original. Man is Chinese with composition-type head, wood body and original. Baby and child are made same as 24". Front: 14" baby with glass eyes, jointed neck and shoulders, rest of body in one piece. Courtesy Frasher Doll Auctions. 24" - $600.00. Man (in this condition) - $100.00. Child - $75.00. Baby (lying down) - $165.00.

6½" made of crushed oyster shell paste, set glass eyes. Comes with three wigs, a fan, bag, paper umbrella and slippers. The wigs denote different stages of a Japanese girl/woman. Box marked "The Hanakor. Trademark: Japan." Courtesy Sandra Cummins. In box: $100.00-150.00.

ORSINI

Jeanne I. Orsini of New York designed dolls from 1916 to the 1920's. It is not known who made the heads for her, but it is likely that all bisque dolls designed by her were made by J.D. Kestner in Germany. The initials of the designer are "J.I.O." and the dolls will be marked with those initials along with a year such as 1919, 1920, etc. Since the middle initial is "I", it may appear as a number 1. Dolls can also be marked "Copy. by J.I. Orsini/ Germany."

Painted Bisque Character: Can be on a cloth body with cloth limbs or a bent limb baby body, a toddler body, have flirty eyes and an open smiling mouth. Can be wigged or have molded hair and be a boy or a girl. Head is painted or painted clay-like material. Prices are for excellent condition, no damage and nicely dressed.**#1429:** 14" - $1,800.00; 18" - $2,200.00.

Bisque Head Baby: Cloth body with bisque head with wide open screaming mouth, eye squinted and marked "JIO." 12" - $1,100.00; 14" - $1,500.00.

Bisque Head Baby: Fired-in color bisque head with sleep eyes (some may be set), open mouth and has cloth body and painted hair. Marked "KIDDIE JOY JIO. 1926." 14" - $1,600.00; 18" - $2,400.00.

All Bisque: See All Bisque section for Didi, Fifi, Dodo, Zizi, etc.

Painted pottery-style head with open smiling mouth, glass eyes, tongue and two upper teeth. 22" tall with cloth body and composition limbs. Marked "J.J. Orsini Germany." Courtesy Frasher Doll Auctions. 22" - $2,800.00.

P.G.

Pintal & Godchaux of Montreuil, France made dolls from 1890 to 1899. They held one trademark - "Bebe Charmount." The heads will be marked "P.G."

Child: 16" - $2,600.00; 21" - $3,200.00; 24" - $3,900.00.

Child, Open Mouth: 16" - $1,400.00; 21" - $2,100.00; 24" - $2,700.00.

22" Bebe by Pintel & Godchaux marked "B/P. 11 G." On French jointed body, pierced ears and closed mouth. Courtesy Frasher Doll Auctions. 22" - $3,400.00.

Left: 17" painted bisque head with flirty eyes that also sleep, open mouth and on five-piece composition body. Dressed in Colonial style. Marked "H 42 I." Right: 14" Effanbee Historical doll of 1939. All composition in costume representing year 1841, Pre-Civil War Period. Courtesy Frasher Doll Auctions. 17" - $450.00. 14" - $450.00.

Rear: 7" Googly by Gobel marked "208-126." Crown mark with W over G. Germany. Painted bisque head on five-piece baby body. Front: 6½" by Alt, Beck & Gottschalck marked "A.B.G./Germany 1360 19/0." Jointed body, open mouth. 29" Teddy Bear of German origin, glass eyes. Courtesy Frasher Doll Auctions. 7" - $650.00. 6½" - $155.00. 29" Bear - $450.00 up.

14" painted bisque head on fully jointed French body. Glass eyes with lashes, open mouth and all original. Tag and mark: "Jumeau." Made after the formation of "S.F.B.J." Courtesy Shirlie Glass. 14" - $575.00. 20" - $850.00.

Papier maché dolls were made in U.S., Germany, England, France and other countries. Paper pulp, wood and rag fibers containing paste, oil or glue is formed into a composition-like moldable material. Flour, clay and/or sand was added for stiffness. The hardness of papier maché depends on the maount of glue that was added.

Many so called papier maché parts were actually laminated paper with several thicknesses of molded paper bonded (glued) together or pressed after being glued.

"Papier maché" means "chewed paper" in French, and as early as 1810, dolls of papier maché were being mass produced by using molds.

Marked "M&S Superior": (Muller & Strassburger) Papier maché shoulder head with blonde or black molded hair, painted blue or brown eyes, old cloth body with kid or leather arms and boots. Nicely dressed and head not repainted, chipped or cracked. 14"- $325.00; 18" - $575.00; 24" - $745.00. Glass eyes: 20" - $750.00. With wig: 18" - $650.00. Repainted nicely: 14" - $125.00; 18" - $300.00; 24" - $500.00. Chips, Scuffs, or Not Repainted Well: 14" - $50.00; 18" - $85.00; 24" - $100.00.

French or French Type: Painted black hair, some with brush marks, on solid dome. Some have nailed-on wigs. Open mouths have bamboo teeth. Inset glass eyes. In very good condition, nice old clothes. All leather/kid body. 15" - $1,200.00; 20" - $1,800.00; 26" - $2,500.00; 30" -$3,400.00.

Early Papier Maché: With cloth body and wooden limbs. Early hairdo with top knots, buns, puff curls or braiding. Ca. 1840's. Not restored and in original or very well made clothes. In very good condition and may show a little wear. 10" - $500.00; 14" - $650.00; 17" - $750.00; 20" - $1,000.00; 24" - $1,300.00.

Marked "Greiner": Dolls of 1858 on: Blonde or black molded hair, brown or blue painted eyes, cloth body with leather arms, nicely dressed and with very little minor scuffs. 18" - $975.00; 23" - $1,400.00; 29" - $1,850.00; 32" - $2,200.00.

Motschmann Types: With wood and twill bodies. Separate hip section, glass eyes, closed mouth and brush stroke hair on solid domes. Nicely dressed and ready to display. 16" - $650.00; 20" - $925.00; 24" - $1,350.00.

18" French papier maché, ca 1830. Black glass eyes, painted hair, cloth body with wooden limbs. All original with original bonnet. Courtesy Pat Timmons. 18" - $1,600.00.

German Papier Maché: 1870-1900's. Molded various hairdos, painted eyes and closed mouth. May be blonde or black hair. Nicely dressed and not repainted: 16" - $475.00; 20" - $650.00; 26" - $1,300.00; 32" - $1,800.00. Glass eyes: 16" - $575.00; 20" - $750.00; 26" - $1,400.00; 32" - $1,900.00. Showing wear and scuffs, but not touched up: 16" - $200.00; 20" - $275.00; 26" - $400.00.

Turned Shoulder Head: Solid dome, glass eyes and closed mouth. Twill cloth body with composition lower arms. In very good condition and nicely dressed. 16" - $575.00; 20" - $825.00.

German Character Heads: These heads are molded just like the bisque ones. Glass eyes, closed mouth and on fully jointed body. In excellent condition and nicely dressed. 16" - $950.00; 20" - $1,200.00.

1920's on - Papier Maché: Head usually has bright coloring. Wigged, usually dressed as a child, or in provincial costumes. Stuffed cloth body and limbs or have papier maché arms. In excellent overall condition. 8" - $80.00; 12" - $125.00; 16" - $225.00.

Clowns: Papier maché head with painted clown features. Open or closed mouth, molded hair or wigged and on cloth body with some having composition or papier maché lower arms. In excellent condition. 12" - $365.00; 16" - $550.00.

18" wax over papier maché with glass eyes, closed mouth and original human hair wig and on jointed composition body. Ca. 1920's. Courtesy Henri & John Starzel. 18" - $800.00.

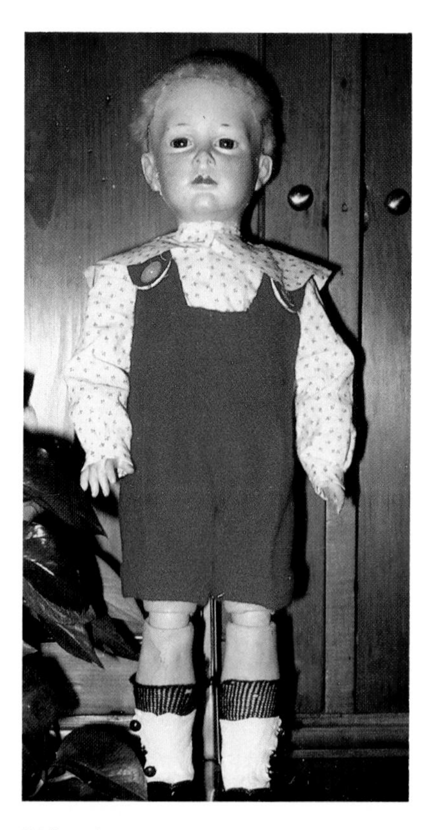

20" character marked on head "C.O.D." Head is made of papier maché with glass eyes and very pouty closed mouth, wigged and German fully jointed body. Courtesy Jane Walker. 20" - $3,000.00.

Back: 10½" early papier maché shoulder head with short curls at side of head and exposed ears, hair combed into a bun at crown of head, kid body with wooden limbs, original. Front left: 9¾" papier maché with center part and three curls on each side of head that is combed into a braided bun in back. Kid body with wooden limbs. Right: 11" papier maché hair modeled wide over ears combed upward in back and braided high knot on top. 9¾" - $500.00. 10½" - $545.00. 11" - $1,000.00.

"Parian-type" dolls were made from the 1850's to the 1880's, with the majority being made during the 1870's and 1880's. All seem to have been made in Germany and if marked, it will be found on the inside of the shoulder plate. There are hundreds of different heads, and it must be noted that the really rare and unique unglazed porcelain dolls are difficult to find and their prices will be high.

"Parian-type" dolls can be found with every imaginable thing applied to the head and shirt tops - from flowers, snoods, ruffles, feathers, plumes, etc. Many have inset glass eyes, pierced ears and most are blonde, although some will have from light to medium brown hair, and a few will have glazed black hair.

Various Fancy Hairstyles: With molded combs, ribbons, flowers, head bands, or snoods. Cloth body with cloth/"parian" limbs. Perfect condition and very nicely dressed. 17" - $1,500.00 up; 21" - $1,800.00 up. Painted eyes, unpierced ears: 17" - $850.00; 21" - $1,100.00.

Swivel neck: 17" - $2,500.00; 21" - $3,200.00.

Molded Necklaces: Jewels or standing ruffles (undamaged). Glass eyes, pierced ears: 17" - $1,500.00; 21" - $1,900.00 up. Painted eyes, unpierced ears: 17" - $1,000.00; 21" - $1,400.00.

Bald Head: Solid domes, takes wigs, full ear detail. 1850's. Per-fect condition and nicely dressed. 14" - $750.00; 16" - $900.00; 20" - $1,400.00.

Very Plain Style: With no decoration in hair or on shoulders. No damage and nicely dressed. 15" - $300.00; 18" - $500.00.

Men or Boys: Hairdos with center or side part, cloth body with

25½" Parian with untinted bisque, black and gold band in front and back, painted features, cloth body and bisque limbs. Courtesy Frasher Doll Auctions. 26" - $1,500.00.

22½" Parian with untinted bisque and applied shirtwaist collar and ribbon bow in hairdo. Cloth body with bisque limbs. Courtesy Frasher Doll Auctions. 23" - $1,500.00.

cloth/"parian" limbs. Decorated shirt and tie. 15" - $700.00; 18" - $1,000.00.

Undecorated Shirt Top: 15" - $300.00; 18" - $450.00; 24" - $750.00.

Molded Hat: 9" - $1,500.00; 14" - $2,400.00.

25" Parian shoulder head, untinted bisque, ears partly exposed with wavy hairdo that has a braid in front, painted features, cloth body with bisque limbs. Courtesy Frasher Doll Auctions. 25" - $950.00.

26" Parian with untinted bisque shoulder head, cloth and bisque limbs. Painted features and sausage curl hair-do and curls around head. Civil War era. Courtesy Frasher Doll Auctions. 26" - $950.00.

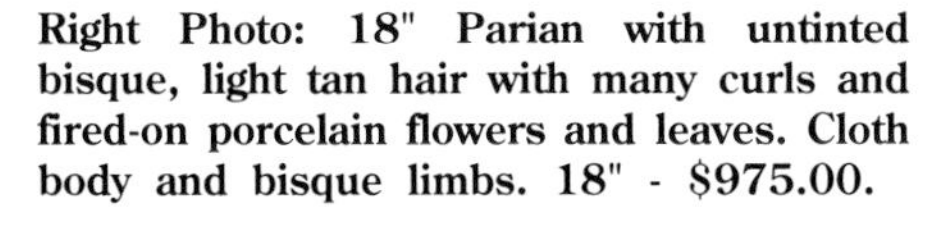

Right Photo: 18" Parian with untinted bisque, light tan hair with many curls and fired-on porcelain flowers and leaves. Cloth body and bisque limbs. 18" - $975.00.

PARIS BÉBÉ

These dolls were made by Danel & Cie in France from 1889 to 1895. The heads will be marked "Paris Bébé" and the body's paper label is marked with a drawing of the Eiffel Tower and "Paris Bébé/Brevete."

Paris Bébé Child: Closed mouth, no damage and nicely dressed. 16" - $3,900.00; 20" - $4,200.00; 24" - $4,800.00; 26" - $5,200.00.

22" marked "Tete Deposee Paris Bébé 9." Jointed French body is also marked "Paris Bébé." Closed mouth and paperweight eyes. Courtesy Frasher Doll Auctions. 22" - $4,600.00

PHENIX

Phenix Bébé dolls were made by Henri Alexandre of Paris who made dolls from 1889 to 1900.

Child - Closed Mouth: 16" - $3,500.00; 18" - $3,800.00; 22" - $4,200.00.

Child - Open Mouth: 16" - $1,900.00; 18" - $2,200.00; 22" - $2,600.00.

18½" marked "Phenix" in red. Open mouth with six teeth, French body with a blue paper label with child and flag. Courtesy Frasher Doll Auctions. 18½" - $2,200.00.

20" Bébé Phenix incised with star 93. Closed mouth, pierced ears, on French jointed body that has the "Jumeau Medaille D' or Paris" stamp. Courtesy Frasher Doll Auctions. 20" - $4,000.00.

**22" - $6,250.00 at auction.*

PIANO BABIES

Piano Babies were made in Germany from the 1880's into the 1930's and one of the finest quality makers was Gebruder Heubach. They were also made by Kestner, Dressel, Limbach, etc.

Piano Babies: All bisque, unjointed, molded hair and painted features. The clothes are molded on and they come in a great variety of positions. Excellent Quality: Extremely good artist workmanship and excellent detail to modeling. 4" - $185.00; 8" - $400.00; 12" - $725.00; 16" - $900.00. Medium Quality: May not have painting finished on back side of figure.

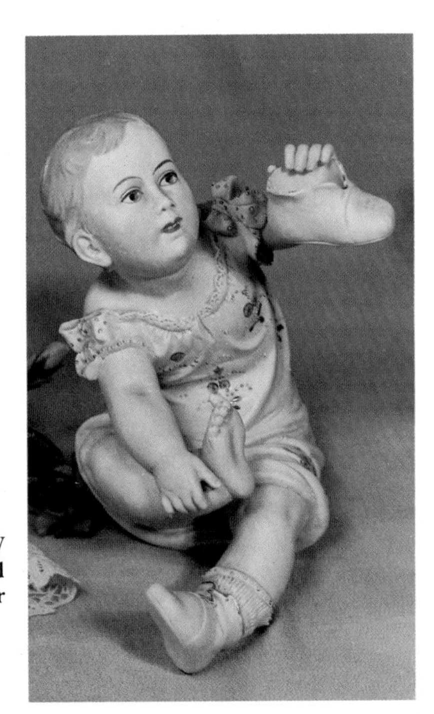

Piano Baby marked "Germany RW Rudolstadt" in blue stamp and incised "5557." 9½" all bisque. Courtesy Frasher Doll Auctions. 9½" - $550.00 up.

4" - $100.00; 8" - $250.00; 12" - $375.00; 16" - $500.00. **With Animal, Pot, On Chair, With Flowers or Other Items:** Excellent quality. 4" - $250.00; 8" - $450.00; 12" - $825.00; 16" - $1,200.00.

12¾" tall Piano Baby with molded eyelids, sitting backward in a chair. A very cute piano baby. Unmarked. Standing: 23" Jumeau marked "1907 9." Open mouth and has pull strings in marked body attached to voice box (Mama - Papa crier.) Courtesy Frasher Doll Auctions. Piano baby - $825.00. 23" - $2,800.00.

RABERY & DELPHIEU

Rabery & Delphieu began making dolls in 1856. The very first dolls have kid bodies and are extremely rare. The majority of their dolls are on French jointed bodies and are marked "R.D." A few may be marked "Bébé de Paris."

Child*: With closed mouth, in excellent condition with no chips, breaks or hairlines in bisque. Body in overall good condition and nicely dressed. 14" - $2,600.00; 17" - $2,900.00; 20" - $3,400.00; 22" - $3,600.00; 25" - $4,200.00.

Child: With open mouth and same condition as above: 14" - $950.00; 17" - $1,600.00; 20" - $2,200.00; 22" - $2,600.00; 25" - $3,000.00.

**24" with fantastic quality - $17,000.00 at auction.*

22½" marked "R 9 D." Open mouth with tiny teeth, paperweight eyes and French jointed body. Courtesy Frasher Doll Auctions. 22½" - $2,600.00.

28" marked "R.D." with excellent quality bisque, large paperweight eyes, closed mouth on fully jointed French body and may have original wig and clothes. Courtesy Barbara Earnshaw-Cain. 28" - $4,800.00.

RALIEGH

Raleigh Dolls were made by Jessie McCutcheon Raleigh of Chicago, IL from 1916 to 1920. Dolls were made of all composition or came with composition head and limbs on cloth body.

Child: 12" - $425.00; 16" - $545.00; 18" - $700.00.

Child - Glass Eyes: 16" - $650.00; 18" - $825.00.

Baby: 12" - $400.00; 16" - $500.00; 18" - $550.00.

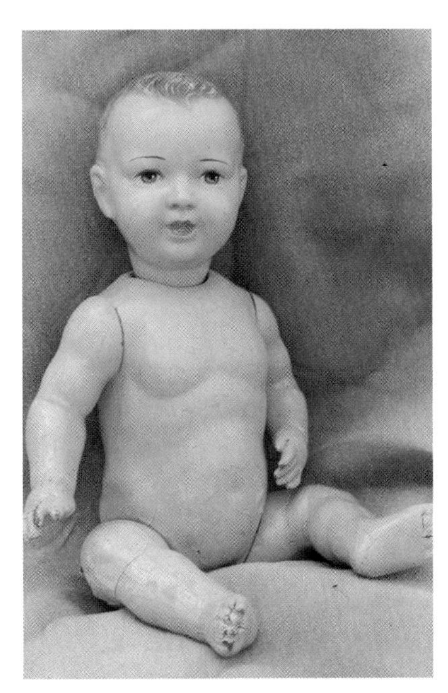

18" Raleigh doll that is all composition, painted eyes, molded, painted hair and open/closed mouth with painted teeth. Courtesy Carole Friend. 18" - $700.00.

Dolls marked with "R.A." were made by Rechnagel of Alexanderinethal, Thur, Germany. The R.A. dolls date from 1886 to after World War 1 and can range from very poor workmanship to excellent quality bisque and artist work. Prices are for dolls with good artist workmanship, such as the lips and eyebrows painted straight, feathered or at least not off center. Original or nicely dressed and no damage.

Child: Set or sleep eyes, open mouth with small dolls having painted-on shoes and socks. 7-8" - $165.00; 12" - $200.00; 15" - $285.00; 19" - $400.00; 21" - $550.00.

Baby: Ca. 1909-1910 on. Five-piece bent limb baby body or straight leg, curved arm toddler body and with sleep or set eyes. No damage and nicely dressed. 9" - $245.00; 12" - $300.00; 16" - $425.00; 19" - $500.00.

Character: With painted eyes, modeled bonnet and open/closed mouth, some smiling, some with painted-in teeth. No damage and nicely dressed. 8" - $600.00; 12" - $800.00.

Character: Glass eyes, closed mouth and composition bent limb baby body. 7" - $625.00; 10" - $750.00; 13" - $825.00.

12" child by Rechnagel marked "21 Germany R 10/0 A." Sleep eyes, open mouth with four teeth. Covered with rabbit fur and fur bunting. This style doll was very popular with the discovery of the North Pole. Courtesy Frasher Doll Auctions. 12" - $200.00.

Dolls marked with "P.M." were made by Otto Reinecke of Hol-Moschendorf, Bavaria, Germany from 1909 into the 1930's. The mold number found most often is the #914 baby or toddler.

Child: Bisque head with open mouth and on five-piece papier maché body or fully jointed body. Can have sleep or set eyes. No damage and nicely dressed. 9" - $150.00; 12" - $275.00; 15" - $395.00; 18" - $565.00; 22" - $675.00.

Baby: Open mouth, sleep eyes or set eyes. Bisque head on five-piece bent limb baby body. No damage and nicely dressed. 12" - $300.00; 16" - $500.00; 22" - $650.00; 25" - $800.00.

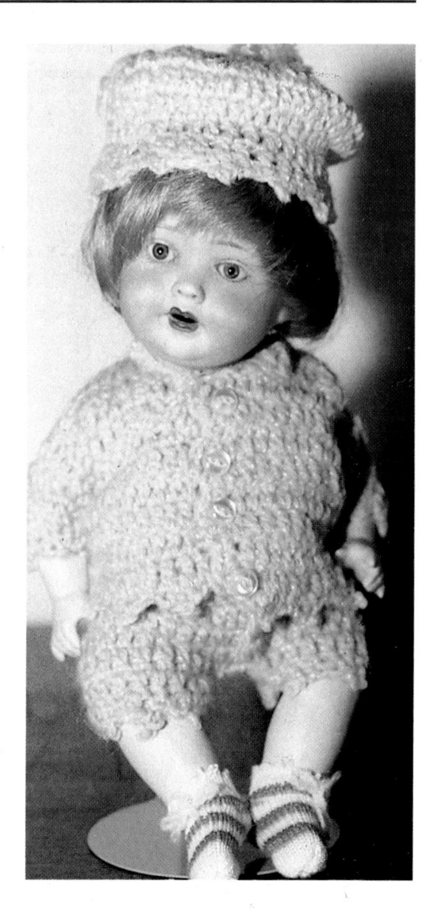

Baby made by Otto Reineke and marked "P.M. 914 Germany." Open mouth with two teeth; bent limb baby body. This one happens to be all bisque and 10" tall, but the face will be the same on larger sizes that are of composition bodies. Courtesy Arthur Boutiette. 9" - $165.00.

REVALO

The Revalo marked dolls were made by Gebruder Ohlhaver of Thur, Germany from 1921 to the 1930's. Bisque heads with jointed bodies, sleep or set eyes. No damage and nicely dressed.

Child: Open mouth. 14" - $385.00; 17" - $550.00; 20" - $625.00; 24" - $725.00.

Molded Hair Child: With or without molded ribbon and/or flower. Painted eyes and open/closed mouth. 11" - $675.00; 14" - $850.00.

Baby: Open mouth, sleep or set eyes on five-piece baby body. 15" - $500.00; 17" - $675.00.

Toddler: 15" - $600.00; 17" - $750.00.

14½" baby marked "Revalo 22.4." Open mouth with two teeth and on five bent limb baby body. Courtesy Frasher Doll Auctions. 14½" - $500.00.

Left: 22" marked "Germany Revalo 7." Open mouth with four teeth and fully jointed body. Right: 20" marked "Armand Marseille 390 A.M." Open mouth with four teeth and on fully jointed body. Courtesy Frasher Doll Auctions. 22" - $675.00; 20" - $425.00.

Bruno Schmidt's doll factory was located in Walterhausen, Germany and many of the heads used by this firm were made by Bahr & Proschild, Ohrdruf, Germany. They made dolls from 1898 on into the 1930's.

Marks:

Child: Bisque head on jointed body, sleep eyes, open mouth, no damage and nicely dressed. 14" - $375.00; 20" - $550.00; 28" - $1,000.00. Flirty eyes: 20" - $650.00; 28" - $1,300.00.

Character Baby, Toddler or Child: Bisque head, glass eyes or painted eyes, jointed body, no damage and nicely dressed. **#2048, 2094, 2096** (called "Tommy Tucker"): Molded, painted hair, open mouth. 17" - $1,300.00; 22" - $1,700.00. **#2048, 2094, 2096:** "Tommy Tucker" with closed mouth. Otherwise, same as above. 17" - $2,500.00; 22" - $3,000.00. **#2072:** Closed mouth, wig. 18" - $3,400.00. **#2097:** Toddler. 14" - $375.00; 16" - $600.00; 20" - $800.00.

Character Child: Closed mouth, painted eyes or glass eyes, jointed child body, no damage and nicely dressed. **Marked "BSW" in heart:** No mold number. 16" - $2,000.00 up; 20" - $2,400.00 up. **#2033 "Wendy"*:** 12" - $12,000.00 up; 16" - $18,000.00 up; 20" - $20,000.00 up.

** 17" - $22,000.00 at auction.*

18" "Tommy Tucker" made by Bruno Schmidt. Molded, painted hair, sleep eyes, open mouth with tongue and on fully jointed body. Courtesy Frasher Doll Auctions. 18" - $1,400.00.

One of the elusive German characters is this Bruno Schmidt "Wendy" with the "BSW" in a heart and mold number "2033." Closed mouth, sleep eyes and on fully jointed body. Courtesy Karen & Paul Johnson. 16" - $18,000.00 up.

30" marked "BSW" in a heart. Open mouth with four teeth, fully jointed body. Courtesy Frasher Doll Auctions. 30" - $1,500.00.

17" rare character doll marked "BSW" in a heart. Intaglio eyes, closed mouth and full cheeks. On fully jointed body. All original. Courtesy Barbara Earnshaw-Cain. 17" - $2,200.00 up.

16" marked "BSW" in heart/2097-4. Open mouth with two upper teeth, sleep eyes and on five-piece bent limb baby body. Courtesy Frasher Doll Auctions. 16" - $500.00.

Franz Schmidt & Co. began in 1890 at Georgenethal, near Walterhausen, Germany. In 1902, they registered the cross hammers with a doll between and also the F.S.&C. mark.

Marks:

1310
F.S. & Co.
Made in
Germany
10

Baby: Bisque head on bent limb baby body, sleep or set eyes, open mouth and some may have pierced nostrils. No damage and nicely dressed. (Add more for toddler body.) **#1271, 1295, 1296, 1297, 1310:** 9" - $325.00; 17" - $650.00; 20" - $750.00; 24" - $1,000.00. Toddler: 9" - $465.00; 16" - $750.00; 20" - $900.00. **#1267:** Open/closed mouth, painted eyes. 16" - $2,000.00; 19" - $2,800.00. Glass eyes: 16" - $2,400.00; 19" - $3,200.00. **#1285:** 16" - $725.00; 20" - $900.00.

Child: Papier maché and composition body with walker machanism with metal rollers on feet. Open mouth, sleep eyes. Working and no damage to head, nicely dressed. **#1250:** 12" - $300.00; 16" - $600.00; 20" - $700.00. **#1266, 1267:** Child with open mouth and sleep eyes. 22" - $2,600.00.

23" marked "F.S. & Co. 1295." Pierced nostrils, open mouth with two upper teeth and on five-piece bent limb baby body. Courtesy Frasher Doll Auctions. 23" - $900.00.

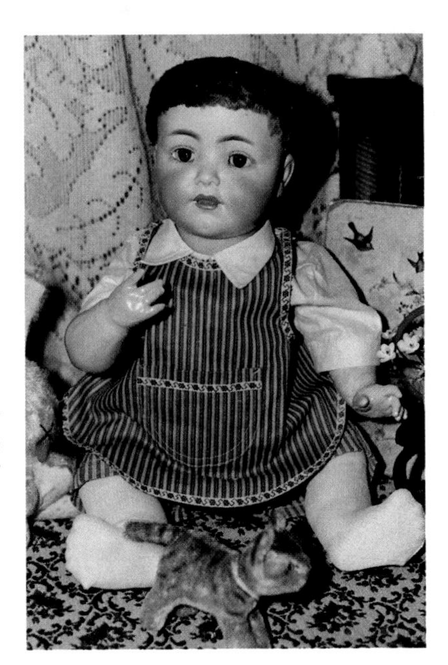

22" baby marked "F.S. & CO. 1295." Sleep eyes, open mouth with two upper teeth, pierced nostrils and on five-piece bent limb baby body. Courtesy Frasher Doll Auctions. 22" - $850.00.

SCHMITT & FILS

Schmitt & Fils produced dolls from 1870's to 1891 in Paris, France. The dolls have French jointed bodies and came with closed mouths or open/closed ones.

Marks:

Child: Bisque head on jointed body with closed mouth or open/closed mouth. No damage and nicely dressed. Marked on head and body. 15" - $8,500.00; 18" - $15,000.00; 20" - $16,000.00; 23" - $19,000.00; 25" - $22,000.00; 30" - $27,000.00. Flange neck: 13" - $14,000.00; 17" - $18,000.00.

23" closed mouth head marked with shield and crossed hammers inside. Body is marked with shield and has free-formed balls at joints with very flat bottom side of torso in back. 23" - $19,000.00.

SCHOENAU & HOFFMEISTER

Schoenau & Hoffmeister began making dolls in 1901 and were located in Bavaria. The factory was called "Porzellanfabrik Burgrubb" and this mark will be found on many of their doll heads. Some of their mold numbers are 21, 169, 170, 769, 900, 914, 1800, 1906, 1909, 1923, 4000, 4900, 5000, 5300, 5500, 5700, 5800 and also Hanna.

Marks:

Princess Elizabeth: Smiling open mouth, set eyes, bisque head on jointed five-piece body and marked with name on head or body. 16" - $2,000.00; 20" - $2,500.00; 24" - $3,200.00.

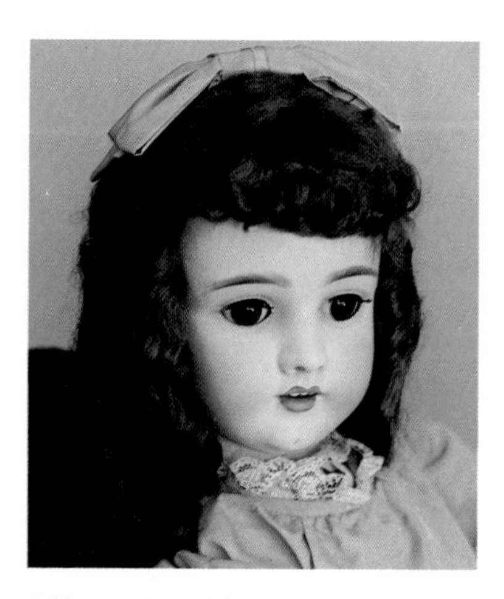

34" marked "S, pb" in star "H 1906 16." Open mouth with four teeth and on full jointed body. Courtesy Frasher Doll Auctions. 34" - $1,400.00.

Hanna: Child with black or brown fired-in color to bisque head. Sleep or set eyes, five-piece body or jointed body. Marked with name on head. 8" - $325.00; 14" - $425.00.

Hanna Baby: Bisque head, open mouth, sleep eyes and on five-piece bent limb baby body. 14" - $625.00; 17" - $750.00; 24" - $1,300.00.

Character Baby: #169, 769, etc. Bisque head on five-piece bent limb baby body. 12" - $325.00; 17" - $575.00; 20" - $645.00; 24" - $800.00. Toddler Body: 17" - $700.00; 20" - $850.00.

Child: #1909, 5500, 5900, 5800, etc. Bisque head with open mouth, sleep or set eys, jointed body. No damage and nicely dressed. 10" - $150.00; 15" - $365.00; 18" - $475.00; 21" - $575.00; 26" - $800.00; 30" - $1,000.00; 34" - $1,400.00.

Painted Bisque: Painted head on five-piece body or jointed body. 10" - $135.00; 13" - $200.00.

Das Lachende Baby (My Laughing Baby): 20" - $2,000.00; 25" - $2,500.00.

Left: 23" marked "S, pb" in star, "H 1909." Jointed body , open mouth with four teeth and on fully jointed body. Right: 22" marked "Made in Germany Floradora A. 7M." Open mouth with four teeth and on fully jointed body. Courtesy Frasher Doll Auctions. 23" - $650.00. 22" A.M. - $400.00.

Hide-covered horse pulling wooden wagon with four bisque head dolls marked "S", "pb" in star, "H 4600." The dolls have glass eyes, open mouth, cardboard torsos, wire upper limbs and carved wood lower limbs. Dolls attached to wood planks on side of wagon. 25" closed mouth Simon & Halbig 949 on fully jointed body. Courtesy Frasher Doll Auctions. Wagon & dolls - $800.00 up. 25" - $3,200.00 up.

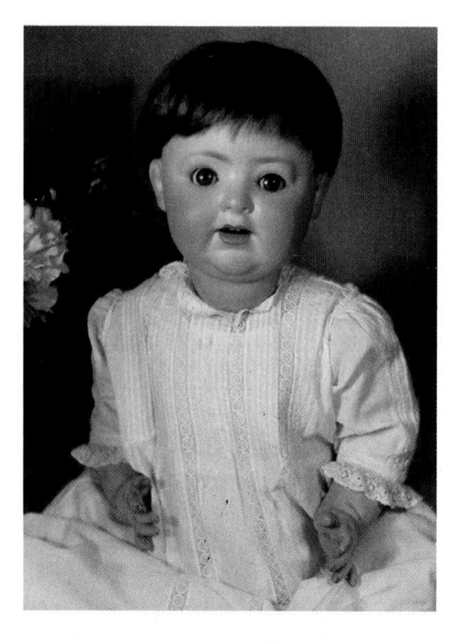

28" baby marked "Porzellanfabrik-Burggrub 169 8." Open mouth with two upper teeth and on five-piece bent limb baby body. Courtesy Frasher Doll Auctions. 28" - $1,200.00.

SCHOENHUT

The Albert Schoenhut & Co. was located in Philadephia, PA from 1872 onto the 1930's. The dolls are all wood with spring joints, have holes in bottom of feet to fit in a metal stand.

Marks:

(1911 - 1913)

SCHOENHUT DOLL
PAT. JAN. 17, '11, USA
& FOREIGN COUNTRIES
(Incised - 1911 on)

(1913 - 1930)

Child With Carved Hair: May have comb marks, molded ribbon, comb or bow. Closed mouth. Original or nice clothes. Excellent condition : 14" - $2,000.00; 21" - $2,500.00. Very good condition with some wear: 14" - $1,200.00; 21" - $1,800.00. Poor condition with chips and dents: 14" - $500.00; 21" - $600.00.

Baby Head: Can be on regular body or bent limb baby body. Bald spray painted hair or wig, painted decal eyes. Nicely dressed or original. Excellent condition: 12" - $550.00; 16" - $700.00; 17" - $800.00. Good condition: 16" - $450.00; 17" - $550.00. Poor condition: 16" - $200.00; 17" - $250.00.

Toddler: Excellent condition. 14" - $800.00; 16" - $875.00.

Cap Molded To Head: 14" - $2,800.00 up.

Tootsie Wootsie: Molded, painted hair, toddler or regular body. 14" - $2,800.00 up; 16" - $3,000.00 up.

"Dolly" Face: Common doll, wigged, open/closed mouth with painted teeth, decal painted eyes. Original or nicely dressed. Excellent condition: 14" - $650.00; 21" - $875.00. Good condition: 14" - $425.00; 21" - $650.00. Poor condition: 14" - $150.00; 16" - $200.00.

Sleep Eyes: Has lids that lower down over the eyes and has an open mouth with teeth or just slightly cut open mouth with carved teeth. Original or nicely dressed. Excellent condition: 16" - $1,300.00; 21" - $1,500.00. Good condition: 16" - $650.00; 21" - $800.00. Poor condition: 16" - $200.00; 21" - $275.00.

Walker: One-piece legs with "Walker" joints in center of legs and torso. Painted eyes, open/closed or closed mouth. Original or nicely dressed. Excellent condition: 14" - $850.00; 17" - $1,000.00; 20" - $1,300.00. Good condition: 17" - $500.00; 20" - $700.00. Poor condition: 17" - $175.00; 20" - $225.00.

All Composition: Molded curly hair, "Patsy" style body, paper label on back, 1924. 14" - $450.00.

16½" baby face boy with Schoenhut label on head and body. 17" "dolly" face with the incised Schoenhut mark. 15" baby face with label on body. All have painted features. Girl has open/closed mouth with painted teeth. 16½" - $800.00. 17" - $725.00. 15" - $650.00.

21" character girl, open/closed mouth with painted teeth, painted features and has paper label on body. 22" sleep eyes, open/closed mouth with painted teeth, has paper label on body. 8" wood Felix the Cat. All wood segments with leather ears. Marked "Felix copr. 1922, 1924 by Pat. Sullivan. Pat. June 23, 1925." Courtesy Frasher Doll Auctions. 21" - $875.00. 22" sleep eyes - $1,600.00. 8" Felix - $150.00.

18" sleep eye Schoenhut in mint, unplayed with condition. Open/closed mouth with carved teeth. 15" carved hair with carved, painted head band, closed mouth and on original stand. (She also has original box.) Courtesy Frasher Doll Auctions. 18" - $1,400.00. 15" - $2,000.00.

17" all wood Schoenhut that is all original except shoes and socks. Painted features, open/closed mouth with painted teeth. Courtesy Jeanne Maudin. 17" - $800.00.

Left: Very rare 16" Schoenhut "Tootsie Wootsie." Doll came out in 1911 both as a toddler and child. Has open/closed mouth with pronounced tongue and two upper teeth, carved baby fuzz hair and blue intaglio eyes. Marked "Schoenhut Doll/Dates (unreadable)/Foreign Countries." Came out same year as boy "Schnickle Fritz." Courtesy Marlowe Cooper. 16" - $3,000.00 up.

Left: 23" baby marked "K star R - Simon & Halbig 126." Sleep eyes, open mouth, bent limb baby body. Middle: 20" baby marked "201 S.Q. Germany." Open mouth, sleep eyes and on five-piece bent limb baby body. Right: 18" baby by Otto Reinecke, sleep eyes and open mouth. Courtesy Frasher Doll Auctions. 23" - $1,300.00. 20" - $675.00. 18" - $565.00.

Schuetzmeister & Quendt made dolls from 1893 to 1898. This short term factory was located in Boilstat, Germany.

Marks:

Child: Can have cut pate or be a bald head with two string holes. No damage and nicely dressed, open mouth. 16" - $450.00; 20" - $575.00; 24" - $700.00.

Baby: Includes mold #201 & 301. Five-piece bent limb baby body. Not damaged and nicely dressed. Open mouth. 12" - $350.00; 14" - $475.00; 17" - $585.00; 22" - $750.00.

Simon & Halbig began making dolls in the late 1860's or early 1870's and continued until the 1930's. Simon & Halbig made many heads for other companies and they also supplied some doll heads from the French makers. They made entire dolls, all bisque, flange neck dolls, turned shoulder heads and socket heads.

Marks:

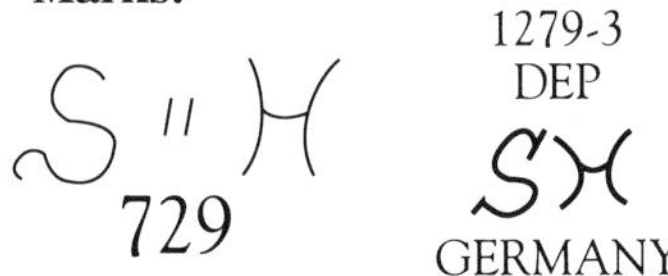

Prices are for dolls with no damage to the bisque and only minor scuffs to the bodies, well dressed, wigged and have shoes. These dolls should be ready to place into a collection.

Child: 1889 to 1930's. Open mouth and jointed body. **#719, 739, 749, 939, 949, 979, etc.:** 16" - $1,200.00; 20" - $2,100.00; 25" - $2,500.00; 30" - $3,000.00.

#130, 540, 550, 1039, 1040, 1078, etc: Open mouth. (More for flirty eyes.) 12" - $475.00; 15" - $525.00; 18" - $625.00; 22" - $725.00; 26" - $1,000.00; 30" - $1,300.00; 33" - $1,900.00; 36" - $2,200.00; 40-42" - $3,000.00 up.

#1009, 1079: Open mouth. 16" - $585.00; 20" - $785.00; 25" - $1,050.00; 30" - $1,500.00.

#1009: With fashion kid body. 18" - $775.00; 23" - $950.00; 25" - $1,300.00.

#1010, 1040, 1080, etc: Open mouth and kid body. 16" - $500.00;

13" marked "S&H 1039 7 Dep." Bisque swivel head on bisque shoulder plate, open mouth and flirty eyes operated by pull strings in back of head. Kid body with bisque lower arms. Courtesy Frasher Doll Auctions. 13" - $495.00.

42" marked "1079 18 Halbig S&H." Open mouth with accented lips, sleep eyes, factory dress and wig. A very pretty doll for one of this size. Courtesy Frasher Doll Auctions. 42" - $3,600.00.

12" marked "Simon & Halbig 908" on jointed adult body with slim waist. Square porcelain teeth in open mouth. Courtesy Turn of Century Antiques. 12" - $1,600.00.

18" marked "S 12 H 939." Closed mouth and on jointed body with straight wrists. Wears old factory dress and bonnet that may be original. Courtesy Frasher Doll Auctions. 18" - $2,700.00.

21" - $625.00; 25" - $750.00; 30" - $1,000.00.

#1250, 1260: Open mouth, kid body. 15" - $500.00; 18" - $600.00; 21" - $700.00; 24" - $900.00.

Characters: 1910 and after. Wig or molded hair, glass or painted eyes, with open/closed, closed, or open mouth. On jointed child bodies. **#IV:** 19" - $14,000.00 up. **#120:** 14" - $1,600.00; 22" - $2,700.00; **#150:** 15" - $8,500.00; 18" - $10,000.00; 22" - $14,000.00. **#151:** 16" - $9,000.00; 22" - $14,000.00. **#153:** 16" - $8,800.00. **#600:** 14" - $600.00; 18" - $1,000.00; 21" - $1,400.00. **#718, 719*:** 16" - $2,300.00; 20" - $3,000.00. **#720, 740:** Kid body, closed mouth. 10" - $575.00; 16" - $1,300.00; 18" - $1,600.00. **#740:** Jointed body. 10" - $675.00; 16" - $1,400.00; 20" - $2,100.00. **#749*:** Closed mouth, jointed body. 16" - $2,300.00; 20" - $3,000.00. **#905, 908, 924:** Closed mouth. 14" - $1,700.00; 17" - $2,800.00. **#905, 908, 929:** Open mouth. 16" - $1,800.00; 22" - $2,200.00; 30" - $3,000.00. **#939*:** Jointed body. 17" - $2,600.00; 20" - $3,000.00; 25" - $3,600.00. Kid body. 17" - $1,800.00; 20" - $2,400.00; 25" - $3,000.00. **Black, closed mouth:** 17"- $2,400.00; 20" - $3,000.00. Open mouth: 17" - $1,400.00; 20" - $1,800.00. **#949:** Closed mouth. 17" - $2,400.00; 20" - $2,800.00; 25" - $3,200.00; 41" - $4,600.00. Black, closed mouth. 17" - $2,300.00; 20" - $2,900.00. Kid body. 17" - $1,500.00; 20" - $2,000.00; 25" - $2,500.00. Jointed body. 17" - $1,800.00; 20" - $2,400.00; 25" - $3,000.00. **#1248, 1249 Santa:** 16" - $850.00; 20" - $1,100.00; 26" - $1,600.00. **#1279:**

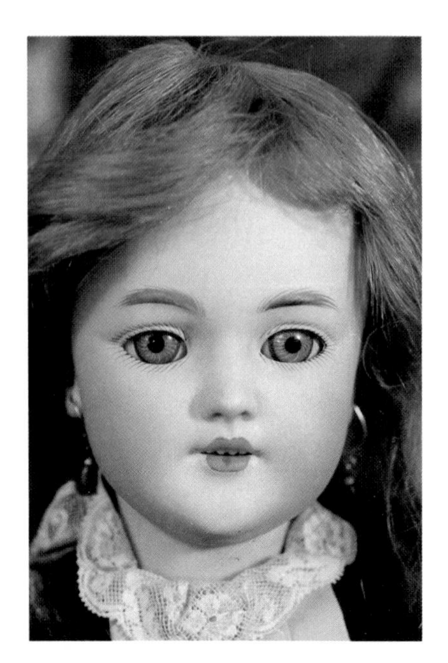

19½" "Santa" marked "S&H 1249 Germany Dep. 7½"." Sleep eyes, open mouth with accented lips and on fully jointed body. Courtesy Frasher Doll Auctions. 20" - $1,100.00.

Left: 23" marked "SH 1279 DEP." Sleep eyes, open mouth with two square cut teeth, accented lips and on fully jointed body. Right: 26" German-made unknown doll with closed mouth, set eyes and on fully jointed body. Marks "630 13." Courtesy Frasher Doll Auctions. 23" - $2,800.00. 26" - $2,700.00.

10" - $800.00; 16" - $1,800.00; 21" - $2,700.00; 25" - $3,300.00; 30" - $5,000.00. **#1299:** 17" - $1,000.00; 21" - $1,300.00. **#1338:** Open mouth, jointed body. 18" - $1,400.00; 24" - $2,600.00; 30" - $3,600.00. **#1339:** Character face, open mouth. 18" - $1,500.00; 24" - $2,800.00. **#1358:** Black. 17" - $5,500.00; 21" - $6,200.00; 24" - $6,900.00. **#1388, 1398:** Lady Doll. 21" - $11,000.00 up; 26" - $17,000.00 up. **#1428:** 20" - $1,900.00. **#1478:** 16" - $6,800.00 up. **#1488:** 16" - $2,900.00; 20" - $3,700.00.

Character Babies: 1909 to 1930's. Wigs or molded hair, painted or sleep eyes, open or open/closed mouth and on five-piece bent limb baby bodies. (Allow more for toddler body.) **#1294:** 15" - $565.00; 18" - $725.00; 22" - $1,000.00; 25" - $1,600.00. With clockwork in head to move eyes. 25-26" - $2,600.00. **#1299:** With open mouth. 10" - $365.00; 16" - $800.00. Toddler: 16" - $900.00; 18" - $1,100.00. **#1428 Toddler:** 12" - $1,400.00; 16" - $1,700.00; 20" - $2,000.00; 26" - $2,600.00. **#1428 Baby:** 12" - $925.00; 16" - $1,400.00; 20" - $1,800.00. **#1488 Toddler:** 17" - $3,400.00; 20" - $3,800.00. Baby: 17" - $2,200.00; 20" - $2,400.00; 24" - $3,000.00. **#1489:** Ericka Baby. 19" - $3,000.00; 21" - $3,700.00; 25" - $4,400.00. **#1498 Toddler:** 16" - $3,200.00; 20" - $3,900.00. **#1039 Walker:** Key wound. 16" - $1,400.00; 18" - $1,700.00; 20" -

$1,900.00. Walking/Kissing: 18" - $975.00; 22" - $1,200.00.

Miniature Dolls: Tiny dolls with open mouth on jointed body or five-piece body with some having painted-on shoes and socks. Fully jointed: 8" - $565.00; 10" - $650.00. Five-piece Body: 8" - $400.00; 10" - $500.00. Little Women Type: Closed mouth and fancy wig. **#1160:** 6" - $385.00; 9" - $485.00.

Ladies: Ca. 1910. Open mouth, molded lady-style slim body with slim arms and legs. **#1159, 1179:** 14" - $1,200.00; 18" - $1,800.00; 25" - $2,800.00.

Ladies: Closed mouth. Ca. 1910. Adult slim limb body. **#1303:** 15" - $7,400.00; 18" - $9,000.00. **#1469:** 15" - $2,800.00; 18" - $4,000.00.

#152 Lady: 17" - $12,000.00 up.

** #729, 20" - $5,000.00 at auction.*

27" marked "S & H 1488." Sleep eyes, open/closed mouth and on jointed toddler body. Courtesy Frasher Doll Auctions. 27" $5,000.00.

Baby: 14" Simon & Halbig marked "1498." Solid dome with painted hair, sleep eyes, open/closed mouth and on five-piece bent limb baby body. Left: 30" Gebruder Heubach marked "11 Heaubach" sunburst mark "Dep. Germany." Glass eyes and closed mouth. Courtesy Frasher Doll Auctions. 14" - $2,200.00; 30" - $8,800.00.

Left: Open mouth Bébé Jumeau stamped on head "Tete Jumeau" and on marked Jumeau body. Right: 22½" child by Simon and Halbig with mold number 758. She is on a marked Jumeau body with "Mama-Papa" pull string talker body. Courtesy Frasher Doll Auctions. 28" Jumeau - $3,900.00. 22½" - $1,900.00.

19½" lady marked "1159 S&H DEP 8." Slender face with open mouth, sleep eyes and on jointed adult body with slim waist, molded bust and slender limbs. Courtesy Frasher Doll Auctions. 19½" - $2,200.00.

17" head circumference baby marked "1489 Erika." Hole cut in bisque, followed by "Simon & Halbig/14." Sleep eyes, open mouth with two lower teeth and on five-piece bent limb baby body. Courtesy Irene Brown. 25" - $4,400.00.

The Societe Française de Fabrication de Bébé St. Jouets (S.F.B.J.) was formed in 1899 and known members were Jumeau, Bru, Fleischmann & Blodel, Rabery & Delphieu, Pintel & Godchaux, P.H. Schmitz, A. Bouchet, Jullien and Danel & Cie. By 1922, S.F.B.J. employed 2,800 people. The Society was dissolved in the mid-1950's. There are a vast amount of "dolly-faced" S.F.B.J. dolls, but some are extremely rare and are character molds. Most of the characters are in the 200 mold number series.

Marks:

S.F.B.J.
239
PARIS

DEPOSE
S.F.B.J.
301

S F
B J

Child: Sleep or set eyes, open mouth and on jointed French body. No damage and nicely dressed. **#60:** 14" - $575.00; 20" - $775.00; 24" - $900.00. **#301:** 8" - $300.00; 14" - $725.00; 18" - $845.00; 22" - $1,200.00; 28" - $1,600.00; 32" - $2,000.00.

Jumeau Type: Open mouth. 16" - $1,200.00; 20" - $1,600.00; 24" - $1,800.00; 28" - $2,300.00. Closed mouth: 16" - $1,600.00; 20" - $2,000.00; 24" - $2,400.00; 28" - $2,800.00.

Lady #1159: Open mouth, adult body. 22" - $2,100.00.

Character: Sleep or set eyes, wigged, flocked, molded hair, jointed body. No damage and nicely dressed. **#211:** 16" - $5,400.00. **#226:** 16" - $1,900.00; 21" - $2,600.00. **Painted eyes:** 14" - $1,200.00. **#227:** 16" - $2,400.00; 21" - $2,900.00. **#229:** 16" -

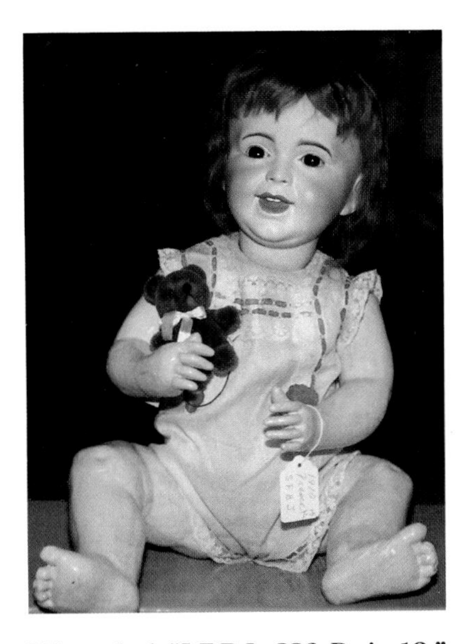

26" marked "S.F.B.J. 236 Paris 12." Sleep eyes, open laughing mouth with two upper teeth, on five-piece bent limb baby body. Holds original "Teddy" and wears one-piece romper. Courtesy Jeanne Mauldin. 26" - $2,400.00.

27" "Twirp" marked "S.F.B.J. 247 Paris." Sleep eyes, open/closed mouth with two tupper teeth. On jointed toddler body. The 24" bear is German made with glass eyes. Courtesy Frasher Doll Auctions. 27" - $4,800.00.

$3,100.00. **#230:** 23" - $2,200.00; 42" - $7,000.00. **#233:** 14" - $2,800.00; 17" - $3,900.00. **#234:** 16" - $3,000.00; 21" - $3,500.00. **#235:** 16" - $2,100.00; 21" - $2,800.00. Painted eyes: 14" - $1,400.00. **#236 Toddler:** 12" - $1,500.00; 16" - $1,900.00; 20" - $2,300.00; 25" - $2,800.00; 27" - $3,000.00. **Baby:** 16" - $1,500.00; 21" - $2,000.00; 25" - $2,500.00. **#237:** 16" - $2,100.00; 21" - $2,400.00. **#238:** 16" - $3,000.00; 21" - $3,400.00. **Lady:** 22" - $4,200.00. **#239 Poubout:** 14" - $16,000.00; 17" - $19,000.00. **#242:** 17" - $4,600.00. **#247:** 14" - $2,800.00; 17" - $4,600.00. **#248:** Very pouty, glass eyes. 14" - $4,400.00; 17" - $4,200.00. **#251 Toddler:** 16" - $1,700.00; 20" - $2,200.00; 26" - $2,900.00. **Baby:** 16" - $1,400.00; 20" - $2,200.00; 26" - $2,800.00. **#252**

Above Photo:
22" marked "Depose S.F.B.J. 8." Flirty eyes, open mouth with six teeth. French walker-type body. Pull string "mama-papa" talker. Courtesy Frasher Doll Auctions. 22" - $1,800.00.

Right Photo:
14" clown incised "S.F.B.J." White, unpainted face with fired-in color design and lips. Sleep eyes and open mouth. Original clothes. Courtesy Barbara Earnshaw-Cain. 14" - $1,000.00.

Toddler: 16" - $5,400.00; 20" - $7,700.00; 26" - $9,000.00. **Baby:** 10" - $2,000.00; 16" - $5,200.00; 20" - $7,500.00; 26" - $8,800.00. **#257:** 16" - $2,300.00. **#266:** 20" - $3,600.00.

Googly: See Googly section.

Kiss Throwing, Walking Doll: Composition body with straight legs, walking mechanism and when walks, arms goes up to throw kiss. Head moves from side to side. Flirty eyes and open mouth. In working condition, no damage to bisque head and nicely dressed. 21-22" - $1,800.00.

Left: 24" marked "S.F.B.J. Paris 11," on head and has blue Jumeau sticker on jointed body. Open mouth. Rear: 26" Jumeau marked "X 230 Paris 12." Has pull string talker "mama-papa" box in torso. Front: 18" Jumeau marked "Tete Jumeau" in red stamp and incised "1907." Blue sticker on body. Courtesy Frasher Doll Auctions. 24" - $1,800.00. 26" - $3,200.00. 18" Jumeau - $1,900.00.

SNOW BABIES

Snow Babies were made in Germany and Japan and they can be excellent to poor in quality from both countries. Snow Babies have fired-on "pebble-textured" clothing. Many are unmarked and the features are painted. Prices are for good quality painted features, rareness of pose and no damage to the piece.

Single Figure: 1½" - $45.00; 3" - $85.00-125.00.

Two Figures: Together. 1½" - $100-125.00; 3" - $150-195.00.

Three Figures: Together. 1½" - $145.00-185.00; 3" - $195.00-245.00.

One Figure On Sled: 2-2½" - $145.00.

Two Figures On Sled: 2-2½" - $175.00.

Three Figures On Sled: 2-2½" - $225.00.

Jointed: Shoulders and hips. 3¼" - $150.00 up; 5" - $350.00 up; 7" - $425.00 up.

Shoulder head: Cloth body with china limbs. 9" - $385.00; 12" - $450.00.

On Sled in Glass: "Snow" scene - $150.00.

With Bear: $175.00.

With Snowman: $165.00.

With Musical Base: $165.00.
Laughing Child: $100.00 up.
Snow Bear with Santa: $265.00.
With Reindeer: $145.00
Snow Baby Riding Polar Bear: $165.00.

Three Snow Babies made to attache to bisque sled by wooden pegs. Larger figure is 4" and smaller ones are 2" tall. Child attached to sled with part of the front broken off. Courtesy Frasher Doll Auctions. Three on sled: $225.00. One on sled: $95.00 in this condition.

Three 2" tall Snow Babies on sled. Pebbly-textured bisque, painted features and sled marked "Germany." Holding a snowball, 2" Snow Baby with fine quality painted features. Courtesy Frasher Doll Auctions. Sled: $225.00. 2" - $60.00.

Steiff started business in 1894 and this German maker is better known for their plush/stuffed animals than for dolls.

Steiff Dolls: Felts, velvet or plush with seam down middle of face. Button-style eyes, painted features and sewn on ears. The dolls generally have large feet so they stand alone. Prices are for dolls in excellent condition and with original clothes. Second price is for dolls that are soiled and may not be original.

Adults: 16-17" - $1,700.00 up; 21-22" - $2,100.00 up.

Military Men: 17" - $3,400.00 up; 21" - $4,400.00 up.

Children: 12" - $950.00; 15-16" - $1,500.00; 18-19" - $1,800.00.

Made is U.S. Zone Germany: Has glass eyes. 12" - $700.00 up; 16" - $900.00 up.

Comic Characters: Such as chef, elf, musician, etc. 14" - $2,400.00 up; 16" - $3,200.00 up.

11" "Harry and Helen," Dutch Fisherpeople. Inset mohair wigs, glass eyes, fully jointed with mitten hands. Both original, but lady is missing apron and bonnet. Both can have variations of headgear. Felt shoes are tacked on the back with thread. The 1913 Steiff catalog also shows them in 14" and 17" size. Courtesy Margaret Mandel. 11" - $2,400.00 each.

STEINER, HERM

Left: 14" baby by Herm Steiner marked "3 HS Germany." Solid dome, closed mouth and sleep eyes. Flange neck on cloth body with composition hands. Right: 16½" marked "Made in Germany 151." Attribuated to Hertal & Schwab. Open mouth, four upper teeth and on bent limb baby body. Courtery Frasher Doll Auctions. 14" - $450.00. 16½" - $575.00.

Left: 14½" Herm Steiner marked "HS" on head. Painted eyes, closed mouth and on fully jointed body. Right: "American School Boy" marked "30 B/5." Bisque shoulder head with set eyes, closed mouth and on kid body with bisque lower arms. Courtesy Frasher Doll Auctions. 14½" - $600.00. School Boy: $850.00.

STEINER, JULES

Jules Nichols Steiner operated from 1855 to 1892 when the firm was taken over by Amedee LaFosse. In 1895, this firm merged with Henri Alexander, the maker of Phenix Bébé and a partner, May Freres Cie, the maker of Bébé Mascotte. In 1899, Jules Mettais took over the firm and in 1906, the company was sold to Edmond Daspres.

In 1889, the firm registered the girl with a banner and the words "Le Petite Parisien" and in 1892, LaFosse registered "Le Parisien."

Marks:

J. STEINER
STE. S.G.D.G.
FIRE A12
PARIS

STE C3
J. STEINER
B. S.G.D.G.

Bourgoin

"A" Series Child: 1885. Closed mouth, paperweight eyes, jointed body and cardboard pate. No damage and nicely dressed. 12" - $3,000.00; 16" - $3,800.00; 20" - $5,300.00; 25" - $6,600.00; 28" - $8,000.00.

"A"* Series Child: Open mouth, otherwise same as above. 16" - $2,200.00; 20" - $2,800.00; 26" - $3,800.00.

"C" Series Child: Ca. 1880. Closed mouth, round face, paperweight eyes, no damage and nicely dressed. 16" - $4,600.00; 20" - $6,000.00; 25" - $7,200.00; 28" - $8,600.00.

Bourgoin Steiner: 1870's. With "Bourgoin" incised or in red stamp on head along with the rest of the Steiner mark. Closed mouth. No damage and nicely dressed. 16" - $4,600.00; 20" - $6,000.00; 25" - $7,200.00.

Wire Eye Steiner: Closed mouth, flat glass eyes that open and close by moving wire that comes out the back of the head. Jointed body, no damage and nicely dressed. Bourgoin: 16" - $4,700.00; 20" - $5,800.00; 25" - $7,000.00. "A" Series: 16" - $4,800.00; 20" - $6,000.00; 25" - $7,200.00. "C" Series: 16" - $4,700.00; 20" - $5,800.00; 25" - $7,000.00.

"Le Parisien" - "A" Series: 1892. 16" - $3,800.00; 20" - $5,300.00; 25" - $6,600.00.

Mechanical: See that section.

Bisque Hip Steiner: Motschmann-style body with bisque head, shoulders, lower arms and legs and bisque torso sections. No damage anywhere. 18" - $5,200.00.

20" "A" Series Steiner, marked "Steiner Paris Fre A 13." Closed mouth and on jointed Steiner body, straight wrists. Body is marked "Le Petit Pariesien Bébé Steiner." Courtesy Frasher Doll Auctions. 20" - $5,300.00.

29" Wire Eye Steiner of the "A" Series. Open mouth and eyebrows that almost meet. Maybe original clothes and wig. Has bisque hands with excellent detail. Courtesy Barbara Earnshaw-Cain. 29" - $8,000.00.

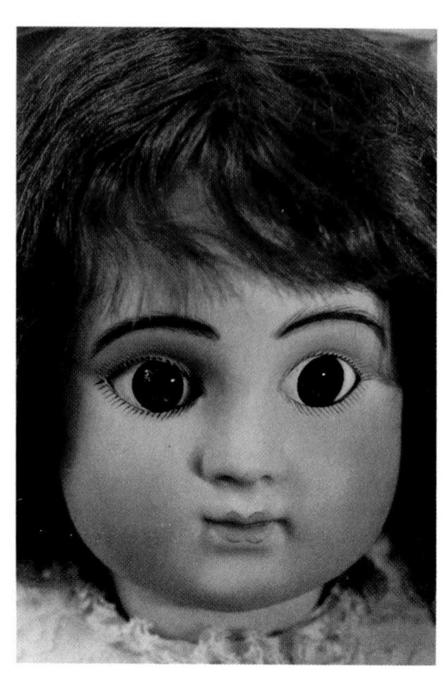

Early White Bisque Steiner: With round face, open mouth with two rows of teeth. Unmarked. On jointed Steiner body, pink wash over eyes. No damage and nicely dressed. **14" - $4,200.00; 18" - $5,900.00.

** 23" - $8,250.00 at auction.*
*** 14" - $5,500.00 at auction.*

25" "C" Series Steiner marked "Ste, C5" and in red "J. Steiner B.S.G.D.G. J. Bourgoin S.D.G.D." The back of the eyes are also incised "Steiner" along with the Steiner patent. Has wire at crown behind ear to move the eyes open or closed. Steiner jointed body. Courtesy Frasher Doll Auctions. 25" - $7,000.00.

TRION

Trion Toy Co. operated from 1911 to 1921 in Brooklyn, NY. Some dolls may have kid bodies.

Child: 14" - $125.00; 18" - $200.00; 22" - $285.00.

Baby: 14" - $100.00; 17" - $175.00; 21" - $265.00.

14" marked "Trion Toy Co. 1915." Name of doll is "Happy" and she has a straw-filled cloth body and composition head and limbs. Clothes are all original. Features are painted. Courtesy Jeanne Mauldin. 14" - $125.00 up.

Tynie Baby was designed by Bernard Lipfert and made by Horsman Dolls in 1924. Sleep eyes, closed mouth with pouty look and modeling of frown between eyes. Cloth body with celluloid or composition hands. Marked "1924/E.I. Horsman, Inc./Made in Germany." Some will be incised "Tynie Baby." No damage and nicely dressed.

Bisque Head: 14" - $775.00; 16" - $895.00.

Composition Head: 14" - $300.00.

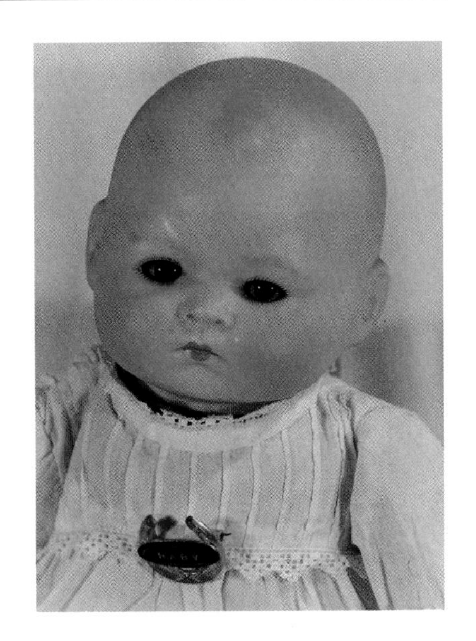

UNIS

"Unis, France" was a type of trade association or a "seal of approval" for trade goods to comsumers from the manufacturers. This group of businessmen, who were to watch the quality of French exports, often overlooked guidelines and some poor quality dolls were exported. Many fine quality Unis marked dolls were also produced.

Unis began right after World War 1 and is still in business. Two doll companies are still members, "Poupee Bella" and "Petit Colin." There are other type manufacturers in this group and they include makers of toys, sewing machines, tile, pens, etc.

Marks:

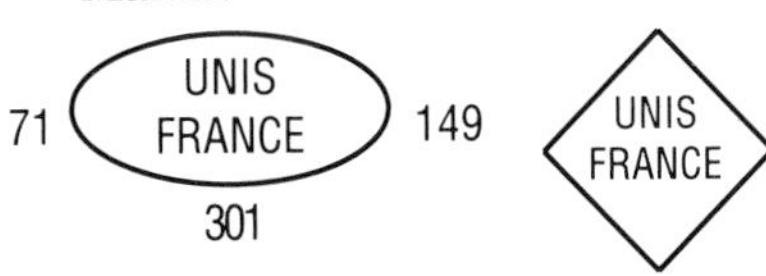

19" "Princess Elizabeth" marked "71 Unis France 149 306 Jumeau 1938 Paris." Bisque head with closed mouth, sleep eyes with hair lashes and on French jointed body. Courtesy Frasher Doll Auctions. 19" - $1,900.00.

#60, 70, 71, 301: Bisque head with papier maché or composition body. Sleep or set eyes, open mouth. No damage and nicely dressed. 14" - $525.00; 17" - $600.00; 21" - $745.00; 24" - $900.00. Black or brown: 14" - $425.00; 17" - $700.00.

Provincial Costume Doll: Bisque head, painted, set or sleep eyes, open mouth (or closed on smaller dolls.) Five-piece body. Original costume, no damage. 6" - $175.00; 12" - $300.00; 14" - $350.00.

Baby #272: Glass eyes, open mouth, cloth body, celluloid hands. 14" - $525.00; 17" - $950.00. Painted eyes, composition hands: 14" - $300.00; 17" - $475.00.

#251 Toddler: 16" - $1,700.00.

Princess Elizabeth: 1938. Jointed body, closed mouth. (Allow more for flirty eyes.) 18" - $1,800.00; 24" - $2,400.00; 32" - $3,400.00.

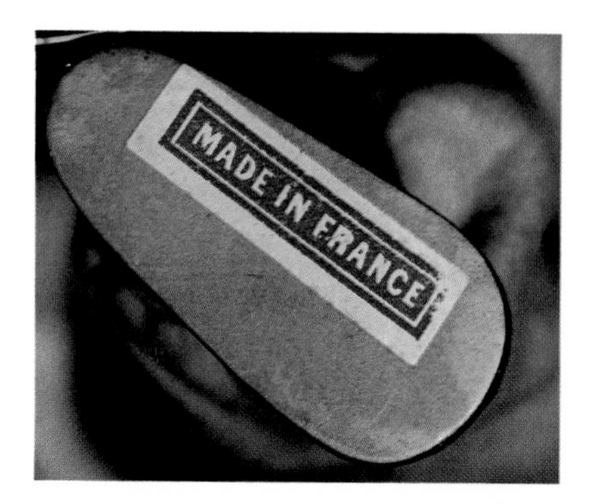

16" "Princess Elizabeth" as young lady in snow suit. Marked "S.F.B.J. Unis 301." Ca. late 1940's. All original including mittens. Has sticker on bottom of shoe "Made in France" and the wrist tag of both "Jumeau" and "Unis." Open mouth, sleep eyes with lashes. Courtesy Barbara Earnshaw-Cain. 16" - $1,600.00.

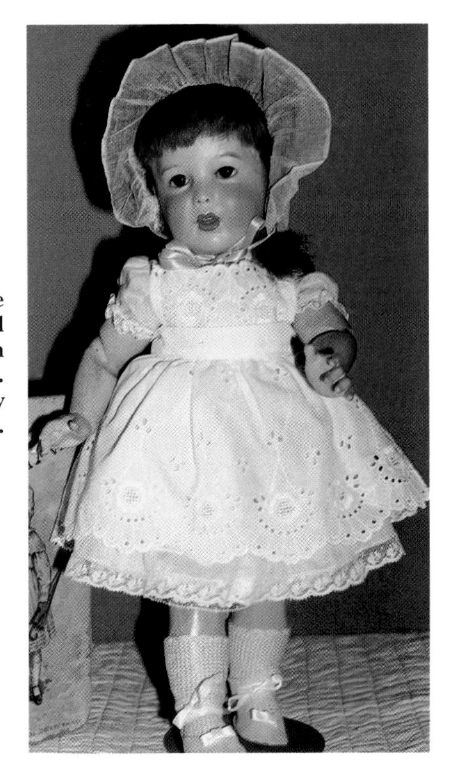

18" called "Twirp" marked "Unis France 251 71 149." This mold also used earlier by S.F.B.J. Sleep eyes, open mouth with two upper teeth and tongue. On jointed toddler body. Courtesy Frasher Doll Auctions. 18" - $1,900.00.

16½" brown bisque head marked "71 Unis France 149 301." Sleep eyes with hair lashes and on jointed French body. Open mouth. 23" marked "France S.F.B.J. 301 Paris." Open mouth and on French jointed body. Courtesy Frasher Doll Auctions. 16½" - $700.00. 23" - $875.00.

J. Verlingue of Boulogne-sur-Mer, France made dolls from 1914 to 1921.

Marks:

J.V. marked child: Bisque head, wig, glass eyes, open mouth, jointed papier maché body. 15" - $585.00; 18" - $675.00; 23" - $875.00.

All Bisque: Swivel neck, sleep eyes, closed mouth, one-piece body and head, jointed shoulders and hips, painted-on hoses and boots. 7" - $300.00; 9" - $385.00.

22" marked "Petite Francaise France JV," anchor mark, "10 Liane." Open mouth with six teeth, set eyes and on French jointed body. 19½" solid dome baby with sleep eyes and open mouth with four teeth marked "151." Attribuated to Hertal and Schwab. Courtesy Frasher Doll Auctions. 22" - $850.00. 19½" - $700.00.

VON BERG

14" marked "H.v.B. 500/2K." Bisque head with flange neck, open mouth with two upper teeth, set eyes and on toddler style kid body with compsoition arms. Hermann von Berg made dolls from 1906 to 1930's near Koppelsdorf, Germany. Courtesy Frasher Doll Auctions. 14" - $425.00. 20" - $650.00.

Poured Wax: Cloth body with wax head, limbs and inset glass eyes. Hair is embedded into wax. Nicely dressed or in original clothes, no damage to wax, but wax may be slightly discolored (evenly all over.) Not rewaxed. 15" - $1,200.00; 18" - $1,500.00; 21" - $1,700.00; 24" - $2,100.00. Lady or Man: 20" - $2,100.00.

25" English slit head wax doll. Ca. 1830-1960. Cloth body with leather hands, glass eyes and has slit in top of head that the wirg fits into. 17½" Parian with untinted bisque, cloth body and bisque limbs. Courtesy Frasher Doll Auctions. 25" - $750.00. 17½" - $500.00.

Front: 13" wax over papier maché boy with painted hair, glass eyes, cloth body with wax over composition limbs. Rear: 21" china with center part, partly exposed ears and could be boy or girl. Cloth body with china limbs. 17" china with center part and sausage curls, cloth body with china limbs. Courtesy Frasher Doll Auctions. 13" - $450.00. 21½" - $575.00. 17" - $575.00.

28" wax over composition doll with glass eyes, closed mouth, mohair wig, cloth body with composition limbs. Courtesy Frasher Doll Auctions. 28" - $900.00.

Wax Over Papier Maché or Composition: Cloth body with wax over papier maché or composition head and with wax over composition or wood limbs. Only minor scuffs with no chipped out places, good color and nicely dressed. **Early Dolls:** *12" - $425.00; 16" - $700.00. **Later Dolls:** 12" - $250.00; 16" - $450.00. **Bonnet or Cap:** (Baby) 16" - $1,100.00.

Lady: 17" - $1,800.00 up.

Slit Head Wax: (English) 1830-1860's. Glass eyes, some open and closed by an attached wire. 14" - $325.00.

** 14" mint - $800.00 at auction.*

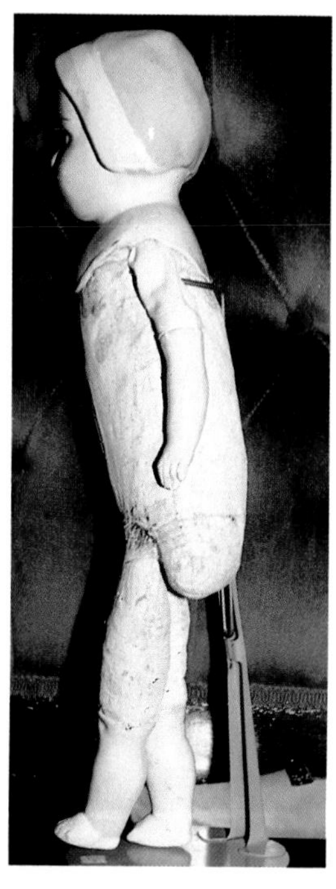

Left Photo: 16" wax over papier maché shoulder head with rare molded on bonnet, glass eyes. Muslin straw stuffed body with wax over composition limbs. Redressed in old materials. Right Photo: Shows the body construction of the wax over papier maché with molded-on bonnet. Courtesy Bonnie Stewart. 16" - $1,100.00.

21" bisque head toddler marked "4703 Weiss Kuhnert & Co. Grafenthal/Made in Germany 4." Has cryer box in torso. Shown with two Steiff animals. Weiss Kuhnert made dolls from 1891 to 1930's. This company also used the initials "W.K.C." Courtesy Frasher Doll Auctions. 15" - $450.00; 21" - $600.00; 25" - $950.00.

Norah Welling's designed were made for her by Victoria Toy Works in Wellington, Shopshire, England. These dolls were made from 1926 into the 1960's. The dolls are velvet as well as other fabrics, especially felt and velour. They will have a tag on the foot "Made in England by Norah Wellings."

Child: All fabric with stitch jointed hips and shoulders and have a molded fabric face with oil painted features. Some faces are papier maché with a stockenette covering. All original felt and cloth clothes, clean condition. Painted eyes: 14" - $400.00; 17" - $600.00; 21" - $800.00; 23" - $1,200.00. Glass eyes: 14" - $500.00; 17" - $700.00; 21" - $900.00.

Mounties, Black Islanders, Scots, and Other Characters: These are most commonly found. Must be in same condition as child. 8" - $90.00; 11" - $125.00; 14" - $175.00.

Glass Eyes: White: 14" - $250.00. Black: 14" - $200.00; 20" - $350.00; 28" - $600.00.

Babies: Same description as child and same condition. 14" - $375.00; 17" - $650.00; 21" - $800.00.

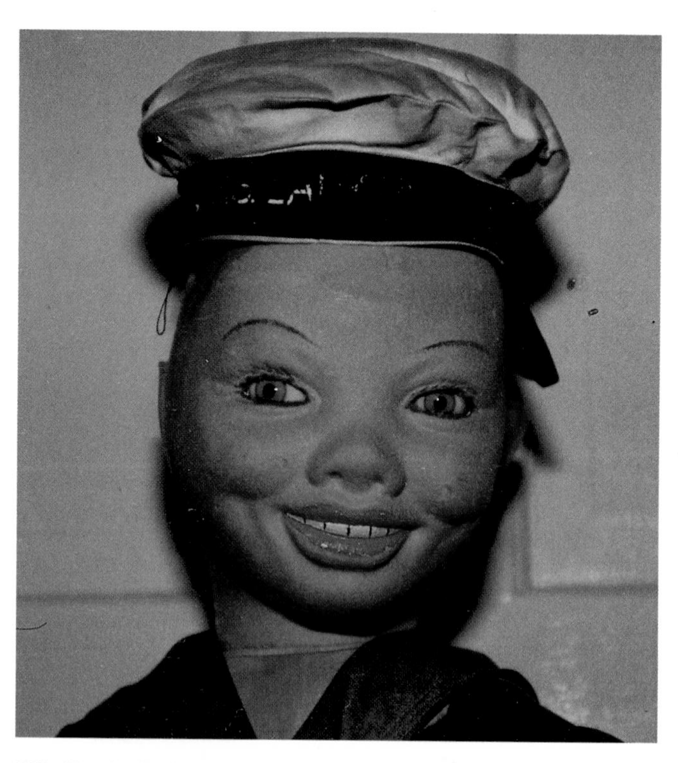

28" Norah Wellings Sailor that is all cloth and velvet, glass eyes and smile painted mouth. Tagged on foot "Made in England by Norah Wellings." Courtesy Jeannie Mauldin. 28" - $600.00.

The Adolpf Wislizenus doll factory was located at Walterhausen, Germany and the heads he used were made by Bahr & Proschild, Ernst Heubach of Kopplesdorf and Simon & Halbig. The company was in business starting in 1851, but it is not known when they began to make dolls.

Marks:

GERMANY
A. W.

Child: 1890's into 1900's. Bisque head on jointed body, sleep eyes, open mouth. No damage and nicely dressed. 16" - $400.00; 21" - $475.00; 24" - $550.00.

Baby: Bisque head in perfect condition and on five-piece bent limb baby body. No damage and nicely dressed. 16" - $425.00; 20" - $565.00; 25" - $900.00.

#115: 16" - $1,100.00.

#110: 17" - $1,300.00.

11" all original soldier with hole in hand for flag. Marked "44.19." Tag: "A.W.S. soldier 1898." Bisque head on five-piece body. Courtesy Henri & John Startzel. 11" - $250.00.

24" marked "A.W. 1." Bisque head with open mouth and four teeth. Sleep eyes and on fully jointed body. The toy washing machine is marked "Louis Marx & Co." Courtesy Frasher Doll Auctions. 24" - $550.00.

MODERN SECTION AND INDEX

Lifesize mechanical "Sweetheart Soap Baby." Excellent quality and very large and heavy (company brochure says 80 lbs.) Marked: "Mechanical Man, Inc. Riverside Dr. and Vanderbilt Ave., N.Y.C." Head turns, raises and lowers, waves arms and kicks legs. Courtesy Frasher Doll Auctions. In Box: $600.00.

18" "Elsie, The Cow" as "Dutch Elsie Doll." Vinyl head with rest all cloth, original outfit, but missing cap. Offered by Carnation Milk Company. Date unknown. Ca. mid-1950's. 18" - $65.00.

17" "Swiss Miss" cloth with painted features, yarn hair and all original. Tag sewn in seam: "1977 Beatrice Foods Co./Made for Beatrice Foods by Product People, Inc. Courtesy Genie Jinright. 17" - $22.00.

Right Photo: Three early 17" "Little Miss Sunbeam" for Sunbeam Bread. First issue doll is sitting and is made of very good quality vinyl. The others are lightweight plastic with vinyl arms and head. Lips are red on early ones and pink on later ones. Later ones also have longer lashes. All marked "Eegee" on head. Variation of print is used. Courtesy Marie Ernst. 17" - $42.00.

17" "Little Miss Sunbeam" in two all original later issues. One has blue ribbon in hair and other has red, with the ribbon being glued to doll. Marked "Eegee" on head. Courtesy Marie Ernst. 17" - $42.00 each.

1953-1954: 7½-8" straight leg, non-walker, heavy hard plastic. **Party Dress:** Mint and all correct - $450.00 up. Soiled, dirty hair mussed or parts of clothing missing - $100.00. **Ballgown:** Mint and correct - $1,000.00 up. Soiled, dirty, bad face color, not original - $200.00. **Nude:** Clean and good face color. $200.00. Dirty and bad face color - $60.00.

1955: 8" straight leg walker. **Party Dress:** Mint and all correct. $425.00. Soiled, dirty, parts of clothes missing - $85.00. **Ballgown:** Mint and all correct - $1,000.00. Dirty, part of clothing missing, etc. - $100.00. **Basic sleeveless dress:** Mint - $285.00. Dirty - $65.00. **Nude:** Clean and good face color - $125.00. Dirty, not original, faded face color - $45.00.

1956-1965: Bend Knee Walker. **Party Dress:** Mint and all correct - $350.00. Dirty, part of clothes missing, etc. - $70.00. **Ballgown:** Mint and correct - $1,200.00. Soiled, dirty, parts missing, etc. - $100.00. **Nude:** Clean, good face color - $100.00. Dirty, faded face color - $35.00. **Basic sleeveless dress:** Mint - $235.00. Dirty, faded face color - $50.00. **Internationals:** $125.00. Dirty, parts missing - $45.00.

1965-1972: Bend Knee, Non-Walkers: **Party Dress:** Mint and original - $300.00. Dirty, parts missing, etc. - $65.00. **Internationals:** Clean and mint - $125.00. Dirty or soiled - $45.00. **Nude:** Clean, good face color - $65.00. Dirty, faded face color - $25.00.

1973-1976: "Rosies" Straight leg, non-walker, rosy cheeks and marked "Alex." **Bride or Ballerina:** Bend knee walker - $325.00. Bend knee only - $250.00. Straight leg - $35.00-40.00. **Internationals:** $100.00. **Storybook:** $75.00.

1977-1981: Straight leg, non-walker marked "Alexander." **Bride or Ballerina:** $50.00-60.00. **International:** $50.00-60.00. **Storybook:** $50.00-60.00.

1982-1987: Straight leg, non-walker with deep indentations over upper lip that casts a shadow and

8" Internationals that are straight leg, but called "Rosies" due to head mold change. These dolls have all been discontinued. 1973-1976. Courtesy Turn of Century Antiques. $100.00 each.

makes the doll look as if it has a mustache. **Bride or ballerina:** $50.00-60.00. **International:** $50.00-60.00. **Storybook:** $50.00-60.00.

1988-1989: Straight leg, non-walker with new face that is more like the older dolls than others and still marked with full name "Alexander." **Bride or ballerina:** $35.00-45.00. **International:** $35.00-45.00. **Storybook:** $35.00-45.00.

Photo Above:
8" "Queen" 1955. Straight leg walker. Courtesy Mike Way. 8" - $900.00.

Right Photo:
1955 Alexander-kin straight leg walker in play suit that is interchangeable with Little Genius. Replaced shoes. Courtesy Margaret Mandel. 8" - $325.00.

Prices are for mint condition dolls.

Baby McGuffey: Composition. 22" - $250.00. Soiled - $85.00.

Bonnie: Vinyl. 19" - $175.00. Soiled - $60.00.

Cookie: Composition. 19" - $275.00. Soiled - $95.00.

Genius, Little: Composition. 18" - $225.00. Soiled - $70.00.

Genius, Little: Vinyl, may have flirty eyes. 19" - $150.00. Soiled - $45.00.

Genius, Little: 8" - $195.00. Soiled - $55.00.

Happy: Vinyl. 20" - $300.00. Soiled - $100.00.

12" "Slumbermate" with composition head with molded hair and painted sleep (closed) eyes. Cloth body with composition legs and gauntlet hands. Original. Courtesy Mike Way. 12" - $425.00.

Honeybun: Vinyl. 23" - $200.00. Soiled - $55.00.

Kathy: Vinyl. 19" - $150.00; 26" - $195.00. Soiled: 19" - $40.00; 26" - $55.00.

Kitten, Littlest: Vinyl. 8" - $185.00. Soiled - $65.00.

Mary Mine: 14" - $145.00. Soiled - $40.00.

Pinky: Composition. 23" - $185.00. Soiled - $65.00.

Precious: Composition. 12" - $145.00. Soiled - $40.00.

Princess Alexandria: Composition. 24" - $200.00. Soiled - $55.00.

Pussy Cat: Vinyl. 14" - $45.00. Black: 14" - $145.00. Soiled: $10.00-30.00.

Rusty: Vinyl. 20" - $450.00. Soiled - $100.00.

Slumbermate: Composition. 21" - $500.00. Soiled - $150.00.

Sunbeam: Vinyl. 16" - $125.00. Soiled - $30.00.

Sweet Tears: 9" - $100.00. With layette - $175.00. Soiled - $45.00.

Victoria: 20" - $60.00. Soiled - $20.00.

23" "Pinky." Cloth with composition head and gauntlet hands, sleep eyes and in original clothes. 1937. Courtesy Phyllis Houston. 23" - $185.00.

20" "Baby Lynn" 1973. Cloth and vinyl, sleep eyes and all original. Courtesy Marge Meisinger. 20" - $125.00.

21" "Genius Baby" 1961 and marked "Alexander 1960" on head. Vinyl and plastic with flirty eyes, original romper, replaced shoes. 13" "Buddy Lee" that is all hard plastic and wears Engineer outfit and has painted-on boots. Courtesy Frasher Doll Auctions. 21" - $225.00. Buddy Lee: $200.00 up.

MADAME ALEXANDER - CISSETE

This 10-11" high heel doll named "Cissette" was made from 1957 to 1963, but it was used for other dolls later. She is made of hard plastic, and clothes will be tagged "Cissette."

First prices are for mint condition dolls; second prices are for soiled, dirty or faded clothes, tags missing and hair messy.

Street Dresses: $225.00, $65.00.
Ballgowns: $400.00 up, $100.00.
Ballerina: $175.00, $55.00.
Gibson Girl: $1,200.00, $250.00.
Jacqueline: $550.00, $150.00.
Margot: $400.00, $100.00.
Portrette: $475.00-550.00, $175.00.
Wigged in case: $650.00, $200.00.

11" Cissette used as 1968 "Godey" of the Portrait series. In mint condition. 11" - $475.00.

MADAME ALEXANDER - CISSY

"Cissy" was made 1955-1959 and had hard plastic with vinyl over the arms, jointed at elbows, and high heel feet. Clothes are tagged "Cissy."

First prices are for mint condition dolls; second prices for dirty, not original, bad face color, and played with dolls.

Street Dress: $350.00, $125.00.

Ballgown: $450.00-900.00, $165.00.

Bride: $450.00, $150.00.

Queen: $600.00, $165.00.

Portrait: "Godey," etc. 21" - $475.00, $150.00.

Scarlett: $375.00-600.00, $100.00 - 250.00.

Flora McFlimsey: Vinyl head, inset eyes. 15" - $500.00, $185.00.

21" "Cissy" with trunk and wardrobe. 1955. All clothes tagged and only item not original to the doll are her shoes. $1,000.00 up.

The Alexander Company made cloth and plush dolls and animals and also oil cloth baby animals in the 1930's, 1940's and early 1950's. In the 1960's, a few were made.

First prices are for mint condition dolls; second prices are for ones in poor condition, dirty, not original, played with or untagged.

Animals: $200.00 up, $75.00.

Dogs: $300.00, $100.00.

Alice in Wonderland: $600.00, $175.00.

Clarabelle, The Clown: 19" - $200.00, $75.00.

David Copperfield or Other Boys: $600.00, $200.00.

Eva Lovelace: $550.00, $165.00.

Funny: $125.00, $35.00.

Little Shaver: 7" - $250.00; 10" - $285.00.

Little Women: $550.00 each, $200.00.

Muffin: 14" - $100.00, $35.00.

So Lite Baby or Toddler: 20" - $300.00, $100.00.

Susie Q: $600.00, $200.00.

Tiny Tim: $600.00, $200.00.

Teeny Twinkle: Has disc floating eyes. $550.00, $165.00.

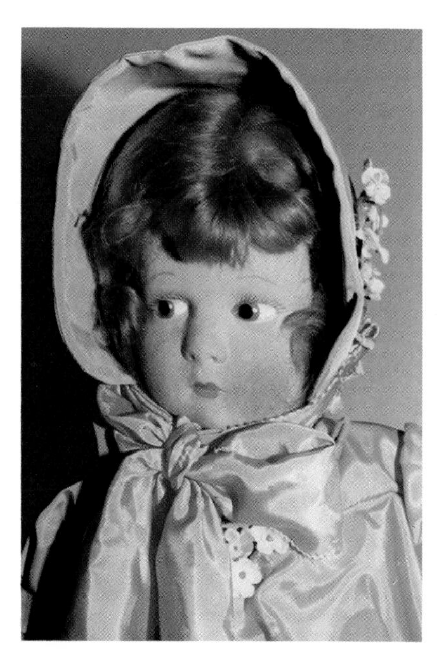

21" "American Tot" with pressed felt-like face that is oil painted, mohair wig, flesh-colored cotton body and limbs with free-standing thumb and mitt-style hands. All original. Courtesy Glorya Woods. 21" - $500.00.

MADAME ALEXANDER - COMPOSITION

First prices are for mint condition dolls; second prices are for dolls that are crazed, cracked, dirty, soiled clothes or not original.

Alice in Wonderland: 9" - $200.00, $60.00; 14" - $350.00, $85.00; 20" - $575.00, $140.00.

Baby Jane: 16" - $700.00, $250.00.

Brides or Bridesmaids: 7" - $175.00, $50.00; 9" - $200.00, $80.00; 15" - $225.00, $95.00; 21" - $425.00, $100.00.

Dionne Quints: 8" - $200.00, $75.00; Set of five - $1,250.00. 11" - $350.00, $125.00; Set of five - $1,700.00. Cloth Baby: 14" - $425.00, $140.00; Set of five - $2,300.00. Cloth Baby: 16" - $475.00, $150.00; Set of five - $2,500.00. 19-20" - $500.00, $200.00; Set of five - $3,200.00.

Dr. DeFoe: 14-15" - $800.00, $300.00.

Flora McFlimsey: (Marked Princess Elizabeth) Freckles: 15" - $600.00, $200.00; 22" - $700.00, $225.00.

Internationals/Storybook: 7" - $175.00, $60.00; 11" - $200.00, $85.00.

Jane Withers: 13" - $650.00, $300.00; 18" - $800.00, $425.00.

Jeannie Walker: 13" - $450.00, $150.00; 18" - $600.00, $250.00.

Kate Greenaway: (Marked Princess Elizabeth) Very yellow blonde wig. 14" - $450.00, $150.00; 18" - $575.00, $200.00.

Little Colonel: 9" - $300.00, $100.00; 13" - $500.00, $200.00; 23" - $800.00, $400.00.

Margaret O'Brien: 15" - $500.00, $200.00; 18" - $650.00, $250.00; 21" - $800.00, $350.00.

Marionettes: Tony Sarg: 12" Disney - $465.00, $165.00. Others: 12" - $325.00, $100.00.

McGuffey Ana: (Marked Princess Elizabeth) 13" - $450.00, $165.00; 20" - $700.00, $300.00.

Portrait Dolls: 1939-1941, 1946: 21" - $1,600.00, $600.00.

Princess Elizabeth: Closed mouth. 13" - $400.00, $150.00; 18" - $575.00, $200.00; 24" - $650.00, $300.00.

Scarlett: 9" - $300.00, $100.00; 14" - $500.00, $200.00; 18" - $675.00, $300.00; 21" - $800.00, $400.00.

Sonja Henie: 17" - $550.00, $225.00; 20" - $600.00, $300.00. Jointed waist: 14" - $475.00, $185.00.

Wendy Ann: 11" - $350.00, $125.00; 15" - $450.00, $175.00; 18" - $500.00, $200.00.

Set of five 19" Dionne Quints that are in mint condition and all original. $500.00 each; $3,200.00 set.

7" "Lollie" Bridesmaid. All composition and original. Also came in yellow. 7" - $175.00.

21" Bridesmaids #451-1945-1946. Gown tagged "Madame Alexander/New York, U.S.A." Came in boxes with pink bows all over them. Both original and in mint condition. 21" - $425.00 each.

First prices are for mint condition dolls; second prices are for dolls that are dirty, played with, soiled clothes or not original.

Alice in Wonderland: 14" - $375.00, $165.00; 17" - $500.00, $200.00; 23" - $750.00, $300.00.

Annabelle: 15" - $425.00, $185.00; 18" - $500.00, $200.00; 23" - $650.00, $300.00.

Babs: 20" - $475.00, $175.00.

Babs Skater: 18" - $500.00, $200.00; 21" - $600.00, $300.00.

Binnie Walker: 15" - $175.00, $90.00; 25" - $375.00, $125.00.

Ballerina: 14" - $375.00, $165.00.

Cinderella: 14" - $575.00, $225.00; 18" - $650.00, $300.00.

Cynthia: Black doll. 15" - $650.00, $300.00; 18" - $725.00, $365.00; 23" - $800.00, $425.00.

Elise: Street dress. 16½" - $350.00, $175.00. Ballgown: $450.00, $200.00.

Bride: 16" - $325.00, $165.00.

Fairy Queen: 14½" - $400.00, $200.00.

Glamour Gals: 18" - $700.00, $350.00.

Godey Lady: 14" - $500.00, $200.00.

Man/Groom: 14" - $800.00, $400.00.

Kathy: 15" - $400.00, $200.00; 18" - $550.00, $265.00.

Kelly: 12" - $400.00, $150.00; 16" (MaryBel): $285.00, $160.00.

Lady Churchill: 18" - $750.00, $325.00.

Lissy: Street dress: 12" - $350.00, $185.00. Bride: $325.00, $185.00. Ballerina: $365.00, $195.00.

Little Women: 8" - $125.00, $60.00; Set of five (bend knee) - $600.00; Set of five (straight leg) - $400.00. 12" Lissy: $350.00, $135.00; Set of five - $1,500.00. 14" - $300.00; Set of five- $1,400.00.

Laurie: 8" - $75.00 up, $30.00; 12" - $475.00, $195.00.

Maggie: 15" - $325.00, $165.00; 17" - $450.00, $225.00; 23" - $600.00, $300.00.

Maggie Mix-up: 8" - $475.00, $200.00; 16½" - $375.00, $175.00. 8" Angel: $1,200.00, $450.00.

Margaret O'Brien: 14½" - $550.00, $250.00; 18" - $750.00, $350.00; 21" - $850.00, $400.00.

Mary Martin: Sailor suit or ballgown. 14" - $500.00, $175.00; 17" - $800.00, $400.00.

Peter Pan: 15" - $500.00, $200.00.

Polly Pigtails: 14" - $450.00, $200.00; 17" - $575.00, $250.00.

Prince Charming: 14" - $625.00, $300.00; 18" - $700.00, $350.00; 21" - $750.00, $350.00.

Prince Phillip: 17" - $550.00, $250.00; 21" - $650.00, $300.00.

Queen: 18" - $700.00, $300.00.

Shari Lewis: 14" - $365.00, $150.00; 21" - $475.00, $200.00.

Sleeping Beauty: 16½" - $475.00, $200.00; 21" - $650.00, $300.00.

Story Princess: 15" - $465.00, $200.00.

Violet, Sweet: 18" - $550.00, $225.00.

Wendy (Peter Pan Set): 14" - $450.00, $150.00.

Wendy Ann: 14½" - $300.00, $150.00; 17" - $400.00, $200.00; 22" - $450.00, $125.00.

Winnie Walker: 15" - $275.00, $100.00; 18" - $300.00, $150.00; 23" - $400.00, $100.00.

16" "Elise Bride." All hard plastic with vinyl over plastic arms and jointed at elbows, knees and ankles. All original. 1957. Marked "MME Alexander" on back. Courtesy Genie Jinright. 16-16½" - $450.00.

18" "Godey" of 1953. Uses the "Maggie" face doll that is all hard plastic. Sleep eyes and is all original. Courtesy Pam Ortman. 18" - $900.00 up.

8" "Maggie Mix-up" of 1960 shown as sold in box. She is a basic doll and separate clothes could be purchased for her. Red nylon hair, freckles and green sleep eyes. Courtesy Mike Way. 8" - $475.00.

First prices are for mint condition dolls; second prices are for dolls that are played with, soiled, dirty and missing original clothes.

Barbara Jane: 29" - $385.00, $100.00.

Caroline: 15" - $350.00, $125.00.

First Ladies: First set of six - $1,000.00. Second set of six - $800.00. Third set of six - $900.00. Fourth set of six - $900.00. Fifth set of six - $900.00.

Fisher Quints: Hard plastic with vinyl heads, set of five - $400.00.

Gidget: 14" - $400.00, $100.00.

Granny, Little: 14" - $325.00, $100.00.

Jacqueline: Street Dress. 21" - $725.00, $300.00. Ballgown: $900.00, $400.00. Riding Habit: $825.00, $375.00.

Janie: 12" - $365.00, $150.00.

Joanie: 36" - $425.00, $200.00.

Jenny Lind & Cat: 14" - $425.00, $150.00.

Leslie: Black doll. Ballgown: 17" - $475.00, $175.00. Ballerina: $325.00, $125.00. Street Dress: $365.00, $150.00.

Madame Doll: 14" - $450.00, $175.00.

Madelaine: 18", jointed knees, elbows and wrists. $475.00, $200.00.

Marlo Thomas: 17" - $525.00, $200.00.

Marybel: 16" - $200.00, $75.00; In case - $275.00; $125.00.

Mary Ellen: 31" - $500.00, $200.00.

Melinda: 14" - $365.00, $150.00; 16" - $450.00, $200.00.

Michael with Bear: Peter Pan set. 11" - $400.00, $150.00.

Mimi: 30" - $500.00, $200.00.

Peter Pan: 15" - $350.00, $150.00.

Polly: 17" - $325.00, $150.00.

Rozy: 12" - $365.00, $150.00.

Smarty: 12" - $365.00, $150.00.

14" "Madame Doll" that is in mint condition and all original. Has pocket under dress that hold a string of pearls. Courtesy Frasher Doll Auctions. 14" - $450.00.

12" "Janie Ballerina," which also came in yellow. Doll is in mint condition with original box. Courtesy Mike Way. 12" - $365.00.

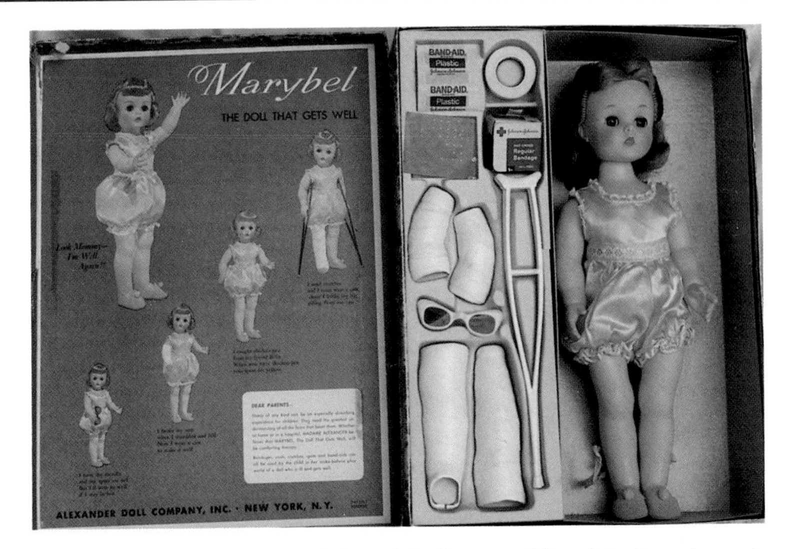

16" "Marybel Get Well" doll in original case with original equipment. Courtesy Mike Way. 16" - $200.00.

Small set of Sound of Music: 8", 11" and 17". All original. Courtesy Mike Way. Small set: $1,400.00.

Sound of Music: Liesl: 10" - $275.00, $95.00; 14" - $250.00, $85.00. **Louisa:** 10" - $350.00, $100.00; 14" - $250.00, $90.00. **Brigitta:** 12" - $225.00, $75.00; 14" - $250.00, $75.00. **Maria:** 12" - $300.00, $80.00; 17" - $350.00, $85.00; **Marta:** 8" - $225.00, $75.00; 11" - $225.00, $75.00. **Gretl:** 8" - $225.00, $75.00; 11" - $225.00, $75.00. **Freidrich:** 8" - $225.00, $75.00; 11" - $250.00, $80.00.

Sound of Music: Small set: $1,400.00. Large set: $1,600.00.

Timmie Toddler: 23" - $200.00, $95.00; 30" - $275.00, $100.00.

Wendy: Peter Pan set. 14" - $300.00, $125.00.

Prices are for mint condition dolls. The 21" Portrait dolls are many and all use the Jacqueline face with the early ones having jointed elbows and then all having one-piece arms. All will be marked "1961" on head.

21" Portrait: Depending upon individual doll. $425.00-800.00.

Coco: 1966. 21" Portrait: $2,500.00. Street Dress: $2,500.00. Ballgown (other than portrait series): $2,500.00.

Back: 21" "Monet." Front left: "Melanie," 1981. Front Right: 21" "Agatha," 1981. All are original and in mint condtion. Courtesy Frasher Doll Auctions. Monet - $375.00. Melanie - $400.00. Agatha - $375.00.

All American Character dolls are very collectible and all are above average in quality of doll material and clothes. Dolls marked "American Doll and Toy Co." are also made by American Character, and this name was used from 1959 to 1968 when the firm went out of business. Early dolls will be marked "Petite." Many will be marked "A.C."

First prices are for mint dolls; second prices are for dolls that have been played with, dirty, with soiled clothes or not original.

Annie Oakley: 17" hard plastic. $300.00, $85.00.

Betsy McCall: See Betsy McCall section.

Front: 19" "Bye-Lo" type newborn infant. Composition head and hands with rest cloth, sleep eyes. Marked "Am. Char. Doll" This same mold was used in 1958 for a vinyl doll and a year later one in vinyl and plastic. 22" - Effanbee "Bubbles" marked "1924." Cloth and composition. Courtesy Frasher Doll Auctions. 19" - $165.00. 22" $325.00.

Butterball: 19" - $165.00, $65.00.

Cartwright: Ben, Joe or Hoss. 8" - $60.00, $25.00.

Chuckles: 23" - $165.00, $85.00. Baby: 18" - $95.00, $40.00.

Composition Babies: Cloth bodies, marked "A.C." 14" - $135.00, $45.00. 22" - $200.00, $75.00. Marked "Petite": 14" - $200.00, $70.00; 22" - $300.00, $100.00.

Cricket: 9" - $20.00, $9.00. Growing hair: $25.00, $10.00.

Freckles: Face changes. 13" - $35.00, $12.00.

Hedda-Get-Betta: 21" - $100.00, $40.00.

19" "Jimmy-John" and used as "Sunny Boy," also. Vinyl head with molded hair. Latex body and limbs have turned dark with age. Also came on stuffed vinyl body and in a 26" size. Character from movie "Easy Way" with Cary Grant, 1954. Courtesy Kay Moran. 19" - $165.00, $80.00.

Miss Echo, Little: 30" Talker: $150.00, $70.00.

"Petite" marked child: Composition. 14" - $185.00, $80.00; 20" - $225.00, $95.00; 23" - $295.00, $125.00.

"A.C." marked child: Composition. 14" - $175.00, $70.00; 20" - $250.00, $100.00.

Popi: 12" - $20.00, $6.00.

Puggy: All composition, painted eyes, frown, marked "Petite." 13" - $500.00, $150.00.

Ricky, Jr.: 13" - $70.00, $25.00; 20" - $100.00, $45.00.

Sally: Composition, molded hair in "Patsy" style: 12" - $175.00, $70.00; 14" - $200.00, $90.00; 16" - $285.00, $100.00; 18" - $325.00, $125.00.

Sally Says: Talker, plastic/vinyl. 19" - $85.00, $35.00.

Sweet Sue/Toni: Hard plastic, some walkers, some with extra joints at knees, elbows and/or ankles, some combination hard plastic and vinyl. Marked "A.C. Amer.Char.Doll," or "American Character" in circle. Ballgown: 15" - $185.00, $60.00; 18" - $250.00, $100.00. Street dress: 15" - $145.00, $45.00; 18" - $200.00, $70.00; 22" - $225.00, $80.00; 24" - $265.00, $80.00; 24" - $265.00, $85.00; 30" - $325.00, $100.00. Vinyl: 10½" - $85.00,

21" "Toni" or "Sweet Sue Sophisticate." Rigid vinyl body and limbs with vinyl head, rooted hair and sleep eyes. All original and in mint condition. Courtesy Margaret Mandel. 21" - $225.00.

18" "Sweet Sue." All hard plastic and original in "After 5" style taffeta dress with flowers at waist. Marked "A.C." on head. 18" - $200.00.

12" "Tina" with clothes designed by Oleg Cassini and made in 1964. Outlined eyes painted to the side, adult body and has many outfits available to the doll which was called "Little Lady of Fashion." Vinyl with rooted hair. Courtesy Marie Ernst. 12" - $95.00 each.

$20.00; 17" - $150.00, $35.00; 21" - $225.00, $70.00; 25" - $300.00, $100.00; 30" - $385.00, $125.00. Groom: 20" - $250.00, $100.00.

Tiny Tears: Hard plastic/vinyl. 8" - $45.00, $15.00; 13" - $95.00, $45.00; 17" - $145.00, $65.00. All vinyl: 8" - $35.00, $10.00; 12" - $55.00, $20.00; 16" - $85.00, $35.00.

Toodles: Baby: 14" - $95.00, $40.00. Tiny: 10½" - $95.00, $40.00. Toddler with "follow me eyes": 22" - $165.00, $70.00; 28" - $265.00, $100.00; 30" - $325.00, $150.00.

Toodle-Loo: 18" - $145.00, $40.00.

Tressy: 12½" - $35.00, $10.00.

Whimette/Little People: 7½" - $28.00, $8.00.

Whimsey: 19" - $110.00, $45.00.

20" "Fanny, The Fallen Angel." Whimsie marked "American Doll & Toy 1960." All stuffed vinyl with modeled closed eyes. All original, wings attached to dress. Courtesy Lee Crane. 20" - $110.00.

The following information courtesy Joan Amundsen.

Tag: First were red woven lettering on white rayon tape. Second tags (around 1969) were red printing on white satin tape. Third tags (around 1976) were red printing on gauze-type cloth.

Hair: From 1934 to 1963, the hair was made of yarn. From 1960-1963, the hair was made of feathers (chicken), hair of yellow or orange. From 1963 to date, the hair is made of synthetic fur in various colors.

Animals: First introduced into the line in 1964. Fabrics are changed each year and often date can be determined by this feature.

Tails: The oldest were made of same felt as the body. From the mid to late 1970's, cotton bias tape was used; the ones of the 1980's are made of cotton flannel.

8" Annalee rabbit in its Easter crate. Felt, soft stuffed, jointed by bendable wire. Hand painted features, pink pompom nose, cloth-lined ears and bandana. 1978. Courtesy Margaret Mandel. 8" - $85.00.

21" "GoGo" boy and girl. Ca. 1966. Al' felt with wire throughout for posing. Hand painted features, cloth clothes. 21" - $365.00.

10" "GoGo" boy and girl. All felt with wire throughout for posing. Oil painted features. Cloth clothes. 10" - $125.00.

ARRANBEE DOLL COMPANY

The Arranbee Doll Company began making dolls in 1922 and was purchased by the Vogue Doll Company in 1959. Vogue used the Arranbee marked molds until 1961. Arranbee used the initials "R & B."

First prices are for mint condition dolls; second prices are for dolls that have been played with, are cracked, crazed, dirty or do not have original clothes.

Babies: Bisque heads. See Armand Marseille section.

Babies: Composition/cloth bodies. 16" - $65.00, $30.00; 22" - $100.00, $45.00.

Bottletot: Has celluloid bottle molded to celluloid hand. 18" - $165.00, $60.00.

Debu-Teen: Composition girl with cloth body. 14" - $185.00, $60.00; 18" - $225.00, $80.00; 21" - $285.00, $125.00.

Dream Baby, My: See Armand Marseille section for bisque heads. Composition: 14" - $185.00, $75.00. Vinyl/cloth: 16" - $75.00, $35.00; 26" - $145.00, $60.00.

Kewty: Composition "Patsy" style molded hair. 10" - $95.00, $30.00.

Littlest Angel: All hard plastic. 10" - $50.00, $15.00. Vinyl head: 10" - $45.00, $15.00. Red hair/freckles: 10" - $85.00, $30.00.

Miss Coty: Vinyl. 10" - $65.00, $20.00.

My Angel: Plastic/vinyl. 17" - $45.00, $15.00; 22" - $65.00, $25.00; 36" - $145.00, $60.00.

Nancy: Composition. Molded hair or wig. 12" - $185.00, $60.00; 17" - $250.00, $85.00; 19" - $300.00, $100.00; 23" - $385.00, $100.00.

Nancy Lee: Composition. 14" - $185.00, $60.00. Hard plastic: 14" -

$185.00, $75.00.

Nancy Lee: Unusual eyebrows/ vinyl. 15" - $100.00, $35.00.

Nancy Lee: Baby, painted eyes and looks as if crying. 15" - $65.00, $30.00.

Nancy Lee: Baby with composition head and limbs, open mouth with upper and lower teeth. 25" - $185.00, $65.00.

Nanette: Hard plastic. 14" - $185.00, $75.00; 17" - $225.00, $90.00; 21" - $300.00, $100.00; 23" - $365.00, $125.00.

Sonja Skater: Composition. 14" - $200.00, $90.00; 18" - $250.00, $100.00; 21" - $300.00, $125.00.

Storybook Dolls: All composition. Molded hair, painted eyes. 10" - $165.00, $45.00.

Taffy: Looks like Alexander's "Cissy." 23" - $75.00, $30.00.

14" "Skippy" by Effanbee. All composition with painted features and in original sailor outfit. 17" all composition "Nancy" by Arranbee and has original clothes, except hair ribbon. Open mouth and sleep eyes. Courtesy Frasher Doll Auctions. 14" - $325.00. 17" - $250.00.

Left: All hard plastic, 17" tall Ideal Doll "Bonnie Walker." Right: 17" all composition "Dream Baby" toddler by Arranbee and marked "R & B." Open mouth and sleep eyes. May be original dress and bonnet. Center: 10" "Littlest Angel" and marked "R & B" on head and body. All hard plastic. 17" Ideal: $70.00. 17" - $250.00. 10" - $50.00.

14" Arranbee's "Princess Juliana." Ca. 1950. Marked "R & B" on head. All original. Courtesy Frasher Doll Auctions. 14" - $250.00.

17" and 15" "Sonja Skater" by Arranbee and both marked "R & B" on head. Both all original and both have sleep eyes. 15" - $215.00. 17" - $245.00.

24" all vinyl, sleep eyes with hair lashes, rooted hair, nail polish, high heel feet and all original.

Marked ◇ 59.

Courtesy Sandra Cummins. 24" - $75.00.

BETSY McCALL

First prices are for mint condition dolls; second prices are for played with, dirty, soiled or not original dolls.

8": All hard plastic, jointed knees. Made by American Character Doll Co. Street Dress: $125.00, $40.00; Ballgown: $150.00, $60.00; Bathing Suit or Romper: $100.00, $30.00.

11½": Brown sleep eyes, reddish rooted hair, vinyl/plastic and made by Uneeda, but unmarked. $85.00, $30.00.

13": Made by Horsman in 1975, although doll is marked "Horsman Dolls, Inc. 1967" on head. $45.00, $20.00.

14": Vinyl with rooted hair, medium high heels, round sleep eyes and made by American Character Doll Company and will be marked "McCall 1958. $200.00, $80.00.

14": Vinyl head, rooted hair, rest hard plastic marked "P-90 body." Made by Ideal Doll Company. $165.00, $60.00.

22": Unmarked. Has extra joints at waist, ankles, wrists and above knees. Made by Uneeda. $185.00, $70.00.

20": Vinyl with rooted hair, slender limbs and made by American Character Doll Company. $250.00, $95.00.

22": Vinyl/plastic with extra joints and made by Ideal Doll Company. $200.00, $80.00.

29-30": All vinyl, rooted hair and made by American Character Doll Company. $300.00, $125.00.

29": Marked "McCall 1961." Has extra joints at ankles, knees, waist and wrists. Made by Uneeda. $285.00, $100.00.

29": Marked "B.M.C. Horsman 1971." $250.00, $80.00.

36": All vinyl with rooted hair and made by American Character Doll Company. $425.00, $185.00.

14" "Betsy McCall" by American Character. All original in original box. Courtesy Sandy Johnson Barts. 14" in box - $285.00 up.

14" "Betsy McCall" made by American Character and is shown in original trunk and all clothes are original. Courtesy Sandy Johnson Barts. 14" doll alone - $200.00 up. In case - $285.00 up.

29" and 8" "Betsy McCall" in original matching clothes. The large doll was made by Uneeda Doll Company and the 8" one by American Character. Courtesy Marie Ernst. 29" - $285.00 up. 8" - $125.00 up.

11½" "Betsy McCall" made by Uneeda with sleep eyes and are plastic and vinyl with rooted hair. Many different outfits were available for the doll. Both these outfits are original. Courtesy Marie Ernst. 11½" - $85.00 up.

Rare 8" "Betsy McCall" furniture in original box. The set is made by Strombecker and can be found in plain oak color or white, but without these decals that make it a McCall item. Courtesy Sandy Johnson Barts. No price available.

Right Photo:
36" "Betsy & Sandy McCall," 1959. Both are rigid plastic and vinyl with the girl having rooted hair and the boy has molded hair. Both have sleep eyes. Both are marked "Amer. Char. Doll Co. 1959." Courtesy Frasher Doll Auctions. 36" girl - $400.00. 36" boy - $425.00.

Photo Below:
14" American Character's "Betsy McCall" in her original suitcase/ trunk. Extra clothes were available to be added to case. Courtesy Sandy Johnson Barts. Doll alone - $200.00 up. In case - $285.00 up.

13" "Buddy Lee," all hard plastic with molded hair, painted features and painted on boots. Jointed at shoulders only. Original clothes. Courtesy Pat Timmons. Composition: original - $275.00 up; not original - $100.00. Hard Plastic: original - $200.00 up; not original - $100.00.

CABBAGE PATCH

The following was written by Betty Chapman, editor of "Dolling Around" (Rt. 1, Box 184; Dekalb Jct., NY 13630.)

Values of Coleco's vinyl face Cabbage Patch Kids vary due to availability, rareness, popularity of certain models and the general economy of the doll market. It should be noted that along with Coleco, the American manufacturer, there were also four foreign licensed producers, so to help explain the Cabbage Patch Kids, the dolls discussed will be mint in box (M.I.B.) COLECOS and then a few words regarding the foreign made ones. Another point of interest to the collector is the fact that there are 21 different faces, many different hairstyles and great many different outfits. It would not be possible to discuss them all here, but we will cover the most desirable.

1983: First year on market. #1: No dimples. #2: Two dimples, large eyes and no freckles. #3: One dimple, large eyes. #4: Two dimples and pacifier. Values from $50.00-75.00.

Red Shag Hairdo Boys: In any face mold. $250.00-600.00.

Freckles #2: With small eyes are regular. #2: Doll with large eyes reduced, has freckles and except for the tan/champagne loop hairdo and Baldie dolls, can bring high second market prices. The highest priced dolls here are the red shag boy, Black dolls with freckles, with the Black girl being the rarest, and the Black shag hair boy, second rarest. The red shag hair boy or Black girl with freckles can bring as high as $800.00. The Black shag hair boy with freckles would be $600.00 and the Black Baldie with freckles is valued at $500.00. When the market is down, these prices will drop to $350.00-$450.00.

More Freckles: Girls with single auburn ponytail, two blonde (lemon) ponytails, two red ponytails, red braids, gold braids or loop hairdo: $175.00-$300.00.

Tan poodle with loop hairdo and two ponytails, brunette braids, brunette poodle hairdo, blonde loop hairdo: $150.00.

Tan poodle with loop hairdo and two ponytails, brunette braids, brunette poodle hairdo, blonde loop hairdo: $150.00.

Tan loop braids, Baldie: $100.00-125.00.

Auburn loop hairdo boy, brunette shag hair boy: $200.00-300.00.

Tan shag hair boy: $150.00 (has been as high as $200.00-225.00.)

1983 - #1: Black with shag hairdo: $125.00-150.00. Black Baldie: $100.00-125.00. Black girl with two ponytails: $75.00-100.00.

1983 - #4 with Pacifiers: Red shag hair boys: $400.00-500.00. Blacks: $175.00-225.00. Auburn single ponytail girl: $150.00. Tan poodle hair girl: $125.00. Remainder of 1983 #4 pacifier dolls range from $50.00-100.00.

1984-1985: Only a few Cabbage Patch Kids of these years are worth more than retail prices. 1985 single tooth brunette with ponytail: $150.00-200.00 up. Rare popcorn hairdos: $100.00-125.00. Grey eye girls, 1985: $50.00-75.00. Grey eye girls, 1983: Very few made. $150.00-275.00. 1985 freckled gold hair girl: $75.00.

Valued from $50.00-75.00: Baldies with eye colors other than blue, 1985 single tooth with brunette side ponytail and blue eyes, popcorn curl with pacifier, red popcorn with single tooth, double gold or double auburn hairdo, 1985 grey eye girls, 1985 gold braided, freckled girls, UT marked tag (body tag indicating the factory where it was made) with high cheek color, pacifiers and/or 1984 dates.

The 16 other molds are not discussed, nor the various types, such as Cornsilk Kids, Splash Kids, preemies, talking Kids, babies, twins, travelers, astronauts, baseball Kids, clowns and ringmasters, as the prices have not risen enough to warrant it. These dolls are collectible due to personal preference. The 1983 dolls with Hong Kong on the body tag or with embroidered tag, with footed terrycloth sleeper or blue flowered corduroy overalls bring slightly higher prices. The powder scent 1983 Colecos are valued $10.00-25.00 above the others of this year.

As for the foreign Cabbage Patch Kids, the rarest seem to be those with freckles made in Mexico by Lili Ledi. Also rare are those made in Spain by Jesmar in 1983, with well placed eyes and the freckle/pacifier combination (notably the red hair boys again.) Rarer ones from the South Africa Triang Pedigree firm are the ones with gaudy yellow hair or freckles and pacifier together. From Japan's Tsukuda firm are ones from 1983 with red or lemon hair and brown eyes or with specialty outfits such as kimonos, Elegance dresses, Samuri outfits, baseball uniforms, Karate outfits and happy coats. Most of these foreign dolls sell for $100.00-$150.00. The Japanese powder scent dolls are valued at $200.00-250.00 up. Also the pacifier/freckle, red hair dolls from Jesmar, Spain are worth $150.00-200.00.

The dolls are stamped on the left buttock with Xavier Roberts's signature. Sometimes a year appears also. There are 6 signature colors to date, 7 Coleco factories and 4 foreign licensed makers, 21 face molds thus far, 7 hair colors, 5 eye colors and 13 basic hairstyles, plus additional hairstyles variations, eye shades and hair color shades. If one considers the large variation in these dolls as compared to any other modern dolls, it becomes obvious why they are an established collector's item only five years after they were introduced. The accompanying photographs, although a good cross section, are a relatively small sampling of the many unique combinations.

Standing: 1983 Coleco #1 Black shag boy and sitting 1984 #1 Black Preemie in rare knit outfit. The #4 (pacifier) Black Preemie of 1983 are valued at $50.00-75.00. Courtesy Betty Chapman. 1983 - $150.00. 1984 - $40.00-50.00.

Standing Left: 1983 Coleco rare small eyed #2, freckles and single auburn ponytail. Right: 1985 Coleco rare #1 freckled with gold braids and sitting 1983 #2 small eyes, freckles, bald in rare blue stripe sleeper. Courtesy Betty Chapman. 1983 - $175.00-200.00. 1985 - $75.00. 1983 Bald - $150.00.

1985 #4 single braid Coleco. 1985 #6 side ponytail Coleco. These dolls show the two pacifiers faces. Smaller #4 has two dimples and larger #6 has one dimple. Courtesy Betty Chapman. #4 braid - $50.00. #6 ponytail - $40.00.

1983 Coleco #4's. Red shag boy and Black shag boy. Courtesy Betty Chapman. Red head - $400.00. Black: $200.00.

Rear: 1983 powder scent red loopy hair, brown eye made in Japan and in rare made in Japan outfit. Black shag hair boy made in Mexico and is #4 with freckles, pacifier and made in Mexico outfit.
Front: 1984 South African #4, freckles, bald in green sleeper with lace, which is rare (not doll's own outfit.) 1983 made in Spain #2 red shag hair, freckles in rare mint green duck romper (not doll's own outfit.) Courtesy Betty Chapman. 1983 Japan - $350.00. Mexico - $150.00. South African - $125.00; Sleeper - $50.00. Spain - $200.00; Romper $25.00.

Standing: 1984 made in Canada Coleco Couture Kid (fur coat) with rare red corduroy snowsuit.
Sitting: 1986 #5 single tooth with rare burgandy twin outfit. Courtesy Betty Chapman.
1984 - $100.00. 1986 - $40.00.

1983 Black shag boy with freckles, #2 small eyes. Made by Coleco. Courtesy Betty Chapman. $600.00.

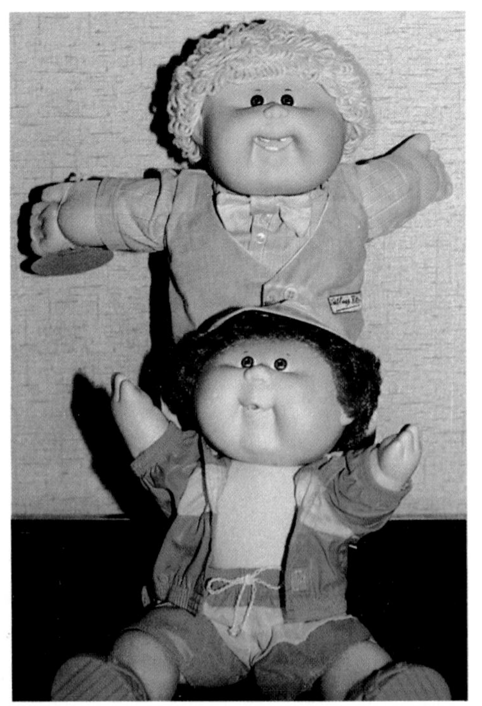

Standing: 1987 Coleco #19 with eight teeth. Doll is original with girl's lemon loop hair in boy's outfit. Sitting: 1987 Coleco #21 with tiny tongue "Splash Kid" with red cornsilk hair and lavender eyes. Courtesy Betty Chapman. #19 - $30.00. #21 - $30.00.

Back: 1986 Coleco double auburn popcorn hair. #14 in Ring Master's outfit. The Ring Masters were not as abundant as some other specialty dolls. Bottom: 1986 Coleco "Cornsilk" #12. Courtesy Betty Chapman. Ring Master - $35.00. Cornsilk #12 - $30.00.

Top: 1987 Coleco Black #15 with smile face and single ponytail poodle loop hair. Bottom: 1986 single champagne popcorn hair, #16 with dimple in chin and hand that holds items. Lavender eyes. Somewhat rare. Courtesy Betty Chapman. 1987 - $30.00. 1986 - $45.00.

Left: 1986 Brunette #10 with two bottom teeth. Popcorn hairdo and holding somewhat rare toothbrush. Right: 1986 single dark gold popcorn hair. #11 with tongue. Clown outfit. Courtesy Betty Chapman. #10 - $35.00. #11 - $40.00.

Left: 1986 #9 Coleco baseball player. There seems to be less #9 dolls than some other molds. Right: 1985 #8 Coleco with glasses. Courtesy Betty Chapman. #9 Baseball player - $40.00. #8 with glasses - $30.00.

Annie Rooney, Little: All composition, legs painted black, molded shoes. 16" - $675.00.

Baby Bo Kaye: Bisque head, open mouth. 17-18" - $2,800.00. Celluloid head: 15-16" - $600.00. Composition head, mint: 18" - $600.00. Light craze and not original: 18" - $350.00.

Baby Mine: Vinyl/cloth, sleep eyes. Mint: 16" - $100.00; 19" - $55.00. Slightly soiled and not original: 16" - $150.00; 19" - $65.00.

Betty Boop: Composition head, wood jointed body. Mint: 12" - $600.00. Light craze and a few paint chips: 12" - $275.00.

Champ: Composition/freckles. Mint: 16" - $600.00. Light craze, not original: 16" - $300.00.

Giggles: Composition, molded loop for ribbon. Mint: 11" - $325.00; 14" - $525.00. Light craze: 11" - $200.00.

Ho-Ho: Plaster in excellent condition. 4" - $50.00. Vinyl in excellent condition: 4" - $15.00.

Joy: Composition, wood jointed body. Mint: 10" - $325.00; 15" - $450.00. Slight craze: 10" - $175.00; 15" - $295.00.

Kewpie: See Kewpie section.

Margie: Composition. Mint: 6" - $195.00; 10" - $275.00. Slight craze and not original: 6" - $95.00; 10" - $150.00.

Miss Peep: Pin jointed shoulders and hips. Vinyl. Mint and original: 1960's. 18" - $60.00. Black: 18" - $85.00. Slightly soiled and not original: 18" - $28.00. Black: 18" - $35.00.

Miss Peep, Newborn: Plastic and vinyl. Mint and original: 18" - $50.00. Slight soil and not original: 18" - $20.00.

Peanut, Affectionately: Vinyl. Mint and original: 18½" - $90.00. Slight soil and not original: 18½" - $40.00.

Pete the Pup: Composition, wood jointed body. Mint: 8" - $200.00. Slight craze and few paint chips: 8" - $100.00.

Pinkie: Composition, 1930's. Mint and original: 10" - $345.00. Slight craze: 10" - $125.00. Wood jointed body: 10" - $365.00. Vinyl/plastic: 1950's. Mint: $185.00. Slight soil and not original: 10" - $60.00.

Scootles: Composition. Mint and original: 8" - $350.00 up; 12" - $450.00 up; 15" - $550.00 up. Light craze and not original: 8" - $100.00; 12" - $225.00; 15" - $285.00. Composition with sleep eyes: Mint: 15" - $650.00; 21" - $850.00. Slight craze: 15" - $300.00; 21" - $400.00. Black, composition: Mint: 15" - $750.00. Slight craze: 15" - $300.00. Vinyl: Mint and original: 14" - $165.00 up; 19" - $300.00 up; 27" - $400.00 up. Lightly soiled and not original: 14" - $45.00; 19" - $85.00; 27" - $125.00.

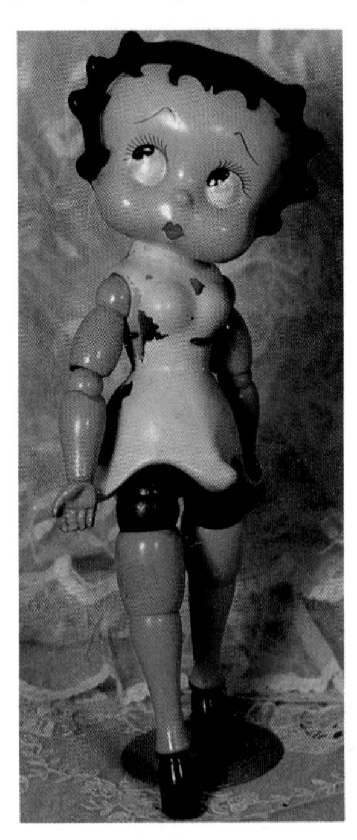

12" "Betty Boop" by Cameo Doll Company. Composition head and body with wood jointed limbs. Dark green paint has flaked off the dress on this doll. Courtesy Frasher Doll Auctions. 12" mint - $600.00. Paint flakes: $275.00.

Two 16" "Scootles" with variations of molded hair and eye painting. 9" all bisque "Kewpie" that is signed "O'Neill" on bottom of foot and has label on chest. Also shown is 8" Dionne Quint by Madame Alexander that is all original. Courtesy Frasher Doll Auctions. 16" - $550.00. 9" - $395.00. 8" - $200.00.

Cameo Doll Company dolls, left to right: "Little Annie Rooney" marked on jacket tag "Little Annie Rooney copyright 1925 by Jack Collins. Pat. Applied for." "Giggles," who is unmarked. "Margie" of 1929 marked with sticker on chest. "Joy," also marked on chest. Courtesy Jeannie Maudin. Annie - $675.00. Giggles - $200.00. Margie - $275.00. Joy - $450.00.

17" "Snow White," all cloth with face mask and painted features, mohair wig. All original. The "Seven Dwarfs" are rubber and marked "Walt Disney Sieberling Latex Made in Akron, O. U.S.A." Courtesy Frasher Doll Auctions. 17" - $300.00. Dwarfs: $55.00 each.

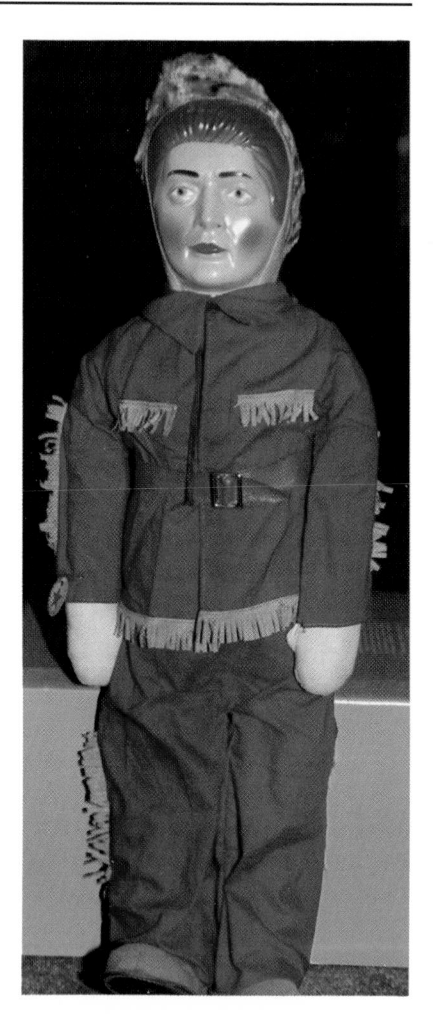

Above Photo:
26" "Davy Crockett," all cloth with face mask and painted features. Felt shoes sewn on. All original with coonskin-style cap on back of head. Tag on arm: "Star Novelty Co. Atlanta Ga." Courtesy Jeannie Mauldin. 26" - $165.00.

Left Photo:
20" "Eloise," 1950's all cloth with painted features, yarn hair. Face mask with cloth in back. All original. Made by Cameo and distributed by American Character Doll Company. Courtesy Jeannie Mauldin. 20" - $250.00.

8" "Ginger" from the Character Series and all original. All hard plastic with sleep eyes. Courtesy Maureen Fukushima. 8" - $45.00 up.

"Ginger" in Activity Series #556, Fireman. Courtesy Maureen Fukushima. 8" - $65.00 up.

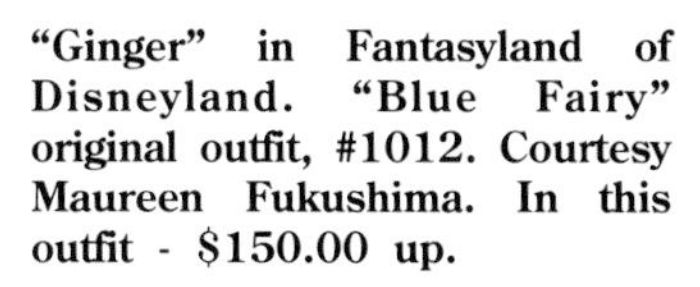

"Ginger" in Fantasyland of Disneyland. "Blue Fairy" original outfit, #1012. Courtesy Maureen Fukushima. In this outfit - $150.00 up.

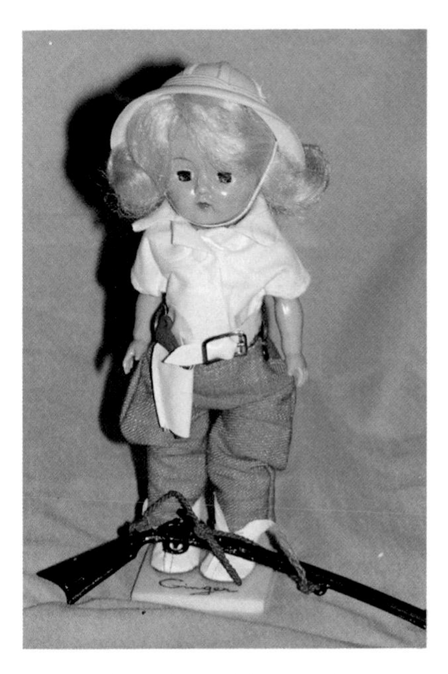

"Ginger" visits Adventureland in Disneyland, #1005 "Safari Girl." Courtesy Maureen Fukushima. In this outfit - $125.00 up.

"Ginger" in masquerade outfit #554. Courtesy Maureen Fukushima. 8" - $95.00 up.

"Ginger," all hard plastic and in #1011 of the Disneyland series: Fantasyland. Courtesy Maureen Fukushima. In this outfit - $125.00 up.

"Ginger" in #772 Trousseau Series. All hard plastic. Courtesy Maureen Fukushima. 8" - $65.00.

25" "Sarah" with bisque shoulder head, cloth body and bisque limbs. Modeled and designed by Nicholas Bramble and is destined to be one of the true antiques of the future. Deeply sculptured and painted eyes. "Sarah" was designed to sit in swing and looks her best in that type setting, such as this chair. Note barefeet in left photo and hands in the photo below. Both are beautifully modeled. Courtesy Barbara Earnshaw-Cain. 25" - No price available.

20" "Patty O'Day" as portrayed by Jane Withers. Bisque with cloth body and a very excellent quality character doll. Glass eyes and open/closed laughing mouth. Modeled and made by Judith Turner. Courtesy Green Museum. 20" - $700.00 up.

24" "Mountain Children" commemorates the May 18, 1980 eruption of Mt. St. Helens. Each doll is incised with number (limited to 100 each), date and "Mt. Babies." Designed and made by Beverly Saxton & Denise Lemmon of Mountain Babies Doll; Graham, Washington. No prices available.

Center: 14" bonnet "Snow Baby" with bisque shoulderplate, cloth body and bisque limbs. Painted features. Marked "Patti Jene. 1966." Left: Gebruder Heubach "Coquette" marked #7768. Molded hair and painted features and on jointed body. 7½" bisque head marked "3." Right: Flapper-style five-piece body, painted-on shoes and long stockings. Courtesy Frasher Doll Auctions. 14" - $200.00. #7768 - $600.00. 7½" - $245.00.

Center: 12½" Faith Wick original incised "Lil Apple 1979." Souvenir doll from national convention for United Federation of Doll Clubs. Left: 9½" Armand Marseille "Just Me" mold #310 with bisque head and composition body. Right: 5" all bisque with open mouth and glass eyes, unmarked. Courtesy Frasher Doll Auctions. 12½" - $175.00. 9½" - $1,200.00. 5" - $265.00.

These unique and fantastic characters were made by Paul Spencer of Texas, who also makes wood carven sleep-eyed babies and jointed children. Figures are hand carved wood with wood left natural except clothes and other areas which are lightly stained. Left Photo: "Fishing" - $250.00 up. Right Photo: "Playing" - $250.00 up.

24" "Tonto and Lone Ranger" tagged "Doll Craft, Brooklyn. N.Y. 1938." Both all original with composition heads and hands, rest is cloth stuffed. Both have painted features. Courtesy Jeannie Mauldin. 24" - $200.00 up.

EEGEE DOLL COMPANY

The name of this company was made up from the name of the founder E.G. Goldberger. Founded in 1917, the early dolls were marked "E.G.", then E. Goldberger" and now the marks of "Eegee" and "Goldberger" are used.

Andy: Teen type. 12" - $25.00.

Annette: Teen type. 11½" - $28.00.

Annette: Plastic and vinyl walker. 25" - $35.00; 28" - $42.00; 36" - $65.00.

Baby Luv: Cloth/vinyl. Marked "B.T. Eegee." 14" - $40.00.

Baby Susan: Name marked on head. 8½" - $12.00.

Baby Tandy Talks: Foam body, rest vinyl, pull string talker. $45.00.

Ballerina: Foam body and limbs, vinyl head. 1967. 18" - $38.00.

Ballerina: Hard plastic/vinyl head. 20" - $45.00.

Boy Dolls: Molded hair, rest vinyl. 13" - $35.00; 21" - $45.00.

Composition: Sleep eyes, open mouth girls. 14" - $125.00 up; 18" $165.00 up. Babies: Cloth and composition. 16" - $100.00 up; 20" - $160.00 up.

Debutante: Vinyl head, rest hard plastic, jointed knees. 28" - $85.00.

Dolly Parton: 1980. 12" - $18.00.

Flowerkins: Plastic/vinyl. Marked "F-2" on head. 16" - $65.00 in box.

Gemmette: Teen type. 14" - $20.00.

Gorgette or Gorgie: Redhead twins. Cloth and vinyl. 22-23" - $45.00.

Gigi Perreaux: Hard plastic, early vinyl head. 17" - $200.00 up.

Granny: from "Beverly Hillbillies." Old lady modeling, grey rooted hair, painted or sleep eyes. 14" - $55.00.

Miss Charming: All composition Shirley Temple look-alike. 19" - $250.00 up. Pin - $12.00.

Miss Sunbeam: Plastic/vinyl, dimples. 17" - $45.00.

Musical Baby: Has key wind music box in cloth body. 17" - $18.00.

My Fair Lady: All vinyl, jointed waist, adult type. 10½" - $30.00; 19" - $65.00.

Posey Playmate: Foam and vinyl. 18" - $18.00.

Susan Stroller: Hard plastic/vinyl head. 20" - $45.00; 23" - $55.00; 26" - $65.00.

Tandy Talks: Plastic/vinyl head, freckles, pull string talker. 20" - $60.00.

32" "Tammy" plastic and vinyl with rooted hair, sleep eyes. All original, has original box which read "Eegee doll - Tammy the little playmate." Came out the same years as the Ideal Patty Play Pal. Courtesy Patricia Wood. 32" - $95.00.

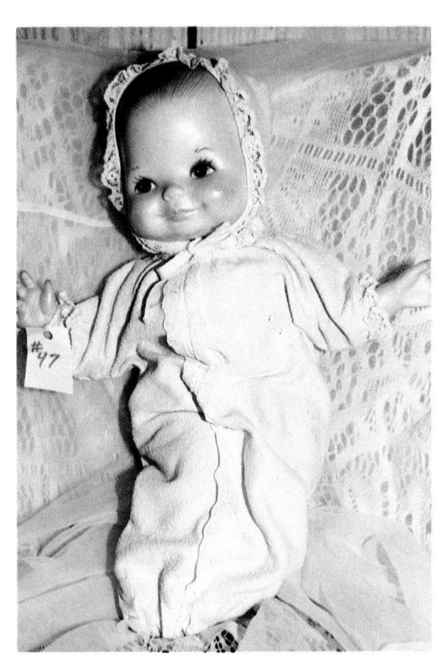

13½" "Bundle of Joy" marked on head "Eegee Co. 1975/14 PT." Cloth body with vinyl head and limbs. Painted features, molded hair. Courtesy Nancy Prestosh. 13½" - $20.00.

First prices are for mint condition dolls; second prices for dolls that are played with, soiled, dirty, cracked or crazed or not original. Dolls marked with full name or "F & B."

American Children: Marked with that name, some have "Anne Shirley" marked bodies, others are unmarked. All composition, painted or sleep eyes. Closed Mouth Girls: 18-19" - $1,300.00. Closed Mouth Boy: 15" - $1,400.00; 17" - $1,300.00. Open Mouth Girl: 15" (Barbara Joan) - $650.00; 18" (Barbara Ann) - $800.00; 21" (Barbara Lou) - $1,000.00.

Anne Shirley: Marked with name. All composition. 15" - $245.00; 21" - $375.00; 27" - $485.00.

Babyette: Cloth/composition. 9-12" - $200.00.

Babykin: All composition. 9-12" - $175.00, $85.00. All vinyl: 10" - $45.00.

Baby Cuddleup: 1953, vinyl coated cloth body, rest vinyl. Two lower teeth. 20" - $60.00, $30.00.

Baby Dainty: Marked with name. Composition/cloth. 17" - $165.00, $95.00.

Baby Evelyn: Marked with name. Composition/cloth. 17" - $165.00, $95.00.

Baby Grumpy: See Grumpy.

Baby Tinyette: Composition. 8-9" - $225.00, $80.00. Toddler: 8-9" - $225.00; $90.00.

Betty Brite: Marked with name.

17" "Barbara Ann." All composition with open mouth and human hair wig. Original clothes and metal Effanbee wrist tag. Sleep eyes, dates from 1936-1939. Designed by Dewees Cochran. Courtesy Turn of Century Antiques. 17" - $800.00.

8" "Baby Tinyette" of 1940. All composition and original, painted features. Courtesy Frasher Doll Auctions. 8" - $225.00.

All composition, fur wig, sleep eyes. 16-17" - $250.00, $100.00.

Bicentennial Boy & Girl: (Pun'kin) 11" - $125.00.

Bridal Sets: 1970's. 4 dolls. White: $200.00, $100.00. Black: $350.00, $165.00.

Bright Eyes: Same doll as Tommy Tucker and Mickey. Composition/ cloth, flirty eyes. 18" - $265.00; 22-23" $365.00.

Brother or Sister: Composition head and hands, rest cloth, yarn hair, painted eyes. 12" - $165.00, $65.00; 16" - $185.00, $70.00.

Bubbles: Marked with name. Composition/cloth. 1924. 16" - $250.00, $95.00; 20" - $325.00, $125.00; 26" - $450.00, $165.00. Black: 16" - $400.00; 20" - $650.00.

Button Nose: Composition. 8-9" - $175.00, $60.00. Vinyl/cloth: 18" - $50.00, $20.00.

Candy Kid: All composition. White: 12" - $285.00, $80.00. Black: 12" - $350.00, $100.00.

Carolina: Made for Smithsonian, 1980. 12" - $65.00, $30.00.

Charlie McCarthy: Composition/ cloth. 19-20" - $400.00, $125.00.

Composition Dolls: Molded hair, all composition, jointed neck, shoulders and hips. Painted or sleep eyes. Open or closed mouth. Original clothes. All composition in perfect condition. Marked "Effanbee." 1930's. 9" - $150.00, $50.00; 15" - $185.00, $80.00; 18" - $245.00, $100.00; 21" - $300.00, $125.00.

Composition Dolls: 1920's. Cloth body, composition head and limbs, open or closed mouth, sleep eyes. Original clothes and in perfect condition. Marked "Effanbee." 18" - $165.00, $70.00; 22" - $200.00, $95.00; 25" - $300.00, $100.00; 27-28" - $350.00, $150.00.

Currier & Ives: Plastic/vinyl. 12" - $50.00, $25.00.

Disney Dolls: Cinderella, Snow White, Alice in Wonderland and Sleeping Beauty. 1977-1978. 14" - $165.00, $65.00.

Emily Ann: 13" puppet, composition. $145.00, $50.00.

Dydee Baby: Hard rubber head, rubber body. Perfect condition. 14" - $125.00, $40.00. Hard plastic/vinyl: 15" - $145.00, $60.00; 20" - $225.00, $100.00.

Fluffy: All vinyl. 10" - $45.00, $15.00. Girl Scout: 10" - $50.00, $15.00. Black: 10" - $50.00, $15.00.

Grumpy: Frown, painted features, cloth and composition. 12" - $225.00, $90.00; 14" - $265.00, $100.00; 18" - $400.00, $150.00. Black: 12" - $300.00, $100.00; 14-15" - $400.00, $150.00.

Historical Dolls: All composition and original. 14" - $550.00, $200.00; 21" - $1,550.00, $700.00.

20" "Dydee Baby" with hard plastic head that has a natural shine to it, applied rubber ears and has rubber body and limbs. Original clothes. Courtesy Margaret Mandel. 20" - $225.00.

Honey: All composition. 14" - $250.00, $95.00; 20" - $400.00, $165.00; 27" - $600.00, $250.00.

Honey: All hard plastic, closed mouth. 14" - $225.00, $75.00; 18" - $275.00, $100.00; 21" - $350.00, $125.00.

Ice Queen: Skater outfit, composition, open mouth. 17" - $750.00, $250.00.

Limited Edition Club: 1975: Precious Baby - $500.00. **1976:** Patsy - $365.00. **1977:** Dewees Cochran - $225.00. **1978**: Crowning Glory - $200.00. **1979:** Skippy - $365.00. **1980:** Susan B. Anthony - $200.00. **1981:** Girl with watering can - $200.00. **1982:** Princess Diane - $165.00. **1983:** Sherlock Holmes - $185.00. **1984:** Bubbles - $100.00. **1985:** Red Boy - $145.00.

Left: 19" Effanbee "Lovums." Composition swivel head on composition shoulderplate, arms and legs, cloth body, open mouth with two upper and lower teeth. Caracul wig and original clothes. Shown with 24" "Chubby Baby" made by Ideal and marked "Ideal Doll." Composition/cloth. Courtesy Frasher Doll Auctions. 19" - $300.00. 24" - $285.00.

Little Lady: All composition. 15" - $245.00, $80.00; 18" - $295.00, $95.00; 21" - $365.00, $125.00; 27" - $500.00, $200.00. Cloth body, yarn hair: 21" - $225.00 up. Pink cloth body, wig: 17" - $195.00 up.

Lovums: Marked with name. Composition/cloth, open mouth smiling. 15-16" - $265.00, $100.00. 22" - $365.00, $150.00.

Mae Starr: Marked with name. Composition/cloth. Record player in torso. 30" - $450.00, $200.00.

Marionettes: Composition/wood. 14" - $145.00, $50.00.

Martha and George Washington: 1976. 11" - $200.00.

26" "Mae Starr." Composition shoulder head, sleep eyes, open mouth, tongue and two teeth, cloth body, human hair wig, original clothes. Courtesy Frasher Doll Auctions. 26" - $450.00.

A beautiful example of an Effanbee all composition "Honey" in perfect, mint original state. All original clothes and original box. Courtesy Shirley Dyer. 20" in box - $575.00.

14" "Honey Walker." All hard plastic, sleep eyes and all original. 14" "Toni," all hard plastic doll by Ideal. All original and marked "P-90" on back. Courtesy Frasher Doll Auctions. 14" - $225.00 up. "Toni" - $200.00.

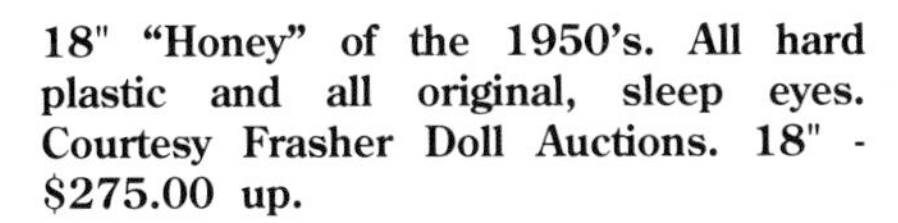

18" "Honey" of the 1950's. All hard plastic and all original, sleep eyes. Courtesy Frasher Doll Auctions. 18" - $275.00 up.

Mary Ann or Lee: Marked with name. Open smile mouth, composition and cloth and all composition. 16" - $185.00, $70.00; 18" - $265.00, $100.00; 20" - $300.00, $125.00; 24" - $365.00, $150.00.

Marilee: 1920's. Marked with name. Composition/cloth, open mouth. 14" - $225.00, $90.00; 22" - $300.00, $125.00.

Mary Jane: Plastic/vinyl, walker and freckles. 31" - $185.00, $85.00.

Mary Jane: 1920's. Composition, jointed body or cloth, "Mama" type. 20-22" - $250.00.

Mickey: (Also Tommy Tucker and Bright Eyes.) Composition/cloth, flirty eyes. 18" - $265.00, $125.00; 22-23" - $365.00, $150.00.

Mickey: All vinyl. Some with molded on hats. 11" - $95.00, $30.00.

Pat-O-Pat: Composition/cloth, painted eyes. Press stomach and pats hands together. 13-14" - $145.00, $50.00.

Patricia: All composition. 14" - $385.00, $110.00.

Patricia-kin: 11" - $285.00, $100.00.

Patsy: All composition. 14" - $300.00, $90.00. Composition/cloth: 14" - $325.00, $150.00.

Patsy Babyette: 9-10" - $245.00, $100.00.

Patsyette: 9" - $250.00, $100.00.

Patsy Ann: 19" - $445.00, $150.00. Vinyl: 15" - $145.00, $50.00.

Patsy Joan: 16" - $385.00, $125.00. Black: 16" - $500.00 up, $250.00.

Patsy, Jr.: 11" - $285.00, $100.00.

Patsy Lou: 22" - $465.00, $175.00.

Patsy Mae: 30" - $685.00, $250.00.

14" Patsy with original box, wrist tag, hair ribbon and shoes/socks. Dress replaced. 14" "Skippy." All composition with painted features. All original, may be missing cap. Shown also is 12" "Fannie Brice" marked "Ideal Doll" on head. Composition with "flexie" metal cable legs. Courtesy Frasher Doll Auctions. 14" - $300.00. 12" - $250.00. "Skippy" - $385.00.

20" "Patsy Ann." All composition, sleep eyes and all original. 14" "Patsy," composition with painted features. Redressed. 9½" "Patsyette," all composition with painted features. Original with replaced shoes. Courtesy Frasher Doll Auctions. 20" - $445.00. 14" - $300.00. 9½" - $250.00.

16" "Patsy" Limited Edition Club doll of 1976. All original. 14" "Skippy" Limited Edition Club doll of 1979. All original. Courtesy Frasher Doll Auctions. 16" - $365.00. 14" - $365.00.

Patsy Ruth: 26-27" - $725.00, $300.00.

Patsy, Wee: 5-6" - $345.00, $125.00.

Polka Dottie: 21" - $185.00, $80.00.

Portrait Dolls: All composition. 12" - $250.00, $100.00.

Prince Charming: All hard plastic. 16" - $275.00 up, $145.00.

Rootie Kazootie: 21" - $185.00, $80.00.

Rosemary: Marked with name. Composition/cloth. 14" - $225.00, $85.00; 22" - $285.00, $125.00; 28" - $465.00, $200.00.

Skippy: All composition. 14" - $550.00, $250.00.

Sugar Baby: Composition/cloth, sleep eyes, molded hair or wig. 16-17" - $225.00, $90.00.

Sunny Toddler: Plastic/vinyl. 18" - $65.00, $30.00.

Suzanne: Marked with name. All composition. 14" - $265.00, $125.00.

Suzette: Marked with name. All composition. 12" - $225.00, $100.00.

Sweetie Pie: Composition/cloth. 14" - $175.00, $50.00; 19" - $250.00, $90.00; 24" - $350.00, $125.00.

Tommy Tucker: (Also Mickey and Bright Eyes.) Composition/cloth, flirty eyes. 22-23" - $365.00, $175.00.

W.C. Fields: Composition/cloth. 22" - $695.00, $200.00. Plastic/vinyl: 15" - $265.00.

14" "Suzanne." All composition and marked "Suzanne" on head, but used as "Little Lady" in original suitcase with wardrobe. Courtesy Frasher Doll Auctions. In case - $365.00 up.

18" "My Fair Baby." All vinyl, open mouth/nurser. All original including blanket. Sleep eyes, baby bracelet with name. Courtesy Jeannie Mauldin. 18" - $50.00.

19" "Champagne Lady" from *The Lawrence Welk Show.* 1957. Rigid vinyl and vinyl with rooted hair, high heel feet, jointed at knees and ankles. All original. Courtesy Frasher Doll Auctions. 19" - $250.00 up.

27" "Little Lady." All composition with sleep eyes, latex, painted arms and fingers. All original, 1948. Courtesy Frasher Doll Auctions. 27" - $500.00.

22¼" Kestner marked "G Made in Germany 13½ 129." Open mouth and on fully jointed body. 10½" "Grumpy" Ca. 1916-1917. By Effanbee and dressed as "Uncle Sam." Composition and cloth, molded hair and painted features. Courtesy Frasher Doll Auctions. 22¼" - $565.00. 10½" - $265.00.

11½" "Mozart" vinyl with rooted hair with braid down the back. All original which are satin.

Marked H C. behind ear.

Ca. 1960's. Clothes are glued on. Courtesy Louise Alonso. 11½" - $85.00.

10" "Farballina" (Little Butterfly) by Sebino, Italy. Vinyl head with rigid vinyl jointed body and limbs. Rooted hair in ponytail and carries storybook about butterflies and has platic butterfly on head. Marked "Sebino Made in Italy" on back. All original. Courtesy Marie Ernst. 10" - $30.00.

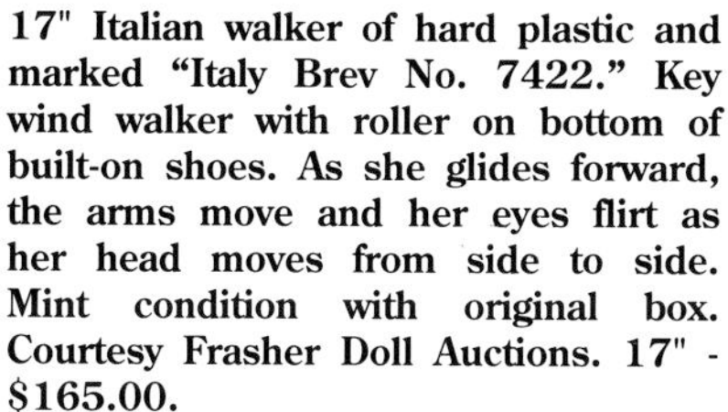

17" Italian walker of hard plastic and marked "Italy Brev No. 7422." Key wind walker with roller on bottom of built-on shoes. As she glides forward, the arms move and her eyes flirt as her head moves from side to side. Mint condition with original box. Courtesy Frasher Doll Auctions. 17" - $165.00.

18" unusual Furga made in Italy doll with open/closed mouth and three teeth. Sleep eyes, rooted hair and with vinyl head and limbs and cloth body. Ca. 1970. Original. Courtesy Lee Crane. 18" - $60.00.

17" Furga unusual mold boy and girl. All vinyl with sleep eyes. He has molded hair and hers is rooted. Both are marked "Furga Italy" and the mark goes from ear to ear. Also marked "Italy" on inside of left thigh and inside upper arm. Both have tiny ears. Courtesy Marie Ernst. 17" - $45.00 each.

Two beautiful Old Cottage Dolls made in England. Composition swivel heads, all felt body and limbs. Painted features. Mitt-style hands with free standing thumb. Both are mint and original. $125.00 each.

CR Club girl "Catocan." 19" vinyl head and limbs, sleep eyes, has extra long lashes and no facial painting. The boy is CR Club "Clement." 19" also. Both are excellent quality European dolls and both are original with quality clothes. Girl has waist length hair held by velvet ribbon. 1976. The CR Club dolls are not available any longer and evolved into the present "Carolle" dolls. Courtesy Margaret Mandel. $150.00 each.

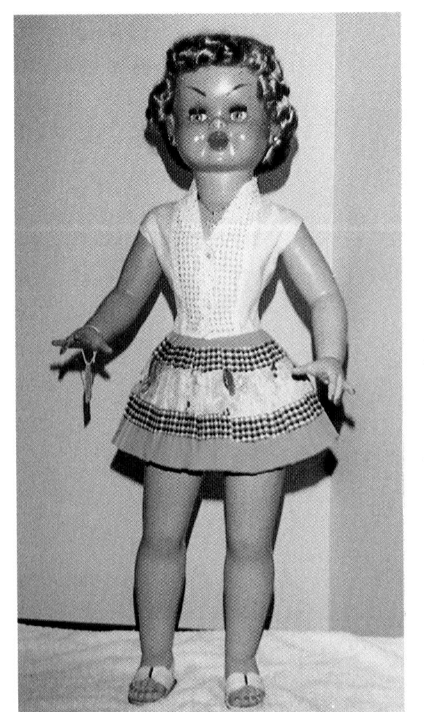

28" most unusual looking doll that was made in Spain. Has flirty eyes, open mouth with tongue and teeth and in original outfit. She has rhinestone earring, painted nails and extra joints at ankles, wrists, waist and upper thighs. Mark on shoes "Fabricado Famosa, Garented Origen. Made In Spain." All hard plastic. Courtesy Ann Wencel. 28" - $200.00.

13" Eskimo doll that is all vinyl, painted features with closed smiling mouth. Purchased in Quebec, Canada in 1973. Courtesy Phyllis Houston. 13" - $45.00.

11½" cloth with painted mask face and has one-piece body. Fine yarn braids. Mexican girl in original clothes. Courtesy Marie Ernst. 11½" - $40.00.

HASBRO

All prices are for mint condition dolls.

Adam: Boy for World of Love series. 9" - $12.00.

Aimee: 1972. Plastic/vinyl. 18" - $60.00.

Defender: One-piece arms and legs. 1974. 11½" - $40.00.

Dolly Darling: 1965. 4½" - $9.00.

Flying Nun: Plastic/vinyl, 1967. 5" - $35.00.

G.I. Joe: 1964, Flocked or molded hair, no beard. Original. 12" - $65.00 up. 1965: Black. 12" - $85.00 up. 1966: Green Beret. $85.00 up. Foreign: $125.00 up each. Nurse: 11" - $600.00 up. 1974: Kung Fu grip. $50.00 up. Eagle eyes: $50.00 up. Talking: $50.00 up.

Leggy: 10" - $14.00.

Little Miss No Name: 1965. 15" - $85.00.

Mamas and Papas: 1967. $35.00 each.

Monkees: Set of four. 4" - $100.00.

Show Biz Babies: 1967. $40.00 each. Mama Cass: $45.00.

Storybooks: 1967. 3" - $25.00-35.00 in boxes.

Sweet Cookie: 1972. 18" - $25.00.

That Kid: 1967. 21" - $85.00.

World of Love Dolls: 9", 1968. White: $8.00. Black: $10.00.

Original set of Foreign G.I. Joes marked "G.I. Joe Copyright 1964/Hasbro/ Patent Pending/Made in USA." There are no scars on the faces and most have different head mold. Back row: (left to right) American, Australian. Front row: Japanese (kneeling), English (with headphones), German and Russian. Courtesy Renie Culp. $125.00 up each.

13" "Fashion By Me" came with materials and patterns, shoes, stand, handbags. No sewing - "just tuck into magic seams." Eight other clothes kits were also available. Marked "Hasbro 1982" on head and "1982 Hasbro Pat. Pend." on back. Doll has vinyl head with painted features and rooted hair. Body made in one piece of plastic, high heel feet and in cutouts along all sides is a soft vinyl lining to hold material. 13" - $20.00 up.

Wide-eyed "Real Baby" designed by Judith Turner. 20" vinyl head and limbs, cloth body, inset eyes with hair lashes. The family has 3 outfits for the "awake" eyes: pink, yellow and lavender, and 3 for the modeled "asleep" eye doll: yellow sleeper, pink and white bunny ears suit and blue two-piece with hood. Each boxed with life-size baby bottle. Made by Hasbro in 1985, copyright Judith Turner 1984. Courtesy Margaret Mandel. Doll - $45.00. Steiff Lamb: $95.00.

21" black "Asleep Baby" (Real Baby). Cloth and vinyl. Eyes modeled asleep with hair lashes. Open/closed mouth and wears original outfit. Marked 1894/J Turner/Hasbro Ind." and on head "Real Baby/H-23/1985 Hasbro Bradley Inc." Courtesy Genie Jinright. 21" - $45.00.

First prices are for mint condition dolls; second prices for ones that have been played with, are dirty and soiled or not original. Marked "Horsman" or "E.I.H."

Answer Doll: Button in back moves head. 1966. 10" - $15.00, $6.00.

Billiken: Composition head, slant eyes, plush or velvet body. 1909. 12" - $365.00, $125.00.

Baby Bumps: Composition/cloth. 1910. 11" - $185.00, $95.00; 16" - $245.00, $100.00. Black: 11" - $275.00, $100.00; 16" - $300.00, $125.00.

Baby First Tooth: Cloth/vinyl, cry mouth with one tooth, tears on cheeks. 16" - $45.00, $15.00.

Baby Tweaks: Cloth/vinyl, inset eyes. 1967. 20" - $35.00, $16.00.

Bedknobs and Broomsticks: Came with plastic and tin bed. Doll has jointed waist, painted eyes. 6½" - $30.00 (complete).

Betty: All composition. 16" - $190.00, $95.00. Plastic/vinyl: 16" - $25.00, $12.00.

12" "Billikin" with Teddy Bear like fur and felt body, composition head, painted features. Courtesy Jeannie Mauldin. 12" - $365.00 up.

19" "Baby Tweaks" marked "3169 18 Horsman Doll Inc. 1970 S18" on head. Vinyl with cloth body. Painted eyes, open/closed mouth. Courtesy Nancy Prestosh. 19" - $35.00.

Betty Jo: All composition. 16" - $190.00, $95.00. Plastic/vinyl: 16" - $25.00, $12.00.

Betty Ann: All composition. 19" - $225.00, $100.00. Plastic/vinyl: 19" - $35.00, $15.00.

Betty Jane: All composition. 25" - $300.00, $125.00. Plastic/vinyl: 25" - $65.00, $25.00.

Betty Bedtime: All composition. 16" - $185.00, $90.00; 20" - $250.00, $100.00.

Body Twist: All composition. Top of body fits down into torso. 11" - $150.00, $50.00.

Bright Star: All composition. 18-19" - $225.00, $90.00. All hard plastic, 1952: 15" - $250.00, $90.00.

Brother: Composition/cloth. 22" - $200.00 up, $120.00. Vinyl: 13" - $35.00, $15.00.

Campbell Kids: Marked "E.I.H." Ca. 1911. Composition/cloth, painted features. 13" - $550.00 up. 12": 1930-1940's. Very "Dolly Dingle" looking face. All composition. $400.00 up.

Celeste Portrait Doll: In frame. Eyes painted to side. 12" - $35.00, $15.00.

Christopher Robin: 11" - $45.00, $20.00.

Child Dolls: All composition: 15" - $175.00, $85.00; 19" - $225.00, $100.00. All composition, very chubby toddler: 16" - $175.00, $70.00. All hard plastic: 14" - $100.00, $50.00; 18" - $225.00 up, $125.00.

Cindy: All hard plastic. 1950's. 15" - $100.00 up, $45.00; 17" - $165.00 up, $70.00. All early vinyl: 18" - $45.00, $15.00. Lady type, jointed waist: 19" - $85.00, $40.00.

15" "Cindy." All hard plastic, sleep eyes and marked "Horsman" on head. Open mouth with four upper teeth and felt tongue. 1955. Courtesy Betty Wood. 15" - $100.00 up.

Cinderella: Plastic/vinyl. Painted eyes to side. 11½" - $30.00, $10.00.

Composition Dolls: 1910's to 1920's "Can't Break Em" composition/cloth body, marked "E.I.H." 12" - $165.00, $60.00; 16" - $195.00, $100.00. 1930's: 16" - $150.00, $60.00; 18" - $200.00, $90.00; 22" - $275.00, $125.00.

Country Girl: 9" - $15.00, $5.00.

Crawling Baby: Vinyl, 1967. 14" - $35.00, $15.00.

Dimples: Composition/cloth. 14" - $165.00, $70.00; 20" - $250.00, $100.00; 24" - $285.00, $125.00. Toddler: 20" - $300.00, $125.00; 24" - $350.00, $150.00. Laughing, painted teeth: 22" - $285.00, $160.00.

Gold Medal Doll: Composition/cloth, upper & lower teeth. 21" - $185.00, $60.00. Vinyl/molded hair: 26" - $175.00, $85.00. Vinyl Boy: 15" - $65.00, $25.00.

Ella Cinders: Comic character. Composition/cloth. 14" - $325.00; 18" - $575.00.

Elizabeth Taylor: 1976. 11½" - $75.00, $40.00.

Flying Nun: (Patty Duke) 1965. 12" - $50.00, $25.00.

Hebee-Shebee: All composition. 10½" - $525.00, $225.00

Jackie Coogan: 1921. Composition/cloth, painted eyes. 14" - $525.00, $200.00.

Jackie Kennedy: Marked "Horsman J.K." Adult body. Plastic/vinyl, 1961. 25" - $165.00, $60.00.

Jeanie Horsman: All composition. 14" - $200.00, $90.00. Composition/cloth: 16" - $175.00, $70.00.

Jojo: All composition. 12" - $200.00, $90.00.

Life-size Baby: Plastic/vinyl. 26" - $225.00, $95.00.

Lullabye Baby: Cloth/vinyl. Music box in body. 12" - $20.00, $8.00. All vinyl: 12" - $15.00, $5.00.

Mary Poppins: 12" - $35.00, $10.00; 16" - $65.00, $20.00; 26" - $175.00, $80.00; 36" - $350.00, $150.00.

Mama Style Babies: Composition/cloth. Marked "E.I.H" or "Horsman." 16" - $175.00, $85.00; 22" - $245.00, $100.00. Hard plastic/cloth: 16" - $75.00; $35.00; 22" - $90.00, $40.00. Vinyl/cloth: 16" - $20.00, $8.00; 22" - $30.00, $15.00.

Peggy Pen Pal: Multi-jointed arms. Plastic/vinyl. 18" - $45.00, $15.00.

Pippi Longstockings: Vinyl/cloth. 1972. 18" - $45.00, $20.00.

18" "Ella Cinder" marked "1925 MNS by Horsman." Composition with cloth body. Painted hair and features. May be original dress. Boy is a German papier mache that is 15" tall with shoulder head, inset glass eyes with open/closed mouth and molded upper teeth. Cloth body. May be original. Courtesy Frasher Doll Auctions. 18" - $575.00. 15" - $365.00.

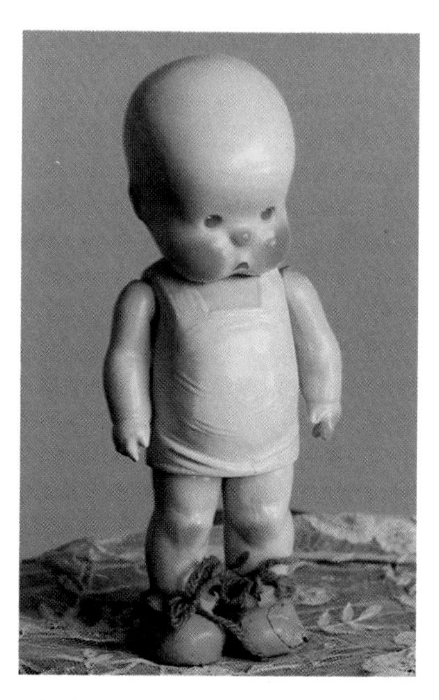

10½" "Hebee" that is all composition, jointed at shoulders and has painted-on booties. Courtesy Frasher Doll Auctions. 10½" - $525.00.

Pipsqueaks: Four in set. 1967. 12" - $20.00 each, $9.00.

Polly & Pete: Black dolls, molded hair. All vinyl. 13" - $200.00, $85.00.

Poor Pitiful Pearl: 12" - $40.00, $15.00; 17" - $85.00, $30.00.

Peterkin: All composition, painted googly-style eyes. 12" - $325.00, $125.00.

Roberta: All composition. Molded hair or wigs, 1937. 14" - $200.00, $90.00; 20" - $300.00, $125.00.

Rosebud: Composition/cloth. Marked with name, dimples and smile. Sleep eyes, wig. 18" - $250.00, $125.00.

Ruthie: All vinyl or plastic/vinyl. 14" - $22.00, $6.00; 20" - $38.00, $12.00.

Ruthie's Sister: Plastic/vinyl. 1960. 26" - $95.00, $40.00.

Sleepy Baby: Vinyl/cloth, eyes molded closed. 24" - $50.00, $25.00.

Tuffie: All vinyl. Upper lip molded over lower. 16" - $75.00, $30.00.

Mary Poppins with Michael and Jane in original box. All are plastic and vinyl. Courtesy Cindy Ruscito. $200.00.

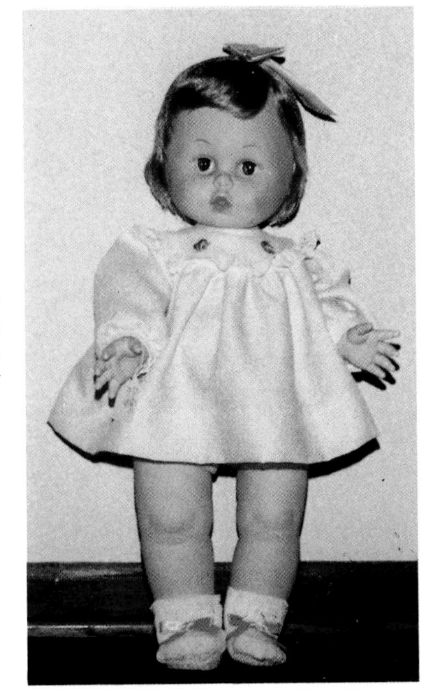

24 "Pudgie Baby." Plastic body with vinyl head and limbs. All original. Marked "Horsman Doll Co. 1980" on head and "Horsman Dolls Inc." on back. Courtesy Jeannie Mauldin. 24" - $65.00.

Left to right: 1973 Eegee Bean Bag with vinyl head and hands. 20" 1973 Eegee vinyl head and hands and cloth body. Back center: 1973 Eegee 12" cloth/vinyl with pull string for mouth. 1950 20" Ideal all cloth with hard plastic head, pull string mouth. 26" 1973 Eegee plastic head and hands, cloth body, pull string mouth. Front: 16" vinyl head, cloth body, felt gloves/ boots. Maker unknown. 28" composition head and hands, sleep eyes by Effanbee. Courtesy Jeannie Mauldin.

All prices are for mint condition dolls.

Howdy Doody Doll: Not a puppet. Cloth body with composition head and hands. 17" - $200.00; 23" - $250.00.

Puppet: Mouth moves, 7 limbs attached to strings. 14" - $95.00; 20" - $150.00.

Marionette: Mouth moves. Sleep eyes, cloth with hard plastic head and hands. Marked "Ideal Doll." 14" - $85.00; 20" - $125.00.

All Vinyl: Molded in one piece. 12½" - $30.00.

All Vinyl: Jointed shoulders, hips and neck. 14" - $50.00.

All Cloth: Printed on clothes and features. 16" - $185.00.

The Mary Hoyer Doll Mfg. Co. operated in Reading, Pa. from 1925. The dolls were made in all composition, all hard plastic, and last ones produced were in plastic and vinyl. Older dolls are marked in a circle on back "Original Mary Hoyer Doll" or "The Mary Hoyer Doll" embossed on lower back.

First price is for perfect doll in tagged factory clothes. Second price for perfect doll in outfits made from Mary Hoyer patterns and third price is for redressed doll in good condition with only light craze to composition or slight soil to others.

Composition: 14" - $400.00 up, 350.00 up, $165.00.

Hard Plastic: 14" - $400.00 up, 265.00 up, $185.00; 17" - $550.00 up, $435.00 up, $325.00.

Plastic and Vinyl: 14-15" (Margie) Marked "AE23." 12" - $100.00, 50.00, $10.00; 14" - $165.00-85.00; $30.00.

17" "Mary Hoyer." All hard plastic and marked "Original Mary Hoyer Doll" in a circle on back. Dress tag "Handmade/Annie Kilborn." Made from 1950's Mary Hoyer pattern. 17" - $550.00.

14" Mary Hoyer that is all composition with sleep eyes and dressed in Mary Hoyer pattern outfit. Courtesy Marie Ernst. 14" - $400.00.

First prices are for mint condition dolls. Second prices are for cracked, crazed, dirty, soiled or not original dolls.

Baby Belly Button: 9" plastic/vinyl. White: $12.00, $5.00; Black: $20.00, $10.00.

Baby Crissy: 24". White: $65.00, $20.00. Black: $85.00, $28.00.

Baby Snooks and Other Flexies: Wire and composition. 12" - $265.00, $95.00.

Bam-Bam: Plastic/vinyl or all vinyl. 12" - $20.00, $6.00; 16" - $25.00, $10.00.

16" "Bam Bam." All vinyl, rooted hair and painted features. Marked "Hanna Barbera Prods. Inc./Ideal Toy Corp. BB-17" and on head "1963". This doll may be on wrong boy as "Bam Bam" has molded first-style right hand to hold a club. 16" - $25.00.

Batgirl and Other Super Women: Vinyl. 12" - $65.00, $25.00.

Betsy McCall: See that section.

Betsy Wetsy: Composition head, excellent rubber body. 16" - $125.00, $20.00. Hard plastic/vinyl: 12" - $75.00, $25.00; 14" - $90.00, $30.00. All vinyl: 12" - $25.00, $9.00; 18" - $75.00, $30.00.

Betty Big Girl: Plastic/vinyl. 30" - $185.00, $90.00.

Betty Jane: Shirley Temple type. All composition, sleep eyes, open mouth. 1941-1943. 14" - $175.00, $70.00; 18" - $275.00, $100.00.

Bizzy Lizzy: Plastic/vinyl. 17" - $30.00, $15.00.

Blessed Event: Called "Kiss Me." Cloth body with plunger in back to make doll cry or pout. Vinyl head with eyes almost squinted closed. 21" - $100.00, $45.00.

Bonnie Braids: Hard plastic/vinyl head. 13" - $60.00, $20.00.

Bonnie Walker: Hard plastic, pin jointed hips, open mouth, flirty eyes. Marked "Ideal W-25." 23" - $95.00, $40.00.

Brandi: Of Crissy family. 18" - $75.00, $40.00.

Brother/Baby Coos: Composition/cloth with hard plastic head. 25" - $125.00, $70.00. Composition head/latex: 24" - $35.00, $10.00. Hard plastic head/vinyl: 24" - $50.00, $15.00.

Bye Bye Baby: Lifelike modeling. 12" - $145.00, $50.00; 25" - $300.00, $135.00.

Cinnamon: Of Crissy family. 12" - $70.00, $30.00. Black: $125.00, $50.00.

Composition Child: All composition girl with sleep eyes, some flirty, open mouth, original clothes and excellent condition. Marked "Ideal" and a number or "Ideal" in a diamond. 14" - $165.00, $70.00; 18" - $225.00,

$90.00; 22" - $275.00, $100.00. Cloth body with straight composition legs. 14" - $145.00, $45.00; 18" - $195.00, $65.00; 22" - $225.00, $75.00.

Composition Baby: Composition head and limbs with cloth body and closed mouth. Sleep eyes (allow more for flirty eyes), original and in excellent condition. 18" - $145.00, $65.00; 22" - $165.00, $75.00; 25" - $185.00, $80.00. Flirty eyes: 16" - $185.00, $70.00; 18" - $200.00, $100.00.

Cricket: Of Crissy family. 18" - $60.00, $30.00. Black: $85.00, $40.00. Look-a-round: $60.00, $30.00.

Crissy: 18" - $60.00, $20.00. Black: $85.00, $35.00. Look-a-round: $60.00, $25.00.

Right: 12" composition head, hands and feet "Flexie" boy marked "Ideal Doll USA." Ca. 1938. Legs and arms are made of flexible metal cable. Original clothes. Left: "Pete the Pup" made by Cameo Dolls. Composition/wood, nose paint chipped. Courtesy Frasher Doll Auctions. 12" - $265.00. Pete - $250.00.

18" "Crissy" and 16" "Velvet" shown in original outfits and both dolls are mint in original condition. Courtesy Marie Ernst. 18" - $60.00. 16" - $60.00.

Daddy's Girl: 42" - $850.00, $300.00.

Deanna Durbin: All composition. 14" - $425.00, $175.00; 17" - $485.00, $185.00; 21" - $585.00, $300.00; 24" - $725.00, $325.00; 27" - $900.00, $400.00.

Dianna Ross: Plastic/vinyl. 18" - $165.00, $80.00.

Dina: Of Crissy family. 15" - $85.00, $40.00.

Dodi: Of Tammy family. Marked "1964-Ideal-D0-9E." 9" - $40.00, $10.00.

Flexies: Composition and wire, soldier, children, Fanny Brice, etc. 12" - $265.00 up, $90.00.

Flossie Flirt: Composition/cloth. Flirty eyes: 22" - $285.00, $90.00. Black: $325.00, $125.00.

Giggles: Plastic/vinyl. 16" - $50.00, $20.00; 18" - $85.00, $30.00. Black: 18" - $150.00, $75.00. Baby: 16" - $50.00, $20.00.

9" "Dodi" shown in original box. All vinyl with bendable arms and legs, painted features with smile mouth and painted teeth. Goes with the Tammy & Pepper family. Courtesy Marie Ernst. 9" in box - $75.00. Doll only - $40.00.

25" "Deanna Durbin." Marked head and body. All composition, sleep eyes, open mouth and all original with original pin. Courtesy Frasher Doll Auctions. 25" - $750.00.

15½" "Harriet Hubbard Ayer" #2901, all original. Hard plastic with early vinyl head and arms. Glued-on wig, sleep eyes. Marked "MK-16/Ideal Doll" on head and on back "Ideal Doll/ P-91." Note beautiful hand and detailed fingernails in photo below. Courtesy Marie Ernst. 15½ - $195.00.

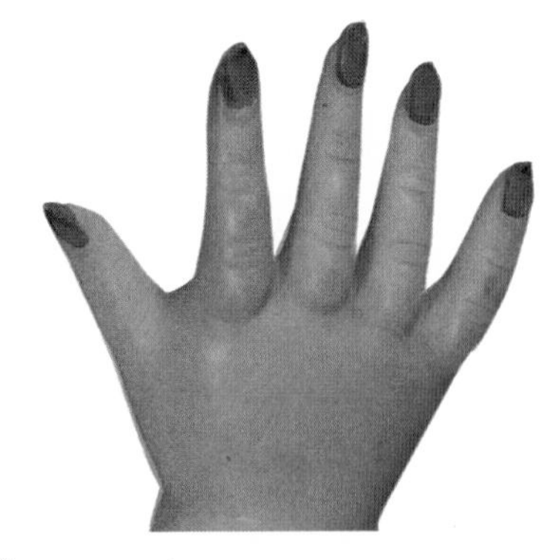

Goody Two Shoes: 18" - $100.00, $45.00. Walking/talking: 27" - $200.00, $65.00.

Harriet Hubbard Ayer: Hard plastic/vinyl. 14½" - $185.00, $50.00; 18" - $250.00, $95.00.

Joan Palooka: 1952. 14" - $65.00, $30.00.

Joey Stivic (Baby): One-piece body and limbs. Sexed boy. 15" - $50.00, $20.00.

Jimmy Cricket: Composition/wood. 9" - $265.00, $100.00.

Judy Garland: All composition. 14" - $1,000.00 up, $400.00; 18" - $1,200.00 up, $500.00. Marked with backward "21": 21" - $500.00, $200.00.

Judy Splinters: Cloth/vinyl/latex, yarn hair, painted eyes. 18" - $100.00, $35.00; 22" - $150.00, $50.00; 36" - $300.00, $100.00.

Kerry: Of Crissy family. 18" - $75.00, $35.00.

King Little: Composition/wood. 14" - $265.00, $95.00.

Kiss Me: See Blessed Event.

Kissy: 22" - $60.00, $30.00. Black: $145.00, $60.00.

Kissy, Tiny: 16" - $55.00, $25.00. Black: $100.00, $50.00.

Liberty Boy: 1918. 12" - $285.00, $100.00.

Little Lost Baby: Three-faced doll. 22" - $65.00, $40.00.

Magic Lips: Vinyl coated cloth/vinyl. Lower teeth. 24" - $85.00, $40.00.

Mama Style Dolls: Composition cloth. 18" - $200.00, $85.00; 23" - $275.00, $100.00. Hard plastic/cloth: 18" - $85.00, $35.00; 23" - $125.00, $45.00.

Mary Hartline: All hard plastic. 15" - $225.00 up, $90.00; 21-23": $350.00 up, $145.00.

Mary Jane or Betty Jane: All composition, sleep and/or flirty eyes, open mouth. Marked "Ideal 18": 18" - $275.00 up, $100.00.

Mia: Of Crissy family. 15½" - $75.00, $30.00.

Miss Curity: Hard plastic. 14" - $225.00 up, $90.00. Composition: 21" - $300.00 up, $100.00.

Miss Ideal: Multi-jointed. 25" - $350.00 up, $125.00; 28" - $400.00, $150.00.

Miss Revlon: 10½" - $95.00, $40.00; 17" - $165.00 up, $75.00. In box - $250.00 up; 20" - $200.00 up, $90.00.

Mitzi: Teen. 12" - $55.00, $30.00.

Mortimer Snerd and Other Flexie Dolls: Composition and wire. 12" - $265.00, $90.00.

Patti Playpal: 30" - $175.00, $90.00; 36" - $265.00, $100.00. Black: 30" - $350.00, $150.00; 36" - $450.00, $200.00.

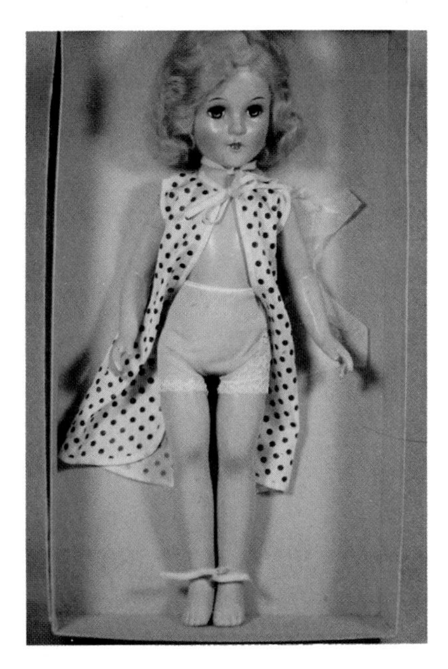

21" all composition doll used for the "Mary Hartline" and "Miss Curity" dolls. Sleep eyes and glued-on wig. This one is all original in original box which is just marked "Ideal Doll." Since she has just basic clothes, the other outfits may have been available separately. 21" in box - $350.00 up.

36" "Patti Playpal" in tagged original dress, sleep eyes and rooted hair. Plastic and vinyl. Shown with 19" "Patti Petite" that is marked "Ideal" and has been nicely redressed. Courtesy Ann Wencel. 36" - $450.00.

Pebbles: Plastic/vinyl and all vinyl. 8" - $15.00, $5.00; 12" - $25.00, $9.00; 15" - $35.00, $15.00.

Penny Playpal: 32" - $185.00, $90.00.

Pepper: 1964. Freckles. Marked "Ideal - P9-3." 9" - $30.00, $15.00.

Pete: 1964. Freckles. Marked "Ideal - P8." 7½" - $30.00, $15.00.

Peter Playpal: 38" - $350.00, $145.00.

Pinocchio: Composition/wood. 11" - $265.00, $95.00; 21" - $465.00, $165.00.

Posey: Hard plastic/vinyl head, jointed knees. Marked "Ideal VP-17." 17" - $100.00, $45.00.

Sandy McCall: See Betsy McCall section.

Sara Ann: Hard plastic. Marked "P-90." Saran wig: 14" - $225.00 up, $90.00. 21" marked "P-93": $350.00 up, $125.00.

Saralee: Cloth/vinyl. Black. 18" - $265.00, $125.00.

Saucy Walker: 16" - $125.00, $50.00; 19" - $165.00, $60.00; 22" - $185.00, $70.00. Black: 18" - $265.00, $100.00.

Shirley Temple: See that section.

Snoozie: Composition/cloth,

12" "Tammy's Mom." Plastic and vinyl with rooted hair, painted eyes to side, high heel feet. Marked "Ideal Toy Corp/W-18-L." on head and on back "Ideal Toy corp/W-13." Dress tag "Petite Fashions/By Dubutante." 12" - $50.00.

molded hair, sleep eyes, open yawning mouth. Marked "B Lipfert." 13" - $150.00, $50.00; 16" - $195.00, $80.00; 20" - $250.00, $120.00.

Snow White: All composition, black wig, on marked Shirley Temple body, sleep and/or flirty eyes. 12" - $475.00, $200.00; 18" - $500.00, $200.00. Molded hair, eyes painted to side: 14" - $185.00, $85.00; 18" - $450.00, $145.00.

Sparkle Plenty: 15" - $60.00, $25.00.

Suzy Playpal: Fat, chubby, vinyl body and limbs. Marked "Ideal O.E.B. 24-3." 24" - $165.00, $60.00.

Tara: Grows hair. Black. 16" - $45.00, $25.00.

Tammy: 1962. 9" - $45.00, $15.00; 12" - $50.00, $18.00. Black: $60.00, $20.00. Grown-up: 12" - $45.00, $15.00.

Tammy's Mom: 1963. Eyes to side. Marked: "Ideal W-18-L." 12" - $50.00, $30.00.

Ted: Tammy's brother. Molded hair. Marked "Ideal B-12-U-2." 1963. 12½" - $50.00, $20.00.

Thumbelina: Kissing: 10½" - $20.00, $8.00. Tearful: 15" - $30.00, $12.00. Wake Up: 17" - $45.00, $20.00. Black: 10½" - $50.00, $20.00.

Tickletoes: Composition/cloth. 15" - $175.00, $85.00; 21" - $285.00, $100.00.

Tiffany Taylor: Top of head swivels to change hair color. 18" - $80.00, $35.00. Black: 18" - $95.00, $50.00.

Tippy or Timmy Tumbles: 16" - $35.00, $15.00. Black: $50.00, $25.00.

Toni: 14" - $225.00 up, $100.00. Walker: $250.00 up, $100.00; 21" - $350.00 up, $150.00.

Tressy: Of Crissy family. 18" - $75.00, $35.00. Black $125.00, $45.00.

Velvet: Of Crissy family. 16" - $60.00, $20.00. Black: $100.00, $45.00. Look-a-round: $60.00, $20.00.

18" "Tiffany Taylor". Both in an original boxed outfit sold for them. Top of head turns to change from blonde to brunette. Painted features. Courtesy Marie Ernst. 18" - $80.00.

15" "Toni" marked "P-91" and all original. 14" pre-Toni called "Peggy" marked "P-90." Side part mohair wig, original clothes. 14" post-Toni called "Sara Ann." Saran wig, eyeshadow. Marked "P-90" and is all original. Courtesy Frasher Doll Auctions. 15" - $225.00 up. Both 14" - $225.00 up

15" mint and original 1956 "Miss Revlon." Marked "Ideal" on head and "Ideal 15" on body. High heel feet, shoes missing. 14" American Character all original 1955 "Toni". Both are all vinyl, sleep eyes, pierced ears. Courtesy Frasher Doll Auctions. 15" - $125.00 up.

Top Left Photo;
16½" "Toni" walker with playwave set. 1951. All hard plastic, sleep eyes, glued-on nylon wig, all original. Wrist tag advertises patterns for Toni: #6895 Advance, #5969 McCalls, #4128 Simplicity. Back marked "P-91/Ideal Doll/ 16. Courtesy Marie Ernst. 16½" - $275.00 up.

Bottom Left Photo:
14" "Toni" that is mint and all original. Sleep eyes and glued-on nylon wig. All hard plastic and marked "P-90 Ideal Doll" on back. Courtesy Marie Ernst. 14" - $225.00 up.

The following information was sent to me by Cecilia Terone of Long Island, NY.

The Juro factory was located near 29th Street on the east side of New York City and the name "Juro" was made up from the name of the two partners - Jupiter and Rosenberg. They made dolls from the 1940's into the late 1960's or early 1970's.

At least we now know this much about the firm.

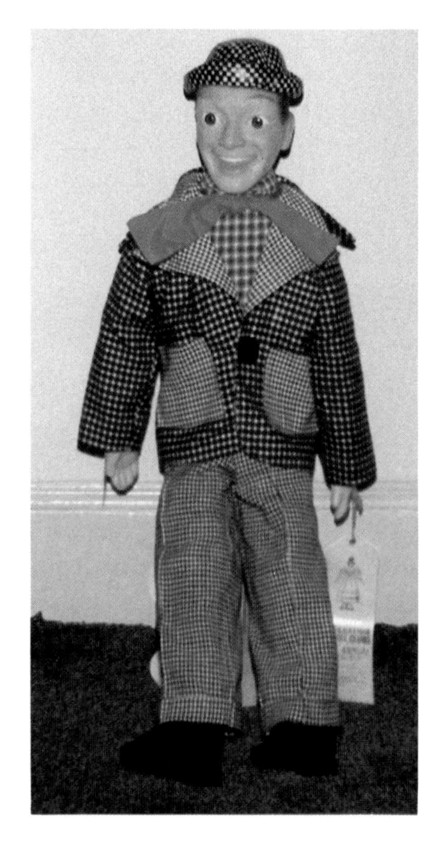

25" 1950 "Pinky Lee." All original, vinyl head with molded hat, inset eyes. Composition hands and rest cloth. Marked "Juro Celebrity Product." Courtesy Jeannie Mauldin. 25" - $225.00 up.

26" "Dick Clark" of 1958. Vinyl head and hands with rest cloth. All original clothes. Marked "Juro Novelty Co." Courtesy Frasher Doll Auctions. 26" - $250.00 up.

First prices are for mint condition dolls; second prices are for played with, dirty or missing clothing and accessories.

Baby Bundles: 16" - $20.00, $10.00. Black: $28.00, $15.00.

Baby Yawnie: Cloth/vinyl, 1974. 15" - $20.00, $10.00.

Big Foot: All rigid vinyl. 13" - $18.00, $7.00.

Butch Cassidy or Sundance Kid: 4" - $15.00, $6.00 each.

Blythe: 1972. Pull string to change the color of eyes. 11½" - $40.00, $20.00.

Charlie Chaplin: All cloth with walking mechanism. 1973. 14" - $70.00, $30.00.

Cover Girls (Darcie, Erica, Dana, etc.): 12½" White: $30.00, $12.00. Black: $35.00, $15.00.

Crumpet: 1970. Plastic/vinyl. 18" - $30.00, $12.00.

Dusty: 11½". $25.00, $10.00.

Gabbigale: 1972. 18" - $35.00, $12.00. Black: $45.00, $15.00.

Garden Gals: 1972. Hand bent to hold watering can. 6½" - $10.00, $4.00.

Hardy Boys: 1978. Shaun Cassidy and Parker Stevenson. 12" - $20.00, $8.00.

Jenny Jones and Baby: All vinyl, 1973. 9" Jenny and 2½" baby: $15.00, $6.00. Set: $25.00, $8.00.

12" Cover Girl "Erica." 12½" tall, all vinyl with bendable arms and legs. Gold face mask came packaged with this all original doll. Marked: "GMFGI 1978" on head. On torso: "C.R.G. Products Corp. 1978/Kenner Cincinnati/47400. Made in Hong Kong." Courtesy Renie Culp. 12" - $30.00.

18" "Sweet Cookie" made by Kenner and shown all original with accessories. Battery operated. Doll is plastic and vinyl with multi-jointed arms. Courtesy Jeannie Mauldin. 18" - $25.00.

11½" "Princess Leia" of the large Star Wars figures. To command the highest price, the hairdo must be in original set as shown here. This is a French packaged doll, but still made by Kenner. Courtesy Karen Heidemann. 11½" - $80.00 up.

15" original all rigid vinyl "Chewbacca" from the Star Wars large action figure series. Courtesy Karen Heidemann. 15" - $85.00 up.

Skye: Black doll. 11½ - $25.00, $10.00.

Sleep Over Dolly: And minature doll. 17" - $35.00, $10.00. Black: $40.00, $15.00.

Star Wars: Large size figures. R2-D2: 7½" - $85.00 up, $25.00. C-3PO: 12" - $85.00 up, $25.00. Darth Vader: 15" - $85.00 up, $25.00. Boba Fett: 13" - $100.00 up, $30.00. Jawa: 8½" - $55.00, $20.00. IG-88: 15" - $100.00 up, $30.00. Stormtrooper: 12" - $85.00 up, $25.00. Leia: 11½" - $80.00 up, $25.00. Hans Solo: 12" - $85.00, $25.00. Luke Skywalker: 13½" - $75.00, $25.00. Chewbacca: 15" - $85.00 up, $25.00. Obi Wan Kenobi: 12" - $90.00, $30.00.

Steve Scout: 1974. 9" - $20.00, $8.00. Black: $30.00, $10.00.

Sweet Cookie: 18" - $25.00, $12.00.

First prices are for mint condition dolls; second prices are for dolls played with, crazed or cracked, dirty, soiled or not original.

Bisque Kewpies: See front Kewpie section.

All Composition: Jointed shoulder only. 9" - $135.00, $50.00; 14" - $195.00, $70.00. Jointed hips, neck and shoulder: 9" - $200.00, $80.00; 14" - $300.00, $110.00.

Talcum Powder Container: 7-8" - $195.00.

Celluloid: 2" - $45.00; 5" - $85.00; 9" - $165.00. Black: 5" - $125.00.

Bean Bag Body: 10" - $45.00, $15.00.

Cloth Body: Vinyl head and limbs. 16" - $185.00, $85.00.

Kewpie Gal: With molded hair/ribbon. 8" - $65.00, $25.00.

Hard Plastic: One-piece body and head. 8" - $95.00, $25.00; 12" - $225.00, $95.00; 16" - $350.00, $145.00. Fully jointed at shoulder, neck and hips: 12-13" - $385.00, $175.00; 16" - $500.00, $200.00.

Ragsy: Vinyl one-piece, molded-on clothes with heart on chest. 1964. 8" - $60.00, $28.00. Without heart, 1971: 8" - $45.00, $19.00.

Thinker: One-piece vinyl, sitting down. 4" - $12.00, $5.00.

Kewpie: Vinyl, jointed at shoulder only. 9" - $55.00, $15.00; 12" - $85.00, $20.00; 14" - $100.00, $30.00. Jointed at neck, shoulders and hips: 9" - $75.00, $25.00; 12" - $125.00, $35.00; 14" - $175.00, $50.00; 27" - $300.00, $165.00. Not jointed at all: 9" - $35.00, $10.00; 12" - $50.00, $15.00; 14" - $65.00, $20.00. Black: 9" - $50.00, $15.00; 12" - $75.00, $25.00; 14" - $125.00, $45.00.

Ward's Anniversary: 8" - $75.00, $25.00.

All Cloth: Made by Kreuger. All one-piece including clothing. 12" - $175.00, $80.00; 16" - $285.00, $100.00; 20" - $425.00, $175.00; 25" - $800.00, $300.00. Removable dress and bonnet: 12" - $225.00, $85.00; 16" - $350.00, $145.00; 20" - $565.00, $200.00; 25" - $1,000.00, $400.00.

Kewpie Baby: With hinged joints. 15" - $195.00, $80.00; 18" - $265.00, $95.00.

Kewpie Baby: With one-piece stuffed body and limbs. 15" - $145.00, $60.00; 18" - $165.00, $65.00.

Plush: Usually red with vinyl face mask and made by Knickerbocker. 1960's. 6" - $60.00, $20.00; 10" - $85.00, $25.00.

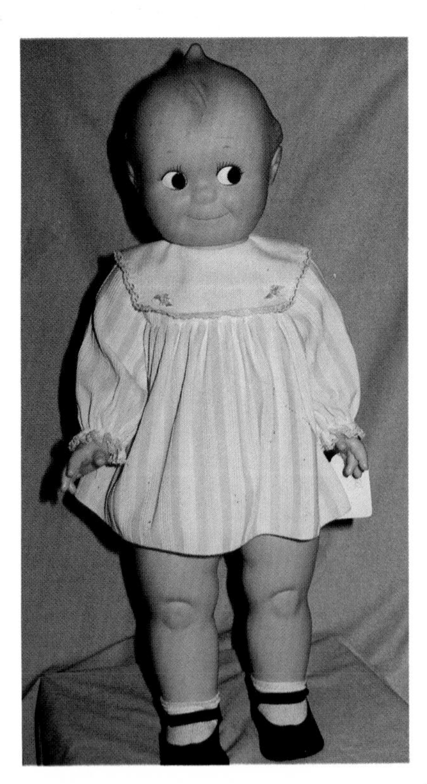

27" "Kewpie" that is marked "Cameo" on head and body. All vinyl head and arms and rigid plastic body and legs. Redressed, although shoes and socks may be original. Courtesy Frasher Doll Auctions. 27" original: $300.00. Redressed - $165.00.

10" Cameo made 1950's "Kewpie" that is all vinyl and jointed at neck only. The dress appears original even if it looks slightly too large. In front is a Kewpie-style bank with blue wings and made of plaster-type material. 10" - $65.00. Bank: $45.00.

13" all composition Kewpie Twins. Jointed neck shoulder and hips. Painted features. 1940's. All original. Courtesy Frasher Doll Auctions. 13" - $300.00 each.

KNICKERBOCKER TOY COMPANY

All prices are for mint condition dolls.

Bozo Clown: 14" - $40.00; 24" - $75.00.

Cinderella: With two heads; one sad; the other with tiara. 16" - $25.00.

Clown: Cloth. 17" - $28.00.

Composition Child: Bent right arm at elbow. 15" - $185.00 up.

Flintstones: 17" - $45.00 each.

Kewpie: See Kewpie section.

Levi Rag Doll: All cloth. 15" - $20.00.

Little House on the Prairie: 1978. 12" - $18.00 each.

Lord of Rings: 5" - $20.00 each.

Pinocchio: All plush and cloth. 13" - $135.00 up. All composition: 13" - $285.00 up.

Scarecrow: Cloth. 23½" - $90.00.

Seven Dwarfs: All composition. 10" - $225.00 up (each).

Sleeping Beauty: All composition, bent right arm. 15" - $250.00 up.

Snow White: All composition, bent right arm. Black wig. 15" - $250.00 up; 20" - $325.00 up.

Soupy Sales: Vinyl and cloth, non-removeable clothes. 13" - $145.00.

Two-headed Dolls: Vinyl face masks; one crying, one smiling. 12" - $20.00.

17" "Bozo the Clown." Vinyl head, painted features, cloth body. Marked "Capitol Records Made in Taiwan 23" and tag "Larry Harmon's/ Bozo the Clown/Capitol Records, Inc./Knickerbocker Toy Co." Courtesy Sandra Cummins. 17" - $45.00.

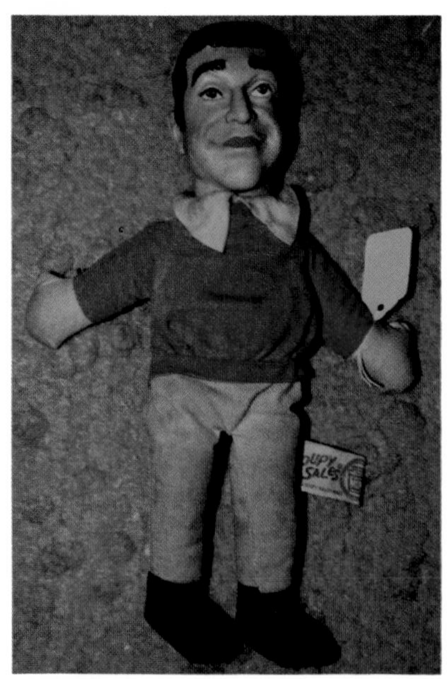

13" "Soupy Sales" with vinyl head, painted features, molded hair, cloth body with non-removable clothes. Tag: "Soupy Sales W.M.C. Knickerbocker Toy Co., 1966." Courtesy Jeannie Mauldin. 13" - $145.00.

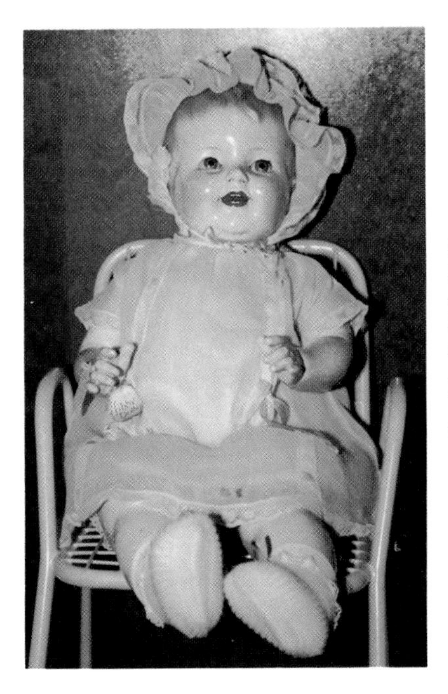

26" baby with cloth body, composition head, arms and legs. Happy, smiling open mouth with two upper and two lower teeth. Sleep tin eyes, molded hair and doll is mint condition with original clothes. Wrist tag: "Libby Dolls New York." Courtesy Jeannie Mauldin. 26" - $225.00.

L.J.N.

12" "Boy George." Marked "L.J.N. 1984" on head. Box: "1984 Sharpegrade Ltd. #7700." All vinyl and bendable. Painted features. Courtesy Cindy Ruscito. 12" vinyl - $45.00. 14½" cloth, vinyl head - $65.00.

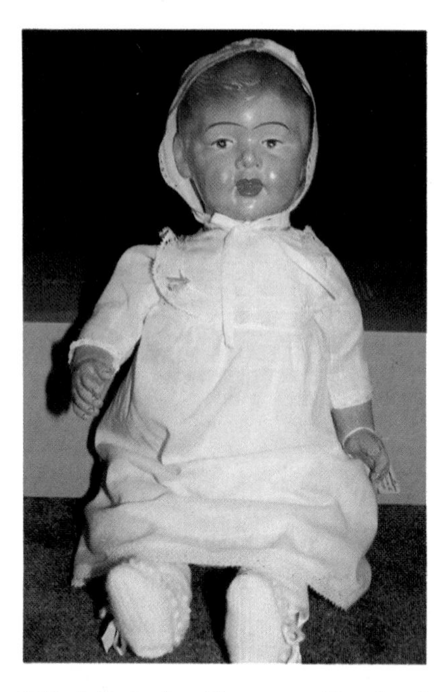

29" cloth body with composition head and arms. Legs are also stuffed cloth. Disc jointed shoulder and hips. Painted features with open/closed mouth and two painted upper teeth. No marks. Wears original clothes. Courtesy Jeannie Mauldin. 29" - $300.00.

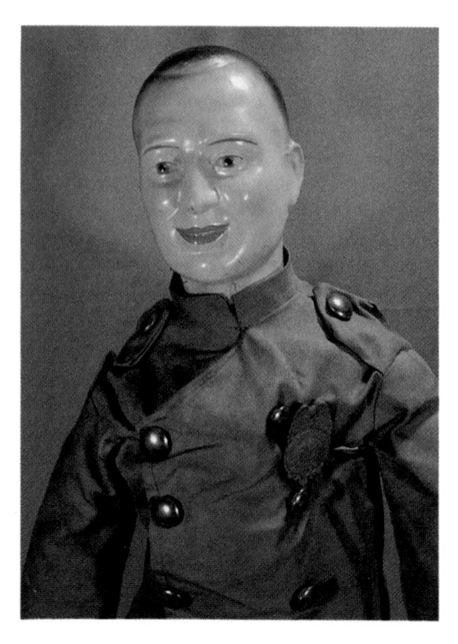

28" composition character head with painted features. Composition hands and rest cloth. In original policeman's uniform of the 1920's or 1930's. Original badge. Unmarked. 28" - $325.00.

14" "Barbra Streisand." All excellent quality vinyl. Jointed low on waist with one-piece torso and legs. Large blue painted eyes and large nose detail. Doll is not marked and original dress has tag "Japanese characters" and "Made in Japan." Courtesy Betty Tait. 14" - $175.00 up.

First prices are for mint condtion dolls; second prices are for dolls that have been played with, are dirty, soiled, not original and/or do not have accessories.

Allen: 12" - $200.00 up (in box.)

Baby First Step: 18" - $30.00, $10.00. Talking: $45.00, $15.00.

Baby Go Bye Bye: 12" - $20.00, $10.00.

Baby's Hungry: 17" - $35.00, $12.00.

Baby Pataburp: 13" - $35.00, $12.00.

Baby Say 'n See: 17" - $30.00, $10.00.

Baby Secret: 18" - $45.00, $15.00.

Baby Small Talk: 11" - $18.00, $8.00. As Cinderella: $25.00, $10.00. Black: $35.00, $15.00.

Baby Tenderlove: Newborn. 13" - $10.00, $5.00.

Baby Walk 'n Play: 11" - $25.00, $10.00.

Baby Walk 'n See: 18" - $30.00, $15.00.

Barbie: 1958-1959: #1, holes in feet with metal cylinders. $2,500.00 in box. Doll only: $1,500.00 up. **1960:** #3, curved brows, marked 1959 body. $300.00 up. **1961:** #4, marked "Pat. Pend. 1961." $250.00 up. **1963:** Fashion Queen with 3 wigs. $200.00 up. **1964:** Ponytail with swirl bangs. No curly bangs. $200.00 up. **1965:** Color 'n Curl, 2 heads and accessories. $450.00 up. **1968:** Spanish Talking - $185.00 up. **1969**: Twist 'n

Left: Barbie "Velveteens" 1965. Rare crushed velvet pants with attached white crepe blouse. Separate jacket lined with white crepe. Right: "Pink Formal" 1965 Sears exclusive, missing white boa stole. Courtesy Margaret Mandel. Velvet - $285.00. Pink Formal - $200.00.

#5 Barbie with ponytail in sausage curl wearing #967 Picnic set. The complete outfit as shown is rare. Courtesy Margaret Mandel. Barbie alone - $200.00 up. Complete outfit - $125.00 up. Fish alone - $50.00 up.

Turn - $85.00 up. **1971:** Growing Pretty Hair, bendable knees. $250.00 up. **1972:** Ward Anniversary - $185.00 up. **1973:** Quick Curl - $85.00 up. **1974:** Newport - $45.00 up. Sun Valley - $75.00 up. Sweet Sixteen - $85.00 up. **1975:** Free Moving - $65.00 up. Funtime - $65.00 up. Gold Medal Skater - $50.00 up. **1976:** Ballerina - $50.00 up. Deluxe Quick Curl - $45.00. Free Moving - $55.00 up. **1978:** Super Size Barbie. $95.00. **1979:** Pretty Changes - $45.00 up. **1980:** Beauty Secrets - $30.00 up. **1981:** Western - $25.00 up. **1983:** Twirly Curls - $25.00 up.

Super Size Barbie. 18" plastic and vinyl with rooted hair, jointed waist and painted features. Different outfits purchased separately, as this gown was. Courtesy Marie Ernst. 18" - $95.00.

Barbie Items: Car Roadster - $265.00 up. Sports car - $150.00. Dune Buggy - $80.00 up. Clock - $40.00. Family House - $65.00. Watches - $20.00-40.00. Airplane - $500.00. Horse "Dancer" (brown) - $100.00 up. Wardrobe - $45.00. First Barbie stand (round with two prongs) - $165.00.

Bozo: 18" - $45.00, $15.00.

Buffie: With Mrs. Beasley. 6" - $45.00, $10.00. 10" - $60.00, $15.00.

Capt. Lazer: 12½" - $250.00, $95.00.

Casey: 1975, 11½". $145.00 up.

Casper, The Ghost: 16" - $40.00, $20.00.

Charming Chatty: 25" - $100.00, $40.00.

Chatty Brother, Tiny: 15" - $40.00, $9.00. Baby: $40.00, $9.00. Black: $55.00, $15.00.

Chatty Cathy: 20" - $85.00, $30.00. Brunette/brown eyes: $100.00, $35.00. Black: $225.00, $55.00.

Cheerleader: 13" - $15.00, $6.00.

Cheerful Tearful: 13" - $25.00, $8.00. Tiny: 6½" - $15.00, $6.00.

Christie: 1968, Black doll. 11½" - $95.00 up.

Cynthia: 20" - $45.00, $15.00.

Dancerina: 24" - $45.00, $20.00. Black: $70.00, $30.00. Baby: Not battery operated. $40.00, $15.00. Black: $60.00, $25.00.

Dick Van Dyke: 25" - $100.00, $50.00.

Fluff: 9" - $60.00 up.

Francie: 11½" - $85.00 up. Black: $400.00 up. Malibu: $30.00.

Grandma Beans: 11" - $20.00, $9.00.

Gorgeous Creatures: Mae West

style body/animal heads, 1979. $18.00 each, $9.00.

Guardian Goddesses: 11½" - $165.00 up (each).

Hi Dottie: 17" - $30.00, $15.00.

Herman Munster: 16" - $45.00, $15.00.

Hush Lil Baby: 15" - $15.00, $5.00.

Jamie Walker with Dog: 1969. 11½" - $295.00 up.

Julia: 11½" Nurse - $185.00 up. Talking: $225.00 up.

15" Chatty Baby. Open/closed mouth with inset teeth. Pull string talker. All original. Courtesy Marie Ernst. 15" - $40.00.

Ken shown in original box, "Ski Champion." Has blonde "crew cut" hairdo. Painted features. Courtesy Pat Timmons. In box - $250.00. Doll only - $125.00.

Lil Big Guy: 13" - $10.00, $4.00.

Kiddles: With cars - $45.00 up. With planes - $50.00 up. In ice cream cones - $20.00 up. In jewelry - $30.00 up. In perfume bottles - $20.00 up. In bottles - $20.00 up. With cup and saucer - $100.00 up. Storybooks with accessories - $100.00 up. Baby Biddle in carriage - $175.00 up. Santa - $50.00 up. Animals - $40.00

Ken: Flocked hair - $125.00 up. Molded hair/non-bending knees - $125.00 up. Malibu - $30.00 up. Live Action - $60.00 up. Mod hair - $30.00 up. Busy - $45.00 up. Talking - $150.00 up.

Midge: 11½", freckles. $150.00 up. Bendable legs, 1965: $85.00 up.

16" "Saucy," 1972. Rotate arms to make face change expression and eyes move position. Both original except black doll has replacement shoes and socks. Courtesy Jeannie Mauldin. 16" - $75.00. Black - $125.00.

14" "Baby Cries For You." Vinyl head and arms, cloth body and legs. Painted features with two tear ducts in left eyes and one in right. Open mouth/ nurser. Pull cord in back makes arm move. Marked "48" in square "1879 Mattel, Inc." Courtesy Genie Jinright. 14" - $30.00.

Mother Goose: 20" - $50.00, $20.00.

Mrs. Beasley: Talking, 16". $50.00, $20.00.

Peachy & Puppets: 17" - $25.00, $10.00.

Randy Reader: 19" - $35.00, $15.00.

Real Sister: 14" - $20.00, $14.00.

Ricky: 1965, red hair and freckles. $100.00 up.

Rockflowers: 6½" - $30.00, $10.00.

Rose Bud Babies: 6½" - $25.00, $10.00.

Saucy: 16" - $75.00. Black: $125.00.

Scooby Doo: 21" - $85.00, $30.00.

Skediddles: 4" - $50.00 up. Disney - $85.00 up.

Skooter: 1963, freckles. $75.00 up.

Skipper: 1963 - $95.00 up. Growing up, 1976: $45.00 up.

Sister Belle: 17" - $45.00, $15.00.

Stacy, Talking: $125.00.

Swingy: 20" - $40.00, $15.00.

Tatters: 10" - $40.00, $15.00.

Teachy Keen: 17" - $35.00, $12.00.

Teeners: 4" - $45.00, $10.00.

Tinkerbelle: 19" - $45.00, $15.00.

Tippy Toes: 16" - $25.00, $9.00. Tricycle or horse: $20.00, $5.00.

Truly Scrumptious: 11½" - $250.00 up. Doll only: $175.00 up.

Tutti: 6" - $40.00 up. Packaged sets: $85.00 up.

Todd: 6" - $50.00 up.

Twiggy: 11" - $145.00 up.

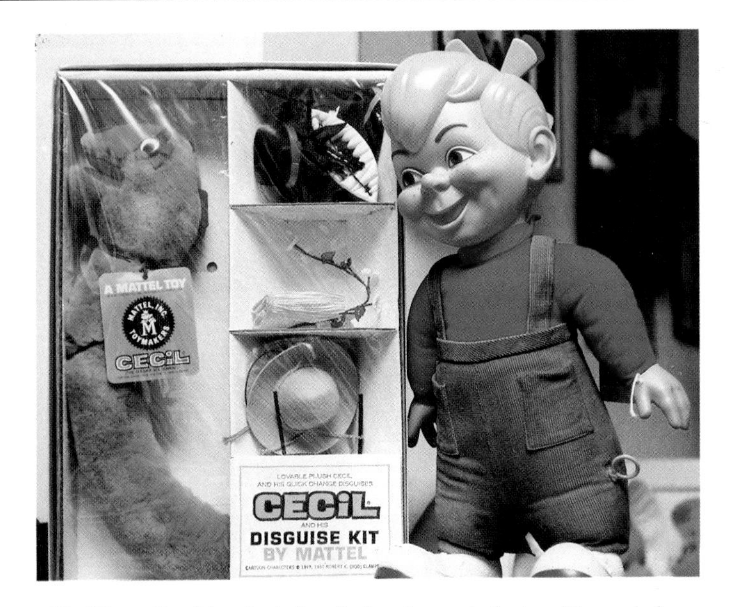

18" "Beany" with vinyl head, hands and feet, with rest foam stuffed cloth. Has molded hair with attached plastic propeller. Pull string talker. Shown with "Cecil" and his disguise kit. Courtesy Jeannie Mauldin. 18" - $100.00 in box.

11½" Guardian Goddess "Sun Spell." Marked "1978 Mattel Inc. Taiwan" on head. At waist "Mattel Inc. 1966 Taiwan." Courtesy Renie Culp. 11½" - $165.00 up each.

22" "Dr. Dolittle" (Rex Harrison) with vinyl head, painted features, rest cloth. Molded hair, removable hat. All original. Pull string talker. Courtesy Jeannie Mauldin. 22" - $95.00 up.

MEGO CORPORATION

First prices are for mint condition dolls; second prices are for ones that are dirty or not original.

Batman: Action figure. 8" - $15.00, $6.00.

Cher: 12" - $15.00 up, $6.00. Dressed in Indian outfit: $20.00, $10.00.

Dianna Ross: 12½" - $45.00 up, $15.00.

Dinah Mite: 7½" - $15.00, $6.00. Black: $20.00, $7.00.

Happy Days Set: Fonzie - $14.00, $6.00. Others - $9.00, $3.00.

Joe Namath: 12" - $75.00, $20.00.

Our Gang Set: Mickey - $22.00, $10.00. Others - $12.00, $6.00.

Planet of Apes: 8" - $15.00, $7.00.

Pirates: 8" - $50.00, $15.00.

Robin Hood Set: $45.00, $10.00.

Sir Lancelot Set: 8" - $50.00, $15.00.

Star Trek Set: 8" - $30.00, $8.00.

Soldiers: 8" - $15.00, $3.00.

Sonny: 12" - $20.00 up, $8.00.

Starsky or Hutch: $10.00, $5.00. Captain or Huggy Bear: $15.00, $7.00.

Super Women: Action figures. 8" - $10.00, $2.00.

Waltons: 8" - $15.00, $6.00.

Wizard of Oz: Dorothy - $20.00, $8.00. Munchkins - $15.00, $5.00. Wizard - $20.00, $7.00. Others - $10.00 - $4.00. 15" size: $100.00, $40.00.

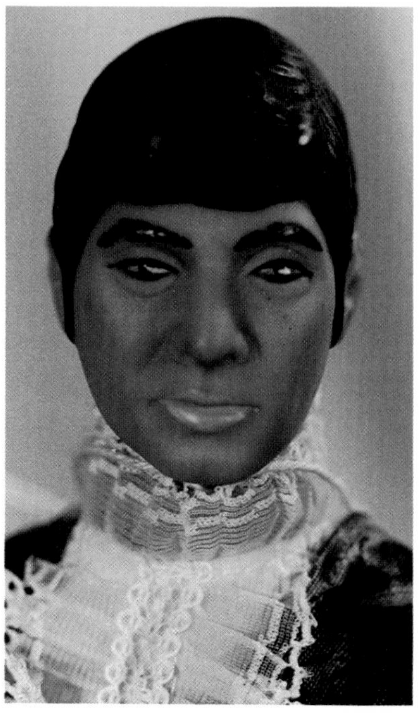

12" "Broadway Joe Namath." All vinyl, extra joints at wrists, elbows, waist, knees and ankles. Outfits is one sold separately #1212 "Jet Set." Marked "Broadway Joe tm/Mego Corp. MCMLXX/Made in Hong Kong." Courtesy Marie Ernst. 12" - $75.00.

MOLLYE DOLLS

First prices are for mint condition dolls; second prices are for crazed, cracked, dirty dolls or ones without original clothes.

Mollye Goldman of International Doll Company and Hollywood Cinema Fashions of Philadephia, PA made dolls in cloth, composition, hard plastic and plastic and vinyl. Only the vinyl dolls will be marked with her name, the rest usually have paper wrist tag. Mollye purchased unmarked dolls from many other firms and dressed them to be sold under her name. She designed clothes for many makers, including Horsman, Ideal and Eegee (Goldberger).

Airline Doll: Hard plastic. 14" -

$200.00 up, $75.00; 18" - $300.00 up, $125.00; 23" - $375.00 up, $100.00; 28" - $500.00 up, $200.00.

Babies: Composition. 15" - $150.00, $65.00; 21" - $225.00, $95.00. Composition/cloth: 18" - $85.00, $40.00. All composition toddler: 15" - $175.00, $80.00; 21" - $250.00, $100.00. Hard plastic: 14" - $95.00, $65.00; 20" - $165.00, $90.00. Hard plastic/cloth: 17" - $95.00, $55.00; 23" - $165.00, $85.00. Vinyl: 8½" - $15.00, $7.00; 12" - $20.00, $8.00; 15" - $35.00, $12.00.

Cloth: Children: 15" - $125.00, $50.00; 18" - $185.00, $75.00; 24" - $225.00, $80.00; 29" - $300.00, $100.00. Young ladies: 16" - $185.00, $80.00; 21" - $275.00, $100.00. Internationals: 13" - $90.00 up, $40.00; 15" - $150.00 up, $50.00; 27" - $275.00 up, $85.00.

Composition: Children: 15" - $150.00, $45.00; 18" - $185.00, $75.00. Young lady: 16" - $350.00, $100.00; 21" - $500.00, $150.00. Jeanette McDonald: 27" - $700.00 up, $250.00. Bagdad Dolls: 14" - $250.00, $85.00; 19" - $425.00, $125.00. Sultan: 19" - $600.00, $200.00. Subu: 15" - $500.00, $200.00.

Vinyl Children: 8" - $25.00, $9.00; 11" - $40.00, $15.00; 16" - $65.00, $20.00.

Hard Plastic: Young ladies. 17" - $185.00 up, $85.00; 20" - $225.00 up, $100.00; 25" - $300.00, $125.00.

Little Women: Vinyl, 9". $35.00, $10.00.

Lone Ranger/Tonto: Hard plastic/latex. 22" - $200.00, $75.00.

Raggedy Ann or Andy: See that section.

Beloved Belinda: See Raggedy Ann section.

27" deluxe size International made by Mollye. All cloth with oil painted face mask. 27" - $275.00.

16" International by Mollye. All cloth with pressed, oil painted face mask. All original. 16" - $150.00.

Tiny 10½" "Monica" by Monica Studios. All composition with rooted human hair, painted features and in original cotton gown. Courtesy Marie Ernst.

10½" - $265.00. 17" - $450.00 up. 21" - $500.00 up. Hard Plastic: (Marion - rooted hair) 17" - $450.00 up.

NANCY ANN STORYBOOK

The painted bisque Nancy Ann Dolls will be marked "Storybook Doll U.S.A." and the hard plastic dolls marked "Storybook Doll U.S.A. Trademark Reg." The only identity as to who the doll represents is a paper tag around wrist with the doll's name on it. The boxes are marked with the name, but many of these dolls are found in the wrong box.

Bisque: 5" - $50.00 up; 7½-8" - $60.00 up. Jointed hips: 5" - $65.00 up; 7½-8" - $75.00 up. Swivel neck: 5" - $75.00 up; 7½-8" - $80.00 up. Swivel neck and jointed hips: 5" - $75.00; 7½-8" - $85.00. Black: 5" - $125.00; 7½-8" - $145.00.

Plastic: 5" - $45.00 up; 7½-8" - $50.00. Black: $60.00.

Bisque Bent Leg Baby: 3½-4½" - $100.00 up.

Plastic Bent Leg Baby: 3½-4½" - $85.00 up.

"June" with socket head and jointed legs from 1941, the first year "month dolls" were on the market. Month dolls had unjointed hips and socket heads. Painted bisque. Courtesy Margaret Mandel. MIB - $75.00.

Nancy Ann Storybooks that are plastic. Back row: "Autumn", "Sabbath", "Princess Monon Minette", "Queen of Hearts". Front row: "March", "Christening", "Little Sister Goes To Play", "Rain, Rain Go Away", "July", "A Pretty Girl is Like a Melody". Courtesy Turn of Century Antiques. All $45.00 except "Princess" and "Christening" - $75.00. "Pretty Girl" - $85.00.

Judy Ann: Incised with name on back. 5" - $300.00 up.

Audrey Ann: 6" heavy doll, toddler legs, marked "Nancy Ann Storybook 12." Actual price not available.

Margie Ann: 6" bisque, in school dress. $125.00.

Debbie: With name on wrist tag and box. Hard plastic in school dress. $125.00.

Debbie: Hard plastic with vinyl head. $80.00.

Debbie: In dressier type Sunday dress and all hard plastic. $150.00. Same with vinyl head. $95.00.

Teen Type: Marked "Nancy Ann." All vinyl. 10½" - $85.00 up.

Muffie: 8", all hard plastic. Dress: $145.00 up. Ballgown: $175.00 up. Riding Habit: $175.00 up.

Muffie: 8" hard plastic, reintroduced doll. $85.00 up.

Nancy Ann Style Show Doll: 17-18" unmarked. All hard plastic. All in ballgown. $450.00 up.

"Muffie" that is walker and in "Muffie Dress Up Styles" Marked "Storybook Dolls/Calif./Muffie. Courtesy Maureen Fukushima. $145.00 up.

A reintroduced "Muffie" doll that is all hard plastic, unmarked and has bend knees. Box is marked "Fairytale Dolls, Inc. San Francisco." Courtesy Maureen Fukushima. $85.00 up.

17½" "Nancy Ann Style Show" doll. All hard plastic, sleep eyes, glued-on wig and is played with but all original. The feet are flat. Courtesy Marie Ernst. Mint: $450.00 up.

A strung "Muffie" with no eyebrows. In "Safari Outfit." Marked "Storybook Dolls" on back. Courtesy Maureen Fukushima. $145.00 up.

A strung "Muffie" with no eyebrows, unmarked. In Special Occasion Styles "Golfer" (rare outfit). Courtesy Maureen Fukushima. $200.00 up.

PARIS DOLL COMPANY

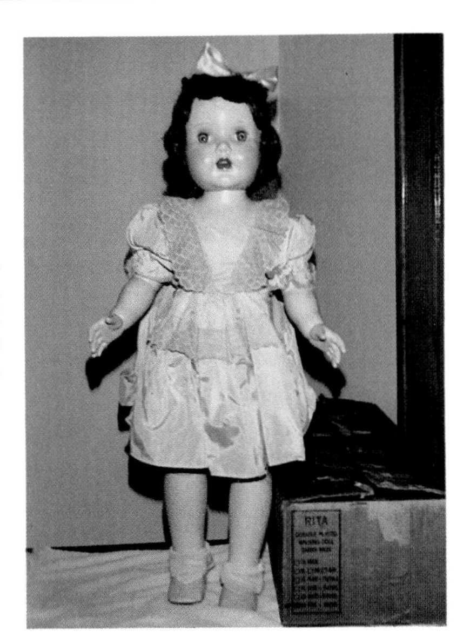

28" "Rita" by Paris Doll Company. All hard plastic, walker with open mouth, sleep eyes, saran wig. All original. Doll unmarked. Box: "Rita Walker by Paris Doll Co." Courtesy Ann Wencel. $250.00.

RAGGEDY ANN and ANDY

First prices are for mint condition dolls; second prices are for played with, dirty, no clothes or redressed dolls.

Designed by Johnny B. Gruelle in 1915, these dolls are still being made. Early dolls will be marked "Patented Sept. 7, 1915." All cloth, brown yarn hair, tin button eyes (or wooden ones), painted lashes below eyes and no outline of white of eyes. Some are jointed by having knees or elbows sewn. Features of early dolls are painted on cloth. 15-16" - $775.00 up, $300.00; 23-24" - $900.00 up, $400.00; 30" - $1,000.00, $500.00.

Averill, Georgene: Red yarn hair, painted feature and have sewn cloth label in side seam of body. Mid-1930's to 1963. 15" - $125.00 up - $45.00.

Beloved Belinda: Black doll. 15" - $800.00 up, $500.00.

Mollye Dolls: Red yarn hair and printed features. Will be marked in printed writing on front of torso "Raggedy Ann and Andy Doll/Manufactured by Mollye Doll Outfitters. 15" - $700.00 up, $185.00; 22" - $900.00 up, $200.00.

Knickerbocker Toy Co.: Printed features, red yarn hair. Will have tag sewn with name of maker. 1963-1982. 12" - $40.00, $10.00; 17" - $55.00; $20.00; 24" - $95.00, $40.00; 26" - $165.00, $70.00; 36" - $225.00, $100.00.

Vinyl Dolls: 8½" - $12.00, $3.00; 12" - $18.00, $6.00; 16" - $22.00, $8.00; 20" - $28.00, $10.00.

Applause Dolls: Will have tag sewn in seam. Still available.

29" and 30" very early Raggedy Ann and Andy. Oil painted features and socks. All cotton dolls. Clothes most likely replacements. 22" composition head and limbs with cloth body, tin sleep eyes, open mouth with two front teeth. Ca. early 1930's. Unmarked. Courtesy Margaret Mandel. 30" - $1,000.00.

22" "Beloved Belinda" from the Raggedy Ann and Andy books. An extremely hard doll to find. Made by Mollye Goldman of International Dolls and licensed by designer John B. Gruelle. 22" - $800.00 up.

First prices are for mint condition dolls; second prices are for played with, dirty or not original dolls.

Adams Family: 5½" - $10.00, $4.00.

Baby Crawalong: 20" - $20.00, $8.00.

Baby Grow A Tooth: 14" - $24.00, $8.00. Black: $35.00, $12.00.

Baby Know It All: 1969. 17" - $25.00, $10.00.

Baby Laugh A Lot: 16" - $15.00, $7.00. Black: $30.00, $15.00.

Baby Sad or Glad: 14" - $20.00, $12.00.

5" Daisy Flower finger puppet. Half of doll has space for child's finger to go into the legs to make her walk. Painted features and rooted hair. Marked "Remco Ind. Inc./1968" on head. Also marked "1969/Remco Ind. Inc./ U.S. & Foreign/Pat. Pend./Hong Kong." Plastic boots are removable. Courtesy Marie Ernst. 5" - $10.00.

5" "Monkees" finger puppets by Remco offered through Kellog's and also sold in stores with a fourth member. Half of the doll is suit with plastic boots and child's fingers go into legs to make doll walk. Marked "1970/Remco Ind. Inc. Harrison N.J. Pat. Pend. Hong Kong." Paper label: "1970 and TM of Columbia Pictures Ind. Inc. Remco Authorized user. Made in Hong Kong." Courtesy Marie Ernst. 5" - $45.00.

Dave Clark 5: 4½" - $45.00, $20.00. Set: $20.00.

Heidi: 5½" - $9.00, $3.00. Herby: 4½" - $12.00, $5.00. Spunky (glasses): 5½" - $14.00, $5.00.

Winking Heidi: $10.00, $4.00.

Jeannie, I Dream Of: 6" - $15.00, $5.00.

Jumpsy: 14" - $15.00, $6.00. Black: $22.00, $10.00.

Laura Partridge: 19" - $45.00, $20.00.

L.B.J.: Portrait, 5½" - $25.00, $10.00.

Little Chap Family: Set of four. $185.00, $60.00. Dr. John: 14½" - $50.00, $20.00. Lisa: 13½" - $40.00, $12.00. Libby: 10½" - $30.00, $10.00. Judy: 12" - $30.00, $10.00.

Mimi: Battery operated singer. 19" - $35.00, $12.00. Black: $60.00, $20.00.

Orphan Annie: Plastic and vinyl. 15" - $35.00, $14.00.

Tumbling Tomboy: 1969. 16" - $15.00, $6.00.

Rainbow and Computer: 1979. 8½" - $35.00, $10.00.

ROBERTA DOLL CO.

20" "Toby Ballerina" made by Roberta Doll Co. Plastic and vinyl, sleep eyes and has two metal keys, one on top of head and the other in back. Makes doll twirl and dance. Courtesy Carmen Moxley. 20" - $100.00.

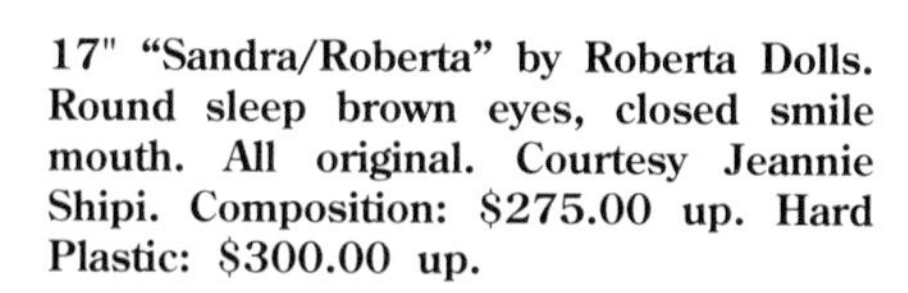

17" "Sandra/Roberta" by Roberta Dolls. Round sleep brown eyes, closed smile mouth. All original. Courtesy Jeannie Shipi. Composition: $275.00 up. Hard Plastic: $300.00 up.

19" "Lonely Liza" 1965-1966. Cloth body with vinyl arms, legs and head with rooted hair and painted features. Wire runs throughout body for posing. In 1966, this same body was used with slightly different head and the eyes are painted to the side. Marked "Royal Doll/ 1965." 19" - $85.00.

SASHA

Sasha dolls are made by Trenton Toys, Ltd., Reddish, Stockport, England from 1965 to 1986, when they went out of business. The original designer of these dolls was Sasha Morgenthaler in Switzerland. The dolls are made of all rigid vinyl with painted features. The only marks will be a wrist tag.

Boy: "Gregor" - $195.00.

Girl: $195.00.

Black Girl: "Cora" - $265.00.

Black Boy: "Caleb" - $265.00.

Black Baby: $195.00.

White Baby: $150.00.

Sexed Baby: $245.00.

Limited Edition Dolls: Limited to 5,000, incised #763, dressed in navy velvet. **1981:** $250.00. **1982:** Pintucks dress: $350.00. **1983:** Kiltie Plaid. $350.00. **1985:** Prince Gregor. $350.00. **1986:** Princess. $1,600.00. **1986:** Dressed in sari from India. $1,000.00.

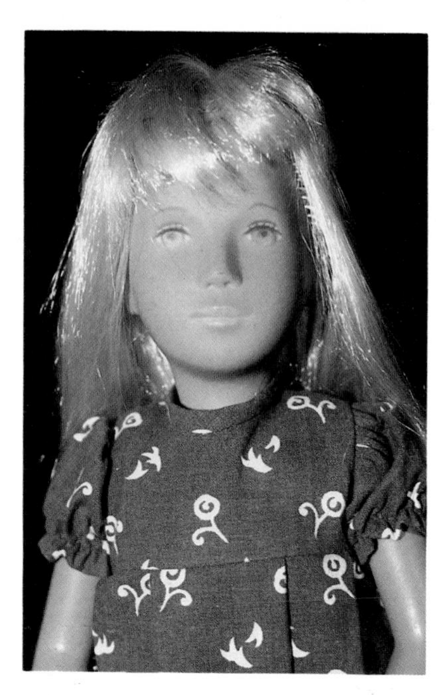

16" Sasha #105. "Made in Serie, England/Trenton Limited Stockport, England SK5 6DU." Rigid plastic with painted features, rooted hair, original dress. Jointed to be very bendable. Courtesy Lee Crane. 16" - $195.00.

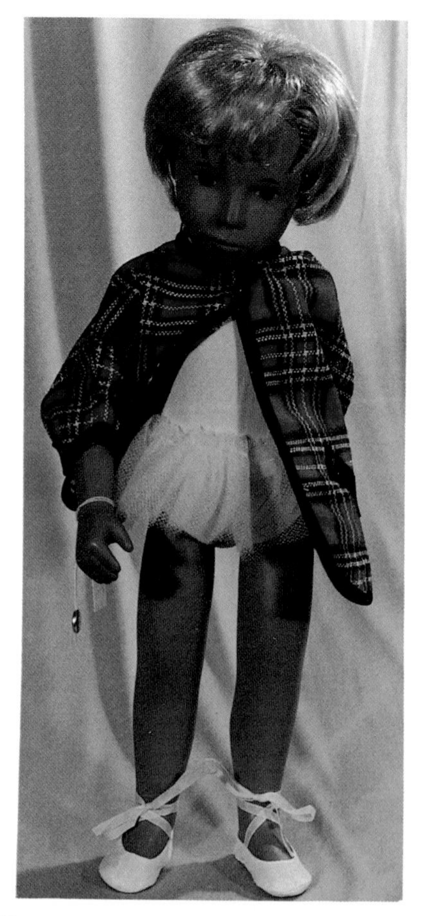

17" Sasha girl with bobbed hair and original outfit called "Dance Rehearsal." Rigid vinyl with very bendable limbs. Rooted hair. Courtesy Marie Ernst. 17" - $195.00.

20" all vinyl Sayco character girl with unusual face. All original in original box. Marked "Sayco." Sleep eyes, high heel feet. Ca. 1958-1960. Courtesy Martha Gragg. 20" - $100.00.

SHINDANA

First prices are for mint condition dolls; second prices are for played with, dirty dolls or not original ones. Dolls will be marked "Div. of Operation Bootstraps, Inc. U.S.A. (year) Shindana." They were in business from about 1968 to 1980.

Baby Janie: 1968. 13" - $35.00, $15.00.

Dr. J (Juluis Erving): Full action figure, 1977. 16" - $35.00, $10.00.

Flip Wilson/Geraldine: All cloth, talker, 1970. 16" - $20.00, $10.00.

J.J. (Jimmie Walker): All cloth talker. 15" - $20.00, $10.00; 23" - $25.00, $12.00.

Kim: Young lady in ballgown, 1969-1972. 16" - $45.00, $20.00.

Lea: Cloth/vinyl face mask and gauntlet hands. 1973. 11" - $20.00, $10.00.

Malaika: Young lady, 1969. 15" - $25.00, $15.00.

O.J. Simpson: Full action figure. 9½" - $35.00, $10.00.

Rodney Allen Rippy: 1979, all cloth talker. 16½" - $20.00, $10.00.

Tamu: Cloth/vinyl talker, 1969. 15" - $25.00, $12.00.

Wanda: 11½": Nurse - $30.00, $10.00. Ballerina - $20.00, $8.00. Disco - $25.00, $10.00. Airline Stewardess: $40.00, $10.00.

Zuri: Sculptured hair baby. All vinyl, 1972. 11½" - $30.00, $15.00.

13" "Baby Janie" by Shindana. 1968 and marked "Shindana Toys." All vinyl with painted features and open/closed mouth with two upper teeth. Rooted hair. 13" - $35.00.

SHIRLEY TEMPLE

First prices are for mint condition dolls; second prices are for played with, dirty, cracked or crazed or not original dolls. Allow extra for special outfits such as "Little Colonel," "Cowgirl," "Bluebird," etc.

All Composition:

11" - $685.00, $425.00. 11" Cowgirl: $700.00, $475.00.

13" - $625.00, $400.00.

16" - $625.00, $425.00.

18" - $675.00, $500.00.

20" - $725.00, $500.00.

22" - $750.00, $550.00.

25" - $850.00, $550.00. 25" Cowgirl: $900.00, $565.00.

27" - $1,100.00, $650.00. 27" Cowgirl: $1,200.00, $70.00.

Vinyl of 1950's: Allow more for flirty eyes in 17" and 19" sizes.

12" in box - $200.00; Mint, not in box - $165.00; Played with, dirty - $35.00.

15" in box - $300.00; Mint, not in box - $265.00; Played with, dirty - $85.00.

17" in box - $400.00; Mint, not in box - $350.00; Played with, dirty - $95.00.

19" in box - $450.00; Mint, not in box - $425.00; Played with, dirty - $100.00.

36" in box - $1,600.00; Mint, not in box - $1,450.00; Played with, dirty - $600.00.

1972: Reissue from Montgomery Ward. In box - $200.00; Mint, not in box - $165.00; Dirty - $45.00.

1973: Has box with many pictures of Shirley on it. Doll in red polka dot dress. 16" in box - $125.00; Mint, no box - $95.00; Played with, dirty - $25.00. Boxed outfits for this doll - $35.00.

Shirley Display Stand: Mechanical doll. $2,000.00 up.

"Hawaiian": Marked Shirley Temple (but not meant to be a Shirley Temple.) 18" - $800.00, $350.00.

Pin Button: Old 1930's doll pin. $90.00. Others - $15.00.

Statuette: Chalk in dancing dress. 7-8" - $245.00.

Japan: All bisque (painted) with molded hair. 6" - $200.00. Composition: 7-8" - $245.00.

Trunk: $145.00 up. Tagged 1930's dress: $100.00 up. Gift set/doll and clothes: 1950's - $300.00 up.

Babies: Marked on head, open mouth with upper and lower teeth, flirty, sleep eyes. 16" - $950.00, $565.00; 18" - $1,000.00, $65.00; 22" - $1,200.00, $700.00; 25" - $1,400.00, $800.00; 27" - $1,600.00, $900.00.

Shirley At The Organ display item. Doll is 15" tall, composition with cloth upper legs and has rods attached to keyboard to make arms move across keyboard. Doll has flirty eyes. Overall size is 38½" tall and 24" wide. Courtesy Frasher Doll Auctions. $2,000.00 up.

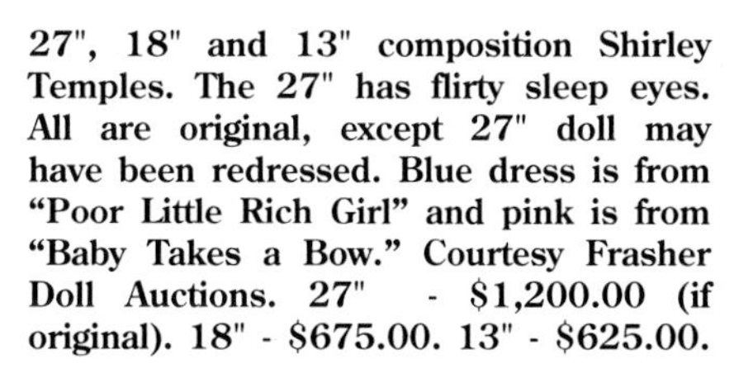

27", 18" and 13" composition Shirley Temples. The 27" has flirty sleep eyes. All are original, except 27" doll may have been redressed. Blue dress is from "Poor Little Rich Girl" and pink is from "Baby Takes a Bow." Courtesy Frasher Doll Auctions. 27" - $1,200.00 (if original). 18" - $675.00. 13" - $625.00.

21", 18" and 11" Shirley Temple dolls. One in red is from "Our Little Girl" and 11" "Cowboy - Texas Centennial Doll." One in navy has original clothes except for shoes and socks. Unknown outfit. Courtesy Frasher Doll Auctions. 21" - $750.00. 18" - $675.00. 11" - $700.00.

18", 13", 11" and 8" Shirley Temple dolls. Three tallest ones are marked on head and body with the 8" one marked on body "Japan." The little one also has painted features and molded hair. The 18" size has flirty eyes. Courtesy Glorya Woods. 18" - $675.00. 13" - $625.00. 11" - $685.00. 8" - $245.00.

12" and 15" Shirley Temple dolls. Left doll is a 1957-1958 issue with original box. Right doll is a 1972 Montgomery Ward doll in nylon flocked dress and velveteen vest with original box. Courtesy Frasher Doll Auctions. 12" - $165.00. 15" - $265.00.

17" and 19" Shirley Temple dolls that are all vinyl with sleep eyes. Both completely original, plus a mint condition "Baby Take A Bow" dress for a composition doll. These dolls date from 1957. Courtesy Frasher Doll Auctions. 17" - $350.00. 19" - $425.00. Dress: $100.00.

19" vinyl and 18" composition Shirley Temple dolls. Both are all original. Composition from the 1930's and vinyl from the 1950's. Courtesy Frasher Doll Auctions. 19" - $425.00. 18" - $675.00.

18" Shirley Temple, all composition and marked head and body. Dressed in "Baby Take A Bow" dress. Ribbons added/ replaced. Shown with 17" Madame Alexander "Elise Ballerina" of the 1950's. Hard plastic with vinyl jointed arms. Ribbon in hair replaces the original flowers. Courtesy Frasher Doll Auctions. 18" - $675.00. 17" - $300.00.

25" Shirley Temple doll. Marked on head and body. All composition with flirty eyes that also sleep. In original tagged outfit from "Stowaway." Ribbon has been added. Courtesy Frasher Doll Auctions. 25" - $850.00.

29" all composition German Shirley Temple doll. Incised 455 72. Flirty eyes, dimpled, smiling open mouth and wears old factory made dress. Courtesy Frasher Doll Auctions. 29" - $1,000.00 up.

First prices are for mint condition dolls, which could be higher due to the outfit on the doll. Second prices are for soiled, poor wig or not original.

Terri Lee: Composition: $285.00, $125.00. Hard plastic: Marked "Pat. Pend." $245.00, $100.00. Others: $200.00, $75.00. Black: $450.00 up, $200.00. Oriental: $375.00, $200.00. Vinyl: $185.00, $90.00. Talking: $450.00, $200.00.

Jerri Lee: 16" hard plastic, caracul wig. $295.00, $165.00. Black: $485.00, $250.00.

Tiny Terri Lee: 10" - $165.00, $85.00.

Tiny Jerri Lee: 10" - $195.00, $95.00.

Connie Lynn: 19" - $365.00 up, $200.00.

Gene Autry: 16" - $1,200.00 up, $600.00.

Linda Baby: (Linda Lee) 10-12" - $185.00 up, $95.00.

So Sleepy: 9½" - $200.00 up, $100.00.

Clothes: Ballgown - $65.00, $15.00. Riding Habit - $65.00, $15.00. Skaters - $65.00, $12.00. School Dresses - $40.00, $10.00. Coats - $35.00, $12.00. Brownie Uniform - $35.00, $15.00.

Clothes for Jerri Lee: Two-piece pants suit - $65.00, $20.00. Short pants suits - $65.00, $20.00. Western shirt/ jeans - $55.00, $20.00.

Mary Jane: Plastic walker, Teri Lee look-alike with long molded eyelids. 16" - $250.00 up.

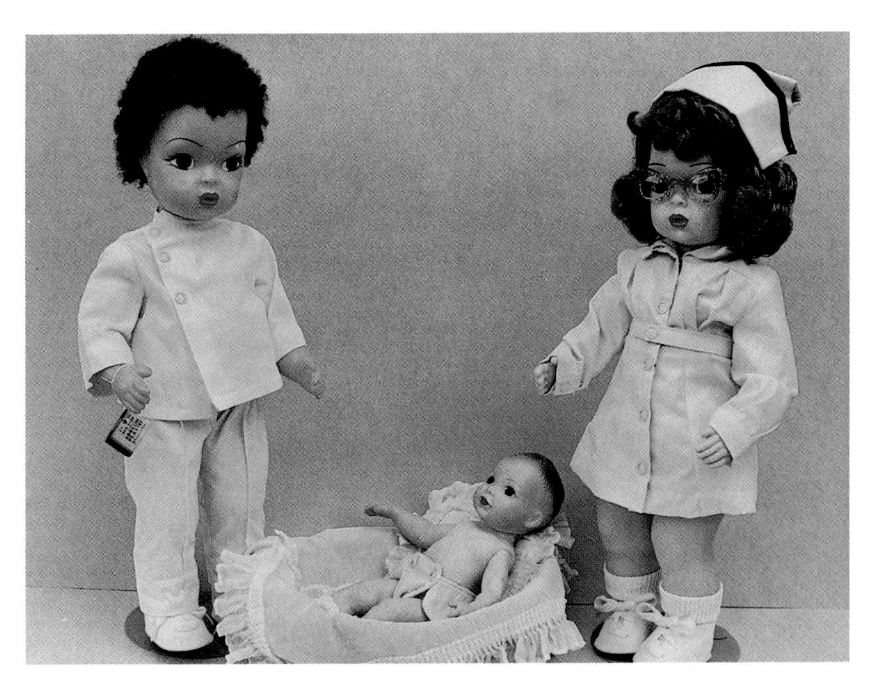

Terri and Jerri Lee in original outfits as Doctor and Nurse. All vinyl 10" Linda Baby in basket. Courtesy Margaret Mandel. Terri - $245.00 up. Jerri - $295.00 up. Linda - $185.00.

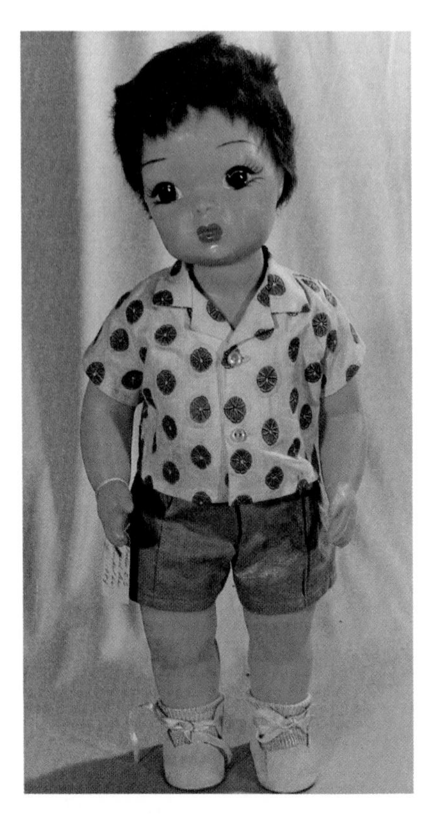

16" "Jerri Lee" with soft caracul wig and in original two-piece suit. Courtesy Marie Ernst. 16" - $295.00.

16" "Terri Lee" in original sunsuit that was a boxed extra outfit. Courtesy Marie Ernst. 16" - $245.00 up.

18½" "Connie Lynn" with curved baby legs, caracul wig, long lashes. Original romper suit tagged and has original soft vinyl baby booties with embossed bow and flowers. Courtesy Margaret Mandel. 18½" - $365.00.

16" Terri Lee in original velvet snowsuit. Wig is matted and sparce. Courtesy Frasher Doll Auctions. 16" - $325.00 (due to clothes).

16" Terri Lee and wears original Ballerina outfit and gold sandals. 10" "Tiny Jerri Lee" with sleep eyes and caracul (lamb's wool) wig. Original with original wrist tag. Courtesy Frasher Doll Auctions. 16" - $250.00 up. 10" - $185.00 up.

TIMELY TOYS

26" "Cindy Snow" with plush, unjointed body. Early vinyl head and hands. Eyes painted in squinting position. Tuff of nylon hair with plush back, inside of pockets match the scarf and cap trim. Tagged "Timely Toys." Sled from 1940's and doll from early 1950's. Courtesy Kay Brandsky. 26" -$250.00 up.

TOMY

16" "Kimberly" 1984 Tomy doll with original price of $24.95. Doll made in Hong Kong and clothes in China. Has many clothes that were sold separately that include soccer, roller skating, ice skating, jogging, sleeping, party, school and jeans outfits. Courtesy Margaret Mandel. 16" - $40.00.

18" "Kimberly" of 1984. Both faces are shown - the closed mouth and the smiling version. Both are all original. Courtesy Sally Bethscheider. 18" - $40.00 each.

TOPPER TOYS

6½" "Combat Kid." All vinyl with wire in arms and legs for posing. Has "action" right arm, which is rigid plastic and hand molded to hold items. Others in set: "Big Ear," "Sarge," "Pretty Boy," "The Rock," "Bugle Ben," "Tex" and "Machine Gun Mike." Also available were tanks and cannons. Doll marked "Deluxe Reading Corp./Elizabeth, N.J./1966/ IA9." Set called "The Tigers" and by Topper Toys, division of Deluxe Reading. 6½" - $15.00 each.

6½" "Spy." All vinyl with wire in arms and legs for posing. Painted features and glued on wig. Original. Marked "4/Deluxe Reading Corp./1965." Belongs to the "Tiger" set. 6½" - $22.00.

TROLLS

12" "Trolls" marked "Dam Things 1964" on feet. Felt clothes on boy and girl. Inset eyes. Courtesy Renie Culp. 12" - $65.00 up.

First prices are for mint condition dolls; second prices are for soiled, dirty or not original dolls.

Anniversary Doll: 25" - $50.00, $20.00.

Baby Dollikins: 21" - $35.00, $15.00.

Baby Trix: 16" - $20.00, $10.00.

Ballerina: Vinyl. 14" - $20.00, $7.00.

Blabby: $20.00, $9.00.

Bare Bottom Baby: 12" - $20.00, $9.00.

Dollikins: 8" - $15.00, $6.00; 11" - $20.00, $8.00; 19" - $30.00, $15.00.

Fairy Princess: 32" - $75.00, $40.00.

Freckles: 32" - $75.00, $35.00.

Freckles Marionette: 30" - $65.00, $30.00.

Lucky Lindy: (Lindbergh) Composition. 14" - $300.00, $175.00.

36" "Mary Poppins." Plastic and vinyl, all original including umbrella and purse. Courtesy Turn of Century Antiques. 36" mint in box - $350.00.

Pollyanna: 10½" - $30.00, $9.00; 17" - $45.00, $15.00; 31" - $100.00, $50.00.

Pri-Thilla: 12" - $20.00, $8.00.

Rita Hayworth: Composition. 14" - $265.00, $150.00.

Serenade: Battery operated talker. 21" - $50.00, $15.00.

Suzette: 10½" - $40.00, $20.00; 11½" - $45.00, $20.00; 11½" Sleep Eyes: $60.00, $30.00.

Tiny Teens: 5" - $8.00.

32" "Freckles." Plastic and vinyl, green eyes, yarn hair, 1982. Also available in red outfit with yellow hair and green eyes. Courtesy Marie Ernst. 32" - $75.00.

First prices are for mint condition dolls; second prices are for played with, dirty, crazed, messed up wig or not original.

Baby Dear: 12" - $55.00, $20.00; 17" - $95.00, $40.00. 1964: 12" - $50.00, $20.00.

Baby Dear One: 25" - $185.00, $85.00.

Baby Dear Two: 27" - $195.00, $95.00.

Brickette: 22" - $95.00, $40.00.

Ginny: Composition "Toddles": $265.00 up, $90.00.

22" "Brickette." Plastic two-piece body, ball jointed at waist. Plastic legs, vinyl arms and head. Rooted hair, green sleep eyes that also flirt. Original clothes. 1960. 22" - $95.00 up.

The 1986 Exclusive "Ginny" made for Shirley's Doll House, Wheeling, IL. Quality of doll and clothes is excellent. Shown with miniture ponys, a personal hobby of Shirley Bertrand, owner of Shirley's Doll House. 1986 - $60.00. 1985 set - $80.00.

Ginny: 8" hard plastic, strung, painted eyes. $350.00 up, $100.00.

Ginny: 8" hard plastic, sleep eyes, painted lashes and strung. $300.00 up, $100.00.

Ginny: Caracul (lamb's wool) wig. Child, not baby. $365.00 up, $185.00.

Ginny: Painted lashes, sleep eyes, hard plastic walker. $265.00 up, $95.00.

Ginny: Hard plastic molded lash walker. $185.00 up, $80.00.

Ginny: Hard plastic, jointed knee, molded lash walker. $165.00 up, $70.00.

Ginny Queen: $1,500.00 up, $400.00.

Ginny Crib Crowd: Bent leg baby with caracul (lamb's wool) wig. $650.00 up, $300.00.

Crib Crowd Easter Bunny: $1,200.00 up, $600.00.

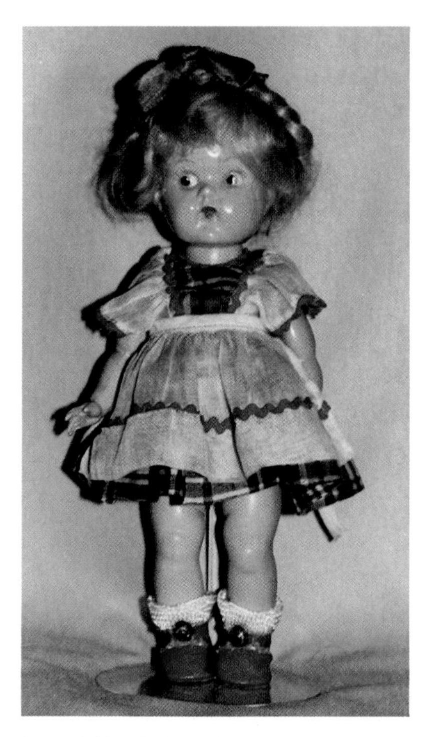

Ca. 1948-1950. Painted eyes, mohair wig. Marked head and body. All hard plastic. Courtesy Maureen Fukuskima. $350.00 up.

Front Left: 7½" "Toddles" marked "Vogue" on head. All composition as "Little Bo Peep." 1944-1945. Front Right: 8" hard plastic "Ginny" tagged "Pamela" of the 1953 "Debutante Series." Back: 8" bride by Madame Alexander. Straight leg, non-walker "Alexander-kins" 1953-1954. Courtesy Frasher Doll Auctions. 7½" - $265.00 up. 8" - $350.00 up. Bride: $250.00 up.

10½" "Little Imp" with the box marked "Vogue Dolls, Inc. #4230 - Country Cousin." All hard plastic with vinyl head, which is marked "R&B/65." Lower back marked "R&B Doll Co." Freckles and sleep eyes. This doll made by Vogue after they purchased the Arranbee company molds. Courtesy Marie Ernst. 10½" - $65.00 up.

Ginny: All vinyl Internationals. $50.00 up. Other: $35.00 up.

Ginny Gym: $265.00 up.

Ginny Pup: Steiff. $165.00 up.

Hug A Bye Baby: 16" - $35.00, $15.00. Black: $45.00, $20.00.

Jan: 12" - $75.00, $25.00.

Jeff: 10" - $50.00, $20.00.

Jill: 10" - $75.00, $25.00.

Lil Imp: 11" - $65.00, $30.00.

Love Me Linda: 15" - $45.00, $15.00.

Star Bright: 18" - $100.00, $40.00. Baby: 18" - $65.00, $25.00.

Welcome Home or Welcome Home Baby Turns Two: 20-24" - $75.00, $30.00.

Wee Imp: 8", red wig. $400.00 up, $100.00.

16" "Brickette." Plastic and vinyl with sleep eyes/lashes and "Mod" hairdo. Marked "Lesney Prod. Corp. 1978/ 71679" on head. Dress tagged "Vogue Dolls, Inc. Made in USA." Doll designed and made after Vogue Dolls sold to Lesney of England. Courtesy Marie Ernst. 16" - $65.00 up.

15" "Littlest Angel." Plastic and vinyl with sleep eyes. All original. Tagged clothes: "Vogue Dolls, Inc. Made in USA." Back of head: "Vogue Dolls 1965." Box: "Melrose Tonka Corp." Doll made after Vogue sold to Lesney of England and then Lesney sold molds to Tonka Toys, Inc. Courtesy Marie Ernst. 15" - $65.00 up.

Front Right: 8" "Ginny." All hard plastic, red tagged velvet dress that is "Ginger" of the Debutante Series. Front Left: 8" "Ginny Hawaiian." Brown skin tones, all hard plastic and original. Back: 16" "Jane Withers" by Madame Alexander. All composition and original. Courtesy Frasher Doll Auctions. Ginger - $300.00 up. Hawaiian - $1,500.00 up. 16" - $675.00.

17" "Marilyn Monroe," a one-year production doll of 1983 and first in the celebrity series by World Doll. Came with diamond necklace which was removed before it stained the vinyl on this doll and the company replaced it with pearls. Doll has no undies and has a form-fitting gown. Courtesy Margaret Mandel. 17" - $95.00.

INDEX

E

F

G

H

I

N

O

P

Q

R

S

NUMBERS

LETTERS AND SYMBOLS

Other Books by
America's Leading Doll Author,
Patricia Smith

French Dolls In Color, 3rd Series	$14.95
German Dolls	9.95
Madame Alexander Dolls	19.95
Madame Alexander Dolls Price Guide #15	7.95
Modern Collector's Dolls I	17.95
Modern Collector's Dolls V	17.95
World of Alexander-kins	19.95

Schroeder's Antiques Price Guide

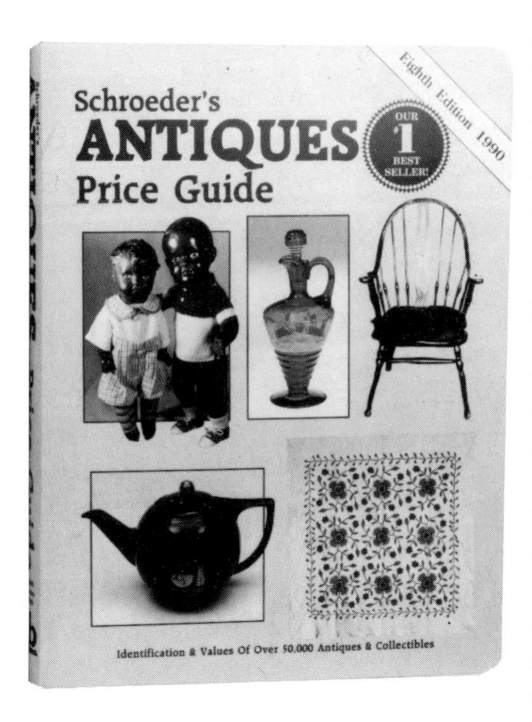

Schroeder's Antiques Price Guide has climbed its way to the top in a field already supplied with several well-established publications! The word is out, *Schroeder's Price Guide* is the best buy at any price. Over 500 categories are covered, with more than 50,000 listings. From ABC Plates to Zsolnay, if it merits the interest of today's collector, you'll find it in Schroeder's. Each subject is represented with histories and background information. In addition, hundreds of sharp original photos are used each year to illustrate not only the rare and the unusual, but the everyday "fun-type" collectibles as well. All new copy and all new illustrations make Schroeder's THE price guide on antiques and collectibles. We have not and will not simply change prices in each new edition.

The writing and researching team is backed by a staff of more than seventy of Collector Books' finest authors, as well as a board of advisors made up of well-known antique authorities and the country's top dealers, all specialists in their fields. Prices are gathered over the entire year previous to publication, then each category is thoroughly checked. Only the best of the lot remains for publication. You'll find the new edition of *Schroeder's Antiques Price Guide* the one to buy for factual information and quality.

No dealer, collector or investor can afford not to own this book. It is available from your favorite bookseller or antiques dealer at the low price of $12.95. If you are unable to find this price guide in your area, it's available from Collector Books, P.O. Box 3009, Paducah, KY 42001 at $12.95 plus $2.00 for postage and handling.